# The History of Modern CYPRUS

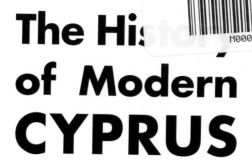

## Dr. Stavros Panteli

Introduced by
Professors:

**Robert Browning**

and

**Robert Holland**

Top*line* Publishing

Published by Topline Publishing
12 The Fairway, New Barnet
Herts. EN5 1HN, England

**www.cyprusbooks.co.uk**

2005

All photographic and textual material was supplied by the author.
The Publishers produced this book in good faith.

ISBN: 0  948853 32 8

Designed and prepared by Toplineart & Design, Barnet
**www.toplineart.co.uk**

Printed in Cyprus by Printco Ltd – Nicosia

History cannot pass judgement.....

It is simply an experience of the past,

possibly a pointer to the future.

*Dedicated to those downtrodden*
*and disposessed peoples of the world*

# CONTENTS

# INTRODUCTION

*by Professor Robert Holland – 2005*

In recent times Cyprus has once again taken a prominent place in 'world news' as fresh attempts are made to bring about the reunification of the island and, with it, a reconciliation between the Greek and Turkish inhabitants of the island. It is therefore a timely moment for such a distinguished history of Cyprus to appear. A repeated theme of Dr Panteli's treatment – that before the aberration of 'modernity' peaceful co-existence between Cypriot communities was often the prevailing norm – is as opposite today as when his earlier works made their first appearance.

In this superbly illustrated account, the author 'begins at the beginning' before the birth of Christ, and proceeds to crisply summarize the main components and problems in Cypriot society through the classical, medieval, and the various sub-periods of the modern era, through to the disaster of 1974, and finally to the end of 2004. In doing so he displays an immensely impressive command of what is a vast associated literature, and often, too, with the relevant primary sources. The treatment avoids pointless rhetoric or generality, but although facts are to the fore, they are presented with admirable clarity, logic and digestability.

Dr. Panteli's coverage of Cypriot events in these pages is by no means narrowly political. It is also social and cultural in a very broad sense, and conveys a strong sense of the changing, but also in some degree changeless, life in an island of such diversity, distinctiveness of atmosphere and physical beauty. A particular quality of the account is its sound, balanced and impartial judgement, without which any history of Cyprus is doomed to fail.

There has been much emphasis with regard to the reconciliation of politically divided societies on the need for history textbooks in schools and universities capable of underpinning a common dialogue. The present volume is equipped to make such a valuable contribution in Cyprus. It is not necessary that everybody should agree with everything Dr. Panteli says. It is after all, about Cyprus, regarding which nobody – Greek, Turkish, English, or anybody else – can expect to be taken quite at the value they might like! But in the following pages there is an endless possibility for future debate, controversy and enjoyable jousting between fellow-scholars and fellow-citizens.

# INTRODUCTION

*by Professor Robert Browning*

Cyprus is among the youngest of nations. Yet it has a longer history than most. Looked at in one way it is a history of rule by foreigners - Assyrians, Egyptians, Persians, Macedonians, Romans, Byzantines, French, Venetians, Turks and British. But in another way it is a history of the meeting and often fruitful mingling of different cultures. Geography and history make the island a bridge between the Mediterranean, Asia Minor and the Fertile Crescent. From the arrival of the Mycenaeans more than three thousand years ago Greek has been the predominant culture. I have deliberately not said 'dominant', because the question of domination rarely arose. For most of the time Greeks and Phoenicians, Greeks and Latins, Greeks and Turks have lived peaceably together, sharing the same cities and villages. Zenon of Kition, the founder of the Stoic school of philosophy and one of the most influential thinkers of the ancient world, was a Phoenician who wrote in Greek - and doubtless thought in Greek. Some of the later Lusignan Kings spoke Greek better than French. During the three centuries of Ottoman rule, Greek and Turkish Cypriots not infrequently joined in protest, or even in revolt, against the government of the Sultan.

Perhaps because of their cosmopolitan backround, Cypriots have never been stay-at-homes. Two of them became Ecumenical Patriarchs and heads of the Orthodox Church. From the fifteenth century many Cypriots settled in Venice. Among these was Thomas Flanginis who in 1626 founded what was for two centuries, the most celebrated Greek school in Europe. Haji Baki Agha, an illiterate Turkish woodcutter from a village in Cyprus, rose after a not entirely reputable career in the service of the Sultan, to become Governor of his native island. Today the Cypriot diaspora stretches from California to the Persian Gulf, and many Cypriots have made their mark as men of science in their adopted homes. In particular, the Cypriot community in Great Britain, which includes Turkish as well as Greek Cypriots, has grown immensely since the Second World War, and London is probably the second Cypriot city in terms of population.

Dr. Panteli in this, his tenth book on the history of Cyprus, concentrates his attention on the period of British rule (1878-1960) and the years of Cypriot independence. There are many paradoxes in the recent history of Cyprus. It has a higher proportion of graduates in its population than any country in Europe, yet until recently it had no university A long struggle, the avowed objective of which was union with Greece, resulted in the establishment of an independent republic. A country with a millenary experience of polyethnic living together has since 1974 been divided by a barrier as impenetrable as that which separates North and South Korea. Dr. Panteli guides his readers through the jungle of tendentious statement and counter-statement, of unrealistic rhetoric and face-saving compromise, of conscientious negotiation and naked exercise of power which marked the gestation and birth of the nation. Fair-minded in his judgements, at home in the sources, both published and unpublished, scrupulous in his handling of them, he provides an admirable introduction to the complex of problems surrounding Cyprus, some of which will not go away but fizzles like time fuses, ready to detonate an international crisis. The problem of Cyprus is the problem of all of us.

The demand for union with Greece was traditional and strong in its appeal to the Greek Cypriots. That it was not realised was due in part to the skill - or the good luck - of successive British governments, who from being the foreign ruler who must be got rid of, gradually transformed themselves into a mediator, and perhaps the arbitrator, between ethnic groups in Cyprus and even between their Greek and Turkish backers. In so doing they helped to create and encourage separatist feelings among the Turkish Cypriots, which soon led to the breakdown of the new constitution. Perhaps it never could have worked. Thus the scene was set for the tragic events of 1974. Some blame for this must fall on the Greek Cypriot people and its leaders, who did not, until it was too late, make a serious attempt to understand and respond to the aspirations and fears of their Turkish fellow-citizens, but tended to regard them as a tiresome minor nuisance. But it was above all the indescribable folly of the military dictatorship in Athens and the eagerness of a weak government in Ankara to show its muscle that led to the invasion and partition of the island

So today Cyprus has sovereignty, but only over part of its territory. Its rise to full nationhood had been interrupted and flawed. If present difficulties are to be overcome - and the key to their solution probably lies far from Cyprus, as far away as Washington and Moscow - it will once again play its historic role as a bridge between east and west. Whether some kind of association with Greece will eventually be sought is a matter for the Cypriot people, Greek and Turkish, to decide. It is no one else's business.

In the meantime British readers need reminding how by its actions - or lack of action -as colonial power, and later as joint guarantor of the independence and territorial integrity of the Republic, their own country has contributed to the present disastrous impasse. Dr. Panteli's book will help them to understand how things came to be as they are, and perhaps to discern what must be done to put them right.

*Professor Robert Browning*
(written in 1990)

# ACKNOWLEDGEMENTS

Acknowledging people who have been instrumental in the production of this work is certainly extremely difficult. I have received much help and encouragement during the writing of this book, and I wish I could find new words to express my gratitude. It is impossible to acknowledge them all, and many may be unaware of the help they have given because it came as a result of my recollections of discussions amongst friends and colleagues over a period of several years.

In a more formal sense I am indebted to my publishers Mrs and Mr Lavithis for reading and making useful comments on the entire typescript and also for providing the maps and photographs.

Above all, I am indebted to the late Professor Robert Browning who read the whole draft of the first edition and made some penetrating and helpful criticisms. The Introduction bears witness to his great wisdom, experience and scholarship.

Professor Holland has also read the script and made some scholarly corrections. My thanks for the Introduction.

I am forever grateful to my sister Thesbo Theophilou for her most efficient typing - a task, I am sure, she would not want to repeat again - which is now being thankfully provided by Anna Lavithis.

Next, I wish to record my deepest gratitude to my wife Floria, not so much for helping me in completing this study but more for her sense of understanding, respect and patience during my many years of research in Britain, Cyprus, Greece and elsewhere.

To conclude, however, I wish to reiterate that the responsibility for any errors or shortcomings in what appears in print is entirely mine.

# THE AUTHOR

## Dr. Stavros Panteli

A Cypriot-born historian now living in London. Stavros has lectured and written extensively on Cyprus and the Greek-world in general - an area where he has in-depth knowledge following some 25 years of research into unpublished documents in the UK (especially), Cyprus, Greece and the US.

He has many publications to his name as author, contributor and editor. Amongst his many publications in English are the following:

- **A New History of Cyprus**: from the earliest times to the present day.
- **The Making of Modern Cyprus**: from obscurity to statehood.
- **Gregoris Afxentiou**: the hero of Machaeras and his statue (English and Greek).
- **Historical Dictionary of Cyprus.**
- **A History of Cyprus**: from foreign domination to troubled independence.
- **Place of Refuge**: the history of the Jews in Cyprus.

He is also a major subscriber to the definitive five-volume **'History of Cyprus'** currently being published by the Makarios Foundation, and to the seven-volume and award winning **"Paithenontas ghia ten Eleftheria" (Dying for Freedom).**

*Forthcoming titles include:*
- **Sir Winston Churchill: an analysis of his Cyprus policy, 1907-65;**
- **The exile and release of Archbishop Makarios, 1956-57;** and
- **Cyprus 1878**: Her Majesty's New Possession.

**About the author:**
The Independent - *"Dr Stavros Panteli, a leading Cypriot historian, tolerant and dispassionate"*

Sir James Wilson K.B.E. M.C - *"I have read with avidity your masterly history of Cyprus and I was most impressed by the quality of your writing and research."*

Hon. Francis Noel-Baker MP - *"I have just read your excellent history of Cyprus first class"*

Professor Richard Clogg (The World Today) - *"The book which is welcome, is well written and based on a wide variety of sources".*

# PREFACE

The period covered by the book extends from the earliest years to the beginning of the 21st century - from *"Obscurity to Statehood"*. The latter years, especially, have not been easy to write. Contemporary history presents many pitfalls to anyone rash enough to record it; Cypriot history incurs extra hazards. In the first place, fewer sources are available than in the case of some other countries. The Turkish invasion of 1974 for example, has been instrumental in either destroying both private and public records or keeping them far away from researchers and writers. Secondly, valuable Cypriot sources either appear years after the event or are simply kept from the public - ostensibly at times, to protect an individual or a group. Thirdly, the problems of statehood and internal strife are certainly not conducive to the presentation of good archival material. There are other reasons which are too numerous to even consider.

What the author has tried to present is not a strict narrative history, following the course of events year by year. Hence at all times statistical data, tables, appendices, maps and photographs have been added to assist the reader. Primarily, it is not intended to be a textbook giving the facts, all the facts and, nothing but tiring details necessary for passing an examination in Cypriot history. It is an unbiased, easy-to-read account aimed at everyone who cares to learn and understand the problems which faced and, still face, this tragic island. This is in the main a political history. The economic, religious, cultural and social sections make no pretence to be comprehensive: they are intended merely to provide the minimum framework within which political events become intelligible.

The reader is invited to study the text and pass his/her own judgement.

# ABBREVIATIONS

AKEL:–     Anorthodiko Komma Ergazomenou Laou – Progressive Party of the Working People

AON:–      Anorthodiki Organosis Neoleas – Reform Youth Organization

BFC:–      British Forces in Cyprus

BMEFC:–    British Middle East Forces in Cyprus

CENTO:–    Central Treaty Organization

CIA:–      Central Intelligence Agency

CRO:–      Commonwealth Relations Office

DEKO:–     Democratico Komma – Democratic Party

DESY:–     Democraticos Synagermos – Democratic Rally

EAK:–      Enosi Agroton Kyprou – Union of Cypriot Agriculturalists

ELDYK:–    Elliniki Dynami Kyprou – Greek Contingent in Cyrpus

EOKA:–     Ethniki Organosi Kyprion Agoniston – National Organization of Cypriot Fighters

EU:–       European Union

FCO:–      Foreign and Commonwealth Office

HMG:–      His(Her) Majesty's Government

KATAK:–    Enosis Tourkikis Meionotitas Kyprou – Cyprus Turkish Minority Association

KKK:–      Kommounistiko Komma Kyprou – Communist Party of Cyprus

NATO:–     North Atantic Treaty Organization

PEK:–      Panagrotiki Enosis Kyprou – All-Farmers Union of Cyprus

PEO:–      Pangypria Ergatiki Omospondia – PanCyprian Federation of Labour

PSE:–      Pangypria Syndehniaki Epitropi – PanCyprian Trade Unions' Committee

SBA:–      Sovereign Base Area

SEK:–      Synomospondia Ergaton Kyprou – Cyprus Workers Confederation

TFSC:–     Turkish Federated State of Cyprus

TMT:–      Türk Müdafaa (or Mukavamet) Teskilati – Turkish Defence or Resistance Organization

TOURDYK:–  Tourkiki Dynami Kyprou – Turkish Contingent in Cyprus

UNFICYP:–  United Nations Peacekeeping Force in Cyprus

# FOREIGN WORDS & PHRASES

ACQUIS COMMUNAUTAIRE: Entire body of legislation ratified by the European Union (EU) since its inception, to which all member states must adhere.

AD HOC: For a particular, usually exclusive purpose.

ANNUS HORRIBILIS: A year of horrors.

ANNUS MIRABILIS: A year of wonders.

ANTE-BELLUM: Occurring or existing before a particular war.

CASUS BELLI: An act or situation provoking or justifying war.

CUL-DE-SAC: A blind alley; a route that leads nowhere

DE FACTO: In fact, whether by right or not.

DE JURE: By right; rightly.

DÉTENTE: The easing of strained relations, especially between states.

DIKTAK: A severe settlement, especially one imposed by a victorious nation on a defeated one.

EX OFFICIO: By virtue of one's position or office.

FAITS ACCOMPLIS: Things that have been done and are past arguing against or altering.

INTER ALIA: Among other things.

IPSO FACTO: By that very fact or act; thereby.

LOCUS STANDI: A recognized or identifiable, especially legal status.

MACHTPOLITIK: Power politics.

MAL DE MER: Seasickness.

MODUS OPERANDI: The way a thing operates.

MODUS VIVENDI: An arrangement whereby those in dispute can carry on pending a settlement.

MUTATIS MUTANDIS: In comparing cases, making the necessary alterations.

NOM DE GUERRE: An assumed name under which a person fights.

NULL & VOID: Invalid; not binding.

PAR EXCELLENCE: As having special excellence; being the supreme example of its kind.

PER SE: By or in itself; intrinsically.

PERSONA NON GRATTA: A person, especially a diplomat, who is not acceptable.

RAISON D'ÊTRE: Purpose, reason, role.

RAPPROCHEMENT: Drawing together; establishment or renewal of cordial relations.

STATUS QUO: The existing state of affairs.

SUI GENERIS: Of its own kind; unique.

QUID PRO QUO: Something for something; a thing given as compensation.

The ruins of the once great Temple of Aphrodite at Kouklia – ancient kingdom of Paleapaphos

# Chapter ONE

---

## THE FORMATIVE YEARS

c.10,000 BC
to AD 1,570

Cyprus, nobly described as a 'paradise par excellence' is situated in the northeastern corner of the Mediterranean Sea. It is its third largest island after Sicily and Sardinia and has an area of some 3,572 sq. miles or 9,250 sq.km. Its greatest length up to Cape Andreas is 140 miles (235 km.) and its greatest breadth is very nearly 60 miles (95 km).

At all times Cyprus has been what she is now - the watchtower and outpost of three continents: Europe, Asia and Africa. Consequently, the advantages of strategic location have made her the envy of more powerful neighbours who had, from most ancient times, practiced a policy of territorial expansion at her expense. Cyprus was always important both for its geographical position linking East and West and for its rich resources of copper, other metals and timber.

According to the Holy Scriptures[1] the 70 nations of the earth may be classified as descended from one or another of Noah's three sons: Shem, Ham, and Japheth. From the latter's descendants we find the Cypriots Elishah and Kittim. In general, therefore, the Bible refers to Cyprus as the *"Land of the Kittim"*. Flowery literary epithets include, *'Cerastia'* because of the many promontories it thrusts into the sea like horns; *'Aspelia'* from the roughness and unevenness of its soil; *'Collinia'* form its numerous hills; *'Aerosa'* or *'Aeria''* because of the mines of copper and other metals which were first said to be found there; *'Makaria'* ('blessed') because of the fruitfulness of the soil and happiness of the climate; as *'Amathusia''*, *'Paphia'*, *'Salaminia'* and *'Lapithia'* from the towns of Amathus, Paphos, Salamis and Lapithos. It was also known as *'Alishiya'* and *'Elishah'* by ancient oriental scholars and described so in sources of the 2nd millennium BC. It was also called *'Latanana'* and *'Iadnana'* by the Assyrians of the 8th century BC, whereas the Greek settlers and traders of the end of the 2nd millennium preferred the name *'Makaria'*. An unjustified name was *'Ophioussa'* (abode of snakes), which was acquired in late antiquity.

So much for terminology. To date, it has been customary to record that human settlement in Cyprus started rather belatedly, in the **NEOLITHIC** (or New Stone Age), around the 7th millennium. However, recent findings[2] from Akrotiri-Aetokremmos (Akrotiri-Eagles Cliff) suggests a much earlier occupation; in fact, a very late Mesolithic presence(or Middle Stone Age, regarded as the transitional between the Palaeolithic and Neolithic Ages) c. 8000BC. In the footsteps of the early settlers (Syropalestinians, Greek Achaeans, Mycenaeans and Phoenicians) came the Assyrians, Egyptians, Persians, Macedonian-Greeks, Romans, Byzantines, Lusignans (Franks), Genoese, Venetians, Ottomans and finally the British in 1878. Cyprus became independent in 1960; the 99th

---

(1) Genesis xx: 2-4
(2) Nature: Volume 333. 9 June 1988. p. 554

*Above:* Remains of the important Neolithic settlement of Khirokitia
*Left:* Grey bowl from Khirokitia, around the 7th millenium BC – Nicosia Museum

member-state of the United Nations. It became the 12th member of the Commonwealth in March 1961 and the 16th member-state of the Council of Europe in April 1961. In May 2004, Cyprus became a full member of the enlarged European Union.

Cyprus' Neolithic culture lasted for over 3,500 years and was developed locally with little apparent influence from abroad. This, of course, is not altogether surprising considering that mastery of the seas lay far into the future, as did also the technological advances which were to drive these self-sufficient food-raisers into a position of dependence upon their neighbours for certain rare and precious commodities. During this period the inhabitants lived in low circular-domed stone huts, similar to igloos, and were very fond of hunting. Their settlements at Khirokitia and Kalavasos, for example were usually near the coast or near streams and were mainly found along the north coast and in the south. The Cypriot 'economy' was based (apart from hunting) on mixed farming and fishing. It also appears that grapes and olives, both characteristic Mediterranean products, were now gathered.

*Above:* The Chalcolithic site of Lemba-Lakkous in Paphos with a reconstructed experimental village
*Right:* Limestone statuette from the same site c.3000 BC – Cyprus Museum

The **CHALCOLITHIC** (or copper-stone) **Age** which spanned the years c. 3900 to c.2500 denotes the period when metal first appeared but was still uncommon. Features of the period include: the western end of the island seems to have been inhabited for the first time; the increasing use of metal; changes in burial customs; a new type of miniature sculpture is developed, and Cyprus, henceforth increasingly takes part in international - in fact, regional commerce.

The transition to the **EARLY BRONZE AGE** (c.2500 to c.2000) shows an unbroken development from the earliest cultures, with an infusion of new and foreign ideas. Paramount amongst these is the knowledge of metal-working whilst the West Anatolian[3] strain in some pottery shapes indicates the source of these new traits. Settlements, which were at first spread around river valleys (e.g. Philia and Vasiliko), soon spread right across the island. The long sequence of red polished pottery which spans the period 2500 to 1650 is remarkable for its variety and power of expression. Furthermore, tools and weapons made from copper and

---

(3) Anatolian settlers arrived in Cyprus c. 2300 - following the disasters which afflicted their homeland.

bronze show the importance of smelting as a main source of income for the people. Therefore, a thriving economy supplemented by an emerging metallurgical industry led to better provision for the dead. They were henceforth buried in rock-cut chambers approached by an open passage known as a '*dromos*' and the cave-like chamber was sealed by a large stone slab. And, in common with most of the ancient world the Cypriots believed in life after death. Hence, even humble burials were equipped with pottery vessels containing food, drink and ointment. The wealthier ones also received utensils, tools and weapons.

Towards the end of the period a small number of imports reached the island and Cypriot products found their way to Egypt and the Near East.

Commercial and cultural contact was continued into the next phase called the **MIDDLE BRONZE PERIOD** c.2000 to c.1650. Settlements, with the exception of the most mountainous regions, were now found right across the island. Trading relations (especially with countries close by) reached new heights and Cyprus became known as the 'trading emporium' of the region. A pottery style known as 'White Painted II' - burnished vessels decorated with dark paint applied in linear motifs direct to a light background - characterises this phase which is often described as "an epilogue to the Early Bronze Age and the prelude to the Late Bronze period". Agriculture, copper-mining and pottery-making continued to be the cornerstones of the Cypriot economy.

The **LATE BRONZE** phase c.1650-c.1050 is characterised by various events that can only be described as "climacteric". Firstly, Cyprus traded freely with neighbouring countries - copper and pottery being the main items. This must have been the heyday of the cosmopolitan coastal towns such as Enkomi, Kition, Hala Sultan Tekke and Maroni. Secondly, and probably the most important event of the Bronze Age, was the arrival of the Achaean-Mycenaeans around 1200 BC. At about the end of the 13th century many of the Mycenaean settlements were afflicted with disaster, in the course of which Pylos was overwhelmed and Mycenae grievously harmed. A considerable dispersal of the mainland population took place, which resulted in the establishment of refugee settlements at widely separated points, from the Ionian Islands and Achaea in the west to Chios in the east. At least one substantial group of these people (the actual number is unknown), fled to Cyprus where their establishment in a number of places (including Enkomi, Kition and Kouklia) was of incalculable significance for the future development of the island.

The arrival of the newcomers was important in two respects: firstly, Cyprus' civilisation was transformed and eventually the ethnological

*Above:* Clay model terracota of red polished ware c. 2900BC from Kotchati
*Right:* "The Horned God" a young god bronze statue from the sanctuary of Enkomi, 12th cent. BC. Both Cyprus Museum

composition of the population changed. From their Peloponnesian home, the Achaean settlers introduced into the island not merely a language but names of places, institutions and cults. Secondly, the island turned towards the west and began to draw away from the east. It has, to date, followed the fortunes and misfortunes of the wider Greek world. This colonisation, it must be stressed, was a slow, peaceful process, achieved through successive waves of newcomers from the Aegean (including Crete, Chios and Asia Minor), and by the close of the 12th century Cyprus was developed into an integral part of the Hellenic world, where Greek was spoken and Greek culture was familiar. Both historians and poets spoke highly of the wealth and culture of the island under kings such as Kinyras, Onasagoras and Philokypros, King of Soloi who entertained Solon, the famous Athenian statesman and lawgiver in 570 BC. Thirdly while the process of Greek settlement was under way, the Mediterranean experienced troubled times. During the late 13th and 12th centuries adventurers known as *"Peoples of the Sea"* were roaming the coasts; Cyprus did not remain unaffected.

The **GEOMETRIC (IRON) AGE** c. 1050-750 which witnessed another so-called "Dark Age" between 1050 and 850, also saw the coming of new settlers. The Phoenicians arrived in the mid-9th century. Called *"Canaanites"* they were great seafarers and traders who were probably the first to explore, colonise and trade in the Mediterranean sea - they came from the Syrian/Lebanese coast. Kition and Amathus were to become Phoenician strongholds. Their temple of Astarte at Kition is one of the largest of its kind in the region. The mid-9th century therefore, saw a substantial revival of Cypriot culture and an increase in population.

The **ARCHAIC PERIOD** (750-475) witnessed the further prosperity of the island due to, amongst other factors, continued and extensive trade with the east and the Greek world. Salamis was probably one of the largest and most prosperous cities of the region, with a cosmopolitan culture (Greeks, Jews, Phoenicians and others) combining the exuberance and wealth of the Near East with Greek undertones.

One point that has to be stressed at the outset is the fact that due to the influx of the **Greeks** (especially) and **Phoenicians**, the older Cypriot inhabitants i.e. the indigenous population, called *"Eteocyprians"*, played only a secondary part in the life of the island. Yet their culture and language was never completely wiped out. The Archaic period was also marked by a swift succession of foreign overlords: Assyria (c.709-c.660), Egypt (c.560-c.545) and Persia from 545 to 333.

The **ASSYRIAN** occupation proved very brief - it was aimed primarily at the defence of its western borders along the coast of Syria and southern Asia Minor. It appears that political subjugation was not intended. The **Egyptian** hold was even shorter. Yet they hold the distinction of being the first to capture the island by recourse to war.

The destiny of Cyprus was henceforth to depend on the rising Persian empire. At the time of the expedition of King Cyrus II the Elder, against Babylon in 538, the Cypriots voluntarily placed their forces at his disposal. The island soon became the western seaward link of this great empire. The Cypriot kings were obliged to pay tribute to the Persians and to supply them with an army and ships for their foreign campaigns.

Internally, the island was organised (during the Archaic period) into autonomous city-kingdoms; seven, and later ten (Salamis, Kition, Soloi, Paphos, Kourion, Lapithos, Kyrenia, Marion, Amathus and Tamassus), are mentioned in Assyrian documents. They grew prosperous and had wide-ranging commercial connections; moreover, towards the end of the 6th century they began to strike their own coinage. However, **Persian** domination was another turning point in the development of the island. During the whole of the 5th century Cyprus joined in a panhellenic struggle for freedom, an event which had far-reaching political effects.

The Greek consciousness of the Cypriots was awakened and closer political and cultural contacts developed between the Greek mainland and Cyprus. It was in this atmosphere that the great king of Salamis **Evagoras I**, appeared on the scene of Cypriot politics, as an advocate of the panhellenic ideals of freedom and Greek culture. For 40 years (from 411 to around 371 BC), Evagora's fate was also the destiny of Cyprus. He fought the Persians (circa 390 to 380) with exceptional bravery against vastly superior odds. Yet, like the earlier Onesilos revolt of 499-98 (when the Ionians revolted against the Persians, all the tiny kingdoms of Cyprus, except Amathus, joined them), internal discord (in part due to the cosmopolitan composition of its cities) and fighting against a more powerful opponent proved decisive.

A point that needs to be mentioned is that under the Persians, satisfactory progress was made in the arts and general culture of the island. In fact, a particular style in sculpture, the so-called "Cypriot character", appeared and made some headway.

Also, some explanation of the island's religious beliefs and practices should be given. The beliefs of archaic Cyprus remain obscure, but the concept of fertility (as shown by scores of human figurines) was evidently paramount. Greater foreign influence is evident during the late Bronze Age when a Syrian type of female figurine is often described as the "Astarte" type, taking the name of the eastern mother goddess. Sanctuary remains are also of this period. During the years 750 to c.325 (the Archaic and Classical eras) the principal deity was the Great Mother Goddess. She was identified above all with **Aphrodite the Cypriot**, goddess par excellence, who was already described as "*the Cyprian*" in the 8th century poems of Homer and in the later works of Hesiod. Aphrodite's sanctuary at Old Paphos was the chief religious centre of the island and famous throughout the ancient Mediterranean world. Dedications to her indicate that she was also known as "*the Paphian*" and "*the Lady*". From the many female figures found it is clear that the worship of a fertility goddess remained supreme in Cyprus. Hylates and perhaps the deified Kinyras, the legendary founder and first kingdom of Paphos, were male gods much revered on the island.

The **PHOENICIANS** also introduced their own deities - the goddesses Astarte and Anat and the gods Baal, Eshmoun, Reshef, Mikal, Melquart and Shed. Egyptian cults were also initiated into the island by the Phoenicians - long before the time of Egyptian rule.

It must be noted that in the Archaic and Classical periods the sanctuaries were hives of activity. Here the gods were believed to be present and even to participate in the sacred banquets accompanied by ritual dancing celebrated in their honour. The priests wore animal and humanlike masks, animals (and at times humans) were sacrificed,

*Left:* Four-sided bronze stand. This shows a worker carrying an ingot of copper, a main trading commodity in ancient Cyprus.

*Right:* Bearded youth - head of a statue  c. 500BC  Cyprus Museum

*Above:* Ivory draughts box from Engomi - late bronze age - showing a hunting scene.

*Right:* Silver coin of Salamis produced by King Evagoras I with his name appearing in both Egyptian script and Greek alphabet  - Obverse shows Hercules wearing a lion skin.  On the reverse is a seated goat.  Cyprus Museum libations were offered and incense burnt. During the 4th century Greek cults became widespread in the island. Also around this time Cypriot and Phoenician gods and goddesses started to become identified with Greek deities. Thus the Cypriot Hylates and the Phoenician Reshef became identified with the Greek Apollo. It is also probable that Zeus became the principal god - at least this was the case at Salamis. Nevertheless, towards the close of the 4th century some kings made great efforts to Hellenise their kingdoms and in so doing propagated Greek sects.

Ptolemaic rule (294-58 BC) naturally affected Cyprus' religious institutions. For 200 years or so of this rule the governor or *"strategos"* (general) received the title of High Priest. This enabled him to collect the revenues from all the sanctuaries and so enrich the royal treasury. The worship of the ruling Ptolemy, the *"Dynastic-Cult"*, became of prime importance and a special organisation known as the **"Koinon ton Kyprion"** (confederation of Cypriots) was set up to promote it. Being Greeks themselves the Ptolemies encouraged Greek cults. Moreover, existing practices were rarely interfered with and worship continued at many of the traditional open sanctuaries and rustic shrines.

With the arrival of the **Romans** (58 BC- AD 330) the dynastic cult gave way to the *"Imperial Cult"*. The "Koinon" became an officially recognised national organisation (centrally based at the sanctuary of Aphrodite), whose principal function was to promote the worship of the Roman Emperors. Some of the traditional rites survived as did the worship of Greek deities. The cult of the Paphian Aphrodite the Goddess of Love and Beauty, remained pre-eminent. Aphrodite, was identified as Venus by the Romans. Of paramount importance was the spread of Christianity during the 1st century AD. The apostles **Paul** and **Barnabas** (a native of Cyprus named Joseph), attended by the latters' young relative **John Mark**, proceeded in AD 45-46 on a teaching mission to proclaim the message of salvation to Jews and Gentiles. From Seleucia they crossed to Salamis and they eventually arrived in Paphos presumably via Kition, Amathus and Kourion. It was in Paphos that the Roman Governor was converted to Christianity. An aristocrat from Rome he was a highly educated person and a very influential man. He was an authority in matters of the physical sciences, open-minded and well-disposed towards philosophy and theology.

According to tradition and before meeting **Sergius Paulus**, Paul had received from the town's Jews[4] the customary 40 stripes save one. A column of white stone about seven feet high is still pointed out to travellers as being the one to which he is said to have been tied for the occasion. From the Holy Bible we learn that the apostles encountered a

---

(4) Excluding 'Hellenised' and 'Crypto' Jews the Jewish community in Cyprus, about this time, numbered between 12,000 and 15,000

Two coins from Paphos showing the Temple of Aphrodite at Paleapaphos (Kouklia)

**MAP OF CYPRUS**

Ancient sites of the island
— Ancient place names are shown in brackets where they coincide with a modern name.

KARPAS

Rizokarpaso
Lythrankomi
Ovgoros
Phlamoudhi
Gastria (Alaas)
Ayios Iakovos
Gypsos
Arnoudhi
Salamis
FAMAGUSTA
Enkomi
Platani
Psilatos
Kaloosidha
Ormidhia
LARNACA (Kition)
Vatyii
Pyla
Arsos
Athienou (Golgoi)
Dhali (Idalion)
Alambra
Hala Sultan Tekke
Arpera
Maroni
Margi
Khirokitia
Kotchati
Kalavassos
Amathus
LIMASSOL
Troulli
Ayios Epiktitos
Kythrea
KYRENIA MTS
NICOSIA
(Ayia Paraskevi)
Vounous
Kazaphani
Karmi
KYRENIA
Lapithos
Philia
Meniko
Akaki
Politiko (Tamassos)
Polemidhia
Erimi
Sotira
Kourion
Episkopi (Phaneromeni)
TROODOS
MOUNTAINS
Salamiou
Koukila (Paleapaphos)
Vasilia
Myrtou (Pigadhes)
Ayia Irini
Morphou
Vouni
Soli
Kalydata
Ambelikou
Mavrovouni
Pctamos tou Kambou
Pomos
Polis (Marion)
AKAMAS
Goudhi
Souskiou
Peyia
Lemba
Maa
PAPHOS (Nea Paphos)

Petra tou Romiou
(Aphrodite's Birthplace)

27

A painting illustrating the famous visit to Paphos of St. Paul and St. Barnabas, preaching the new faith to the Roman Governor. St. Paul is shown blinding Elymas in the presence of the Governor who then became the first Roman official to be converted to Christianity.

sorcerer or magus, a Jew who posed as a prophet, called Bar-Jesus. He withstood them and sought to turn aside the Governor from the new faith. Paul's anger reached boiling point and calling him an "enemy of righteousness" he cast a spell on Bar-Jesus and blinded him. The Governor was truly converted and following the conversion of Constantine the Roman Emperor in AD 313, christianity was henceforth fully embraced by the Cypriots. In the late 4th century it became the official religion of the Roman Empire, and c. 488 the Church of Cyprus was declared autocephalus (independent), a position maintained to this very day.

So much for the development of religion. We must now revert back to the 5th and 4th centuries BC. Throughout the Classical period (c. 475 - 325 BC), Cyprus was poised between Greece and Persia. The failure of the Ionian revolt (499-98), the activities of the Athenian statesman and commander Kimon (485-65), and the heroics of Evagoras I of Salamis all failed to wrest Cyprus permanently from the vice-like grip of Persia. That honour belonged to **Alexander the Great**, King of Macedonia, leader of the Greeks and eventually conqueror of the world. Following Alexander's victory over the Persians at Issus in 333 BC, the Cypriot cities voluntarily submitted to him. Then they helped Alexander take Tyre in 332; this finally set the seal on any hopes the Phoenicians had of dominating Cyprus. Persian control over the island was finally brought to an end. Alexander left the Cypriot kings (pro-Persian and Phoenician were restricted) in undisputed possession of their little kingdoms, honoured them with his friendship and, later on, entrusted them with important duties. Thus Stasanor of Soloi became governor of the Persian province of Drangiana, and other kings were well spoken of. The only administrative change of any significance was that Cyprus became part of the huge system of Alexandrine coinage. Another point of major importance was that commercial relations between the Greek mainland, particularly Athens, and Cyprus were very active. The island's economy reached new heights.

Following Alexander's premature death in 323 BC, his generals struggling to inherit his empire, used the island as a battleground and a number of city kingdoms were destroyed. After 29 bitter years, Ptolemy, one of the seven bodyguards of Alexander, triumphed over Antigonus and annexed Cyprus in 294 BC and claimed Egypt also as his share. He described the island as the "gateway to Phoenicia".

During this period (it lasted for 236 years) Cyprus achieved a fairly high degree of culture and prosperity, with the cities preserving a certain amount of autonomy - similar to the duties performed by local government bodies or communal chambers today. In practice therefore, the masters of the cities were the commanders of the garrisons (strategoi) who gave their orders to the elected organs of native government. The island was however administered by viceroys and regarded as one of the most valuable possessions of the large Hellenistic monarchy of Egypt. The revenues which the Ptolemies drew from Cyprus were enormous. Hence came the copper and corn that Egypt needed so much; here too were built many ships for the Egyptian navy and mercantile fleet. The point that needs to be emphasised is the fact that even though the city kingdoms finally disappeared the Cypriots participated in the regulation of their cultural affairs. Besides "To koinon ton Kyprion", the "League of the Cypriots", a federation of semi-autonomous communities, was a powerful force making for cohesion. The Phoenicians and all other minorities were tolerated but Cyprus became artistically-orientated to the Hellenistic world. This was understandable since the rulers were Macedonian Greeks themselves.

For nearly 400 years (58 BC - AD 330) the **Romans** were the island's rulers although for a brief period, probably from 47 BC to the death of Cleopatra in 30 BC, Cyprus returned to Ptolemaic rule. It is interesting to recall that Mark Anthony, who met Cleopatra at Tarsus in 41 BC and married her at Antioch four years later, presented Cyprus to his wife and her sister Arsinoe because it was, he explained, "supreme in beauty and well above all other places".

Cyprus became part of the province of Cilicia[5] itself Roman since 103 BC and governed by a proconsul. Porcius Marcus Cato became Cyprus' first administrator. During Emperor Octavian's reign (called Augustus from 27 BC) the island became first an imperial province (27 BC) and then, in 22 BC, a senatorial province again governed by a proconsul. Administratively, Cyprus was organised in four districts - Paphos in the west, Amathus in the south, Salamis in the east and Lapithos on the north. Salamis was regarded by the Romans as the commercial centre of Cyprus whilst Paphos was the seat of government (as it had been since early in the 2nd century) under the name of *"Augusta Claudia Flavia"*.

As already pointed out the conversion of Sergius Paulus the Roman proconsul to christianity by the apostles around AD 46 marked the beginning of the penetration of the new religion into the Roman administration. This was an important event which was thereafter accompanied by radical changes in the life of the Cypriots. The island's history, so deeply affected by the new faith, was to be dominated thereafter by religion. In spite of the evident difficulties (for example, the island's Jews were faithful to their religion and system of worship and the Greeks and Phoenicians had their own deeply entrenched deities and methods of worship), the spread of christianity continued steadily during the first three centuries of our era. By the fourth century the new faith had an undisputed dominance. Among those who contributed to this triumph were: Lazarus, who according to religious writings was raised from the dead by Jesus Christ, and later became the patron saint of Larnaca; Spyridon of Tremithus, who took part in the First Ecumenical Council in 325; and St. Epiphanius of Constantia (Salamis) who though not a native of Cyprus distinguished himself as a scholar and played an important part in the various church controversies of the 4th century.

The religious zeal of the Cypriots expressed itself in the establishment of monasteries, the building of churches and the beautification of both with frescoes and icons of the highest artistry. The Byzantine period (330-1191) and the years immediately following are notable in that respect. Important frescoes that survive in the island dating from the 11th century: St. Nicholas of the Roof (tis stegis) in Kakopetria; St. Mary of Araka in the Pitsilia region; St. Neophytos Monastery in Paphos, and so forth.

If we carry the religious theme further it must be stressed that Barnabas visited Cyprus again - once more accompanied by Mark. He was martyred by the Jews in Salamis. Did Elymas (Bar-Jesus), still bitter over his earlier defeat by Paul, incite the Jews himself? Evidence is scanty but the possibilities are certainly there. What is not disputed is that Mark

---

(5) In 58 BC. Cilicia is situated on the southern coast of Asia Minor, now modern Turkey.

*Above:* Salamis, the greatest of all Cypriot kingdoms. This picture shows the gymnasium and public baths

*Right:* Part of the large statue of Emperor Septimius Severus found at Kythrea, at the Cyprus Museum.

*Below*: Roman period mosaic floor (2nd-3rd cent. AD) depicting the Love story/Tragedy of Pyramos and Thisbe. From the House of Dionysos in Paphos.

buried his 'uncle' around June 57, with a copy of the Gospel of St. Matthew, which Barnabas always carried with him. The discovery of the tomb by Anthimius, Archbishop of Constantia, in the reign of Zeno (474-91) proved to be a unique blessing to the church of Cyprus.

The island was found to be, like Syrian Antioch (the cradle of gentile Christianity) an apostolic foundation and hence in c.488 its church became autonomous. The Cypriot church therefore is one of the oldest *"autocephalus and isotimous"* (independent and equal) constituent bodies of the Holy Orthodox Eastern Church. It is senior by hundreds of years to the churches of Russia and Greece and junior only to the four earlier Patriarchates of Constantinople, Alexandria, Antioch and Jerusalem. To this day the Archbishop signs with red ink (a distinction which none but the Emperor enjoyed), wears a purple cloak at church festivals and carries an imperial sceptre instead of a pastoral staff.

Religion and survival undertones were written all over the Jewish rebellion of AD 115-17. The first signs of the rising consisted of clashes between Jews and Greeks in Alexandria and Cyrene. The revolt soon gathered momentum to the extent that it became an open war encompassing Libya, Cyrenaica, Egypt, Cyprus and Mesopotamia. In Cyprus where the Jews were numerous (probably around 15,000) and wealthy, the revolt was headed by one named Artemion (or Arteminius), a person whom we know nothing about.

The causes of the revolt in the island are not entirely clear: apparently, it was due in part to the friction between Jews and non-Jews (gentiles) and not necessarily to their relations with the Roman administration. Yet, in none of the references to the Cypriot Jews during the 1st century is there any hint of friction at any time between them and the Greeks. However, covert hostility must have existed and seems to have been as old as the Apostle's missionary journey to Cyprus in 45-46. Dio Cassius[6] whose father was governor of Cilicia (which included Cyprus), wrote that the Jews were strong enough to massacre their neighbours. His assertion however, that the number murdered amounted to 240,000 is without doubt a ludicrous exaggeration. What is not disputed is the fact that Salamis was destroyed and for a time Artemion controlled a large part of Cyprus. Moreover, there must have been heavy losses on both sides. If we say that around 24,000 died or were unaccounted for then perhaps it will be nearer the truth. Obviously, the margin of error in such guesswork is enormous. We cannot even be certain of the exact number of Jews in Cyprus since the literary evidence is spotty and the archaeological data almost nil. Dio Cassius of course, is supported by other ancient sources

---

(6) Greek historian born c.155 who became a Roman Senator and Consul. He died in AD 235

(the writings of Orosius and Eusebius) which point out that the Jews massacred the inhabitants of Salamis and destroyed the city. In fact, horrible scenes had desolated the peaceful island of Cyprus. Salamis was a great city and it has been calculated that the then existing aqueduct could serve some 120,000 inhabitants. So, was the death toll higher than our estimated figure? Moreover, towns and villages, especially in the northeastern part of the island, suffered extensively. Lapithos and the Karpass district witnessed several bloody clashes, and at Soloi, where a sizeable Jewish community was found, the dedication of a statue to Emperor Trajan between 115 and his death (August 117) suggests that he had inaugurated the repair of damage caused by the revolt. In another honorific inscription, Hadrian was hailed as 'Benefactor of the Salaminians and Saviour of the World.'

The revolt therefore appears to have come out of the blue without prelude or reason. It was put down with bitter severity by the able General Marcius Turbo. A law was passed according to which no Jew might approach the island even if he suffered shipwreck on its coast. The apparent slaughter and consequent emigration must have reduced the island's Jewish population by over 50%. After the rebellion there followed a period of repression and probably the virtual end of the great period of Jewish history in Cyprus - the next distinct stage is after the1570s. No details are preserved of the severity or measures taken against the insurgents. We can only surmise that the Romans repeated their practising methods and exacted reprisals. No doubt the Jewish population of Cyprus was depleted. Yet a thriving Jewish community still lived peacefully in towns and villages - with the exception of the district surrounding Salamis. It is also important to note that some called "Crypto" or "Hellenised Jews", may have embraced the christian faith in order to save their lives but in practice they adhered to their own religious beliefs.

The suppression of the Jewish insurrection was the sole recorded military operation in the history of Roman Cyprus. The tranquillity of the island was again disturbed in 269. The Goths, a Germanic people from the Western Black Sea area, for centuries harassed and proved an embarrassment to the Roman Empire. After their failure in Moesia (part of present day Bulgaria), a section of their fleet made a series of raids through the Aegean, attacking Greece, the Cyclades, Crete, Rhodes and then Cyprus. The damage to the island however was slight and the expedition, ravaged by disease, eventually came to a sudden end.

Further minor incidents with several Byzantine rulers, failed to bring any significant changes to the island. However, its cities were repeatedly ruined by seismic convulsions. Especially serious were those of 15 BC which destroyed Paphos, and AD 76-77 when several cities, amongst them Salamis and Paphos, suffered extensive damage.Like their predecessors, the Romans exacted great booty from the island. However, the material lot of the Cypriot showed a slight improvement. As in their other provinces the Romans paid great attention to the construction of gymnasia and theatres and of course, road building. Thus they encircled the main part of the island with a road running from Salamis in the east diagonally to Kyrenia in the north and from there roughly following the west and south coasts round, and so back to Salamis. Administratively, the cities had their own municipal institutions and were, generally speaking, composed of a *'vouli'* (council) a *'demos'* (popular assembly) and a *'gerousia'* (council of elders).

Before we proceed with the Byzantine period we must round-off our historical introduction by saying something about the 'Cypriot agriculturalist' or 'Cypriot food-raiser' - enough has been written on other issues such as religion, commerce, system of administration and the problems faced by all incoming rulers: In Cyprus' early days the inhabitants were largely self-sufficient, drinking water rather than wine and growing for themselves all they needed to survive. In later years the principal cereal crop grown was wheat, with barley, mainly used for animal fodder, the next largest. Peas, beans, onions and cabbages were also extensively grown. Olives were very important providing not only the principal edible fat but also soap and lamp oil. The honey of Cyprus had a great reputation and its wax was valued as a filler in ointments and remedies for medicines, cooking, cosmetics, perfumes and many other purposes.

Flax was usually raised for manufacture into linen. Cattle were used mainly as draught animals, though some cows were kept for milk and cheese; goats were raised mainly for milk, meat, skin and hair; sheep for their wool, though some mutton was eaten and pigs were the main meat producers.

Ownership of land was very widely dispersed but agriculture remained on the whole in a flourishing condition during the first centuries AD.

However, a sizeable number were landless and could not therefore furnish their basic necessities. During the Roman ascendancy, at least, cattle and vegetable markets (forums boarium and holitorium), were of great importance. In this situation craftsmen and shopkeepers flourished by providing manufactured articles of necessity. Hundreds of other things were also needed by a farming community. Someone had to build houses, temples, bridges, others had to kill animals and sell the meat (where domestic animals were not available), while others had to make and sell cooking utensils, shoes, carts and so forth.

From 330 to 1191 Cyprus was part of the **BYZANTINE** complex. Several events are worth recording:

(1) The earthquakes of 332 and 342 which destroyed Salamis, Paphos (not rebuilt for some time) and the other cities and the 30 to 40 year drought and famine of the first half of the 4th century, when Cyprus was depopulated, left their ugly scars on the island. Salamis was rebuilt a few years later through the material aid given by Constantine, the son and heir to Constantine the Great who renamed the city, Constantia. The new city replaced Paphos as the island's capital and became the seat of the first bishop who thus became Archbishop of Cyprus. His name was **Epiphanius** (later to become Saint Epiphanius) and he led the Cypriot church from 368 to 403.

(2) Around the year 488 Emperor Zeno the Isaurian declared the Cyprus Church *autocephalous*. We have already mentioned the privileges pertaining to the Archbishop. After two centuries the independence of the Church of Cyprus was again confirmed. Justinian II, in his struggle with the Arabs, broke the compact of 689 between Byzantium and Islam by which the tribute of Cyprus was divided and in 691 removed a large proportion of the island's population to the Hellespont (Dardenelles) and other districts in the south and west of Asia Minor. Just as Justinian I had founded the city Nova (New or Nea) Justiniana in the previous century, so in 691 Justinian II founded the city of Nea Justinianopoulis for the Cypriots. The synod[7] (end of 691 to September 692) recognised the Metropolitan of Cyprus, now Bishop of Nea Justinianopoulis, as Metropolitan of the Hellespont and enacted that he should enjoy the same independence of the patriarch as in Cyprus. Once again, therefore, the autocephaly of the Church of Cyprus and the prerogatives of its Archbishop were recognised and definitely asserted.Before the close of the century Cyprus was repeopled when most of the inhabitants of Nova Justinianopoulis were sent back to the island by Leontius, the new Emperor.

(3) Under the Byzantine Empire, Cyprus was a proconsulship and it enjoyed considerable prosperity. However, the **Arab raids** of the 7th to the 10th centuries brought great destruction and the island's development was retarded. Especially severe were those of 632, 647-49, 653, 726, 743, 747, 772-73, 790 and 806. Very briefly the raid of 632 was presumably led by Abu Bakr (father-in-law and successor of the Prophet Mohammed), and he obtained temporary possession of Kition. The one of 647-49 was led by Muawiya I, the Emir of Syria, who commanded a large fleet. In his entourage was Umm Haram, a kin of the Prophet. Alleged to have been attacked by local bandits she fell from her mule and died. Her burial place, now a shrine called

---

(7) Called the Trullan Council because it met in the dome of the Palace of Constantinople. It sanctioned some 102 decrees.

*Left:* One of the "Lambousa Treasures" from the Kyrenia region, a silver plate depicting the marriage of David and Michal. King Saul, in the middle, blessed them. c. 627-630 AD - Cyprus Museum

*Right:* The 7th century AD gold plated cross from Lamboussa

Both at the Cyprus Museum

'*Hala Sultan Tekke*' has become one the most revered sanctuaries of the Islamic faith. So much so that the wife of King Husein of the Hejaz[8] who died in 1930, was buried within its precincts.

In 653 Muawiya dispatched a second but smaller force under Abu'l-Awar. The raiders carried out a systematic policy of senseless cruelty, brutality and destruction. A garrison established in the island was eventually withdrawn around 682 by Caliph Yazid (son of Muawiya I), but it appears that Cyprus continued to pay some form of tribute. From 653 on and for about a generation, very little is heard about Cyprus. It is probable that the island, having been twice plundered within a few years, offered little prospect of further booty; moreover, the tribute seems to have been continuously collected by the Arab authorities. However, there were fresh raids in 726, 743 and 747. In 772-73 it is recorded that the raiders carried off the governor whom they eventually ransomed. Of the 790 raid few details are preserved; one however records a battle which took place in the gulf of Attalia.

Perhaps the most destructive was the one led by Khalif Harum-ar-Rashid in 806. Alleging that the Cypriots had violated the treaty of neutrality which for years had regulated their relations with both Byzantium and Islam, the Arabs landed in Cyprus, laid waste the island and took back to Ragga (a town on the Euphrates) a considerable number of prisoners, including the Archbishop ('*Bishop of Cyprus*') other ecclesiastics and many archons. Once the neutrality treaty was renewed most of them were allowed to return. It is interesting to record that the bishop was ransomed for 2,000 dinars. For those years a considerable amount of money!

---

(8) Region of west Arabia, encompassing Mecca and Medina- major centres of Islam

*Above right:* Details of a mosaic from Kanakaria Church, Lythrankomi, of Jesus as a child. 6th cent.

*Above left:* 6th cent mosaic of Mary and the Child from Panayia Angeloktisti-Kiti.

*Below:* Saint Barnabas monastery first built in 488 - one of Cyprus' most important and revered Greek Orthodox Churches.

In 965, **Emperor Nicephorus Phokas** sent General Nikitas Chalcutzes to Cyprus to repel the Arab raiders once and for all. The Byzantines achieved the final conquest of the island with the defeat of the Egyptian fleet in August 965. Cyprus soon recovered from the suffering inflicted on her by the Arab raids and was turned quietly into a Byzantine '*theme*' or military province.

The Arabs it may be noted, never made any organised attempt to become permanent rulers of Cyprus. They were content with the loot and prisoners their raids yielded. The attacks however caused a marked movement of the population from the coastal towns to the interior of the island, where they sought refuge in caves and fortifications. Thus the three principal castles on the Kyrenia range, St. Hilarion, Kantara and Buffavento were erected during the Arab raids as a defence against the '*barbarian*' onslaughts. Yet, in spite of all these difficulties, Cyprus was still considered a place of refuge by the Christians of Syria and Palestine

(4)  Cyprus was often used as a place of banishment by both the Roman and Byzantine Emperors - not that it hasn't been practiced in later years! During their long hegemony, the Romans made Cyprus a place for '*probationary correction*'. Morally corrupted (or perverts) nobles and senior citizens of Roman society, having disgusted the not-so-sensitive susceptibilities of their professed morality were sent to Paphos "*to finish their sensual studies*". The sanctuaries of the capital were certainly notorious for such moral issues.

Similarly, during the iconoclast persecutions, Cyprus became a place of refuge for iconodule monks. In fact Constantine V, given the nickname of '*copronymous*', gave icon-worshipping monks and nuns the alternative of marrying or being blinded and sent to Cyprus. It must be noted that veneration of icons, previously encouraged was first prohibited by Emperor Leo III (founder of the Isaurian dynasty) in 730 and the resulting persecutions reached their peak in the 740s under Constantine V. Following an acute conflict, the final restoration of icon veneration, promulgated in 843, is still celebrated as the Feast of Orthodoxy in the Eastern Church.

(5)  The two risings of 1042 and 1092 and the attacks on the island which began in 1156 were also significant events. Both risings were attempts by local governors to proclaim Cyprus independent. The first was led by Thephilos Eroticos and the second by Rhapsomates. Both revolts had been planned, allegedly in collaboration with Tzachas, the Emir of Smyrna who had been raiding the Aegean islands and both had been vigorously suppressed by the Grand Duke John Ducas, brother-in-law of Emperor Alexios Comnenos. Nicosia, which played an important part in the second revolt, became the island's capital in the 11th century.

St. Hilarion Castle, a Lusignan fortress extended from an original Byzantine castle.

In 1156, Reynald of Chatillon (husband of Constance, Norman Princess of Antioch since 1153), together with the Armenian Prince Thoros, led a devastating and unprovoked attack on Cyprus from Armeno-Cilicia in southern Asia Minor. It failed. Further raids by Arab bandits in 1158 also proved abortive.

The year 1184 was to prove a turning point in the fortunes of Cyprus. **Isaac Ducas Comnenos**, 'great nephew' of Emperor Manuel Comnenos (the name of a Byzantine family which from 1057 to 1059 and 1081 to 1185 occupied the throne of Constantinople) arrived on the island with a small body of armed men and on the basis of forged documents claimed to be its first governor - just sent out by the Byzantine Emperor. His deception was highly successful and he established himself under the high-sounding title of *'Emperor of Cyprus'*. He ruled the island with great cruelty. His reign ended more by accident than by design - in 1191.

Meanwhile in 1189 **Richard I** was anointed King of England and in the following year he set out for the Holy Land in that remarkable endeavour, semi-feudal, semi-religious but wholly adventurous, known as the Third Crusade. From Lyons they moved to Sicily and after a delay of around six months the crusaders set sail for Jerusalem on 10 April 1191. When they dropped anchor at Crete on 17 April, it was found that 25 transport ships were missing - due to a storm five days earlier. On 18 April they set off for Rhodes where Richard made enquiries about Isaac Comnenos the self-styled emperor of Cyprus. Richard was told that Isaac did everything he could to hold up supplies to the Holy Land and that his missing ships had been driven by the great storm to the island. And so they were.

Among the ships unaccounted for were the three dromonds that carried his affianced bride **Berengaria of Navarre**, his favourite sister

Joan, widow of William the Good of Sicily, the greater part of his treasure and the Great Seal. As it turned out the missing ships had been wrecked trying to put into the port of Limassol (then west of Amathus), and Roger Malcael, the Vice-Chancellor, had been drowned with the Seal hanging round his neck. Those who managed to struggle ashore were disarmed, robbed of their possessions and imprisoned but the ship carrying the Royal ladies had managed to keep clear of the rocks and had put out to sea again in fear of Isaac.

Richard *'Coeur de Lion'* who stayed ten days in Rhodes set sail for Cyprus and the island was sighted distinctly on Sunday 6 May 1191. On the following day Richard sent a courteous message to Isaac requesting him to make amends for all the evil done to the shipwrecked pilgrims. His messengers were insulted by Isaac who then amassed troops on the shore between Richard's fleet and the fortified town beyond. The King's order was *'aux armes'* (to arms). After a brief skirmish the Anglo-Normans marched into the town and on the following day Richard and around 50 knights made a surprise attack on Isaac's camp. The islanders were poor soldiers, badly armed and badly trained and were certainly no match for Richard's men. The *'Griffons'* (a Crusader-Latin term for Greeks) were annihilated but Isaac escaped on his fleet Arab courser 'Fauvel'. The chase of Isaac and the conquest of Cyprus, which was regarded as a *fait accompli* by the crusaders, was temporarily halted.

On 11 May allied crusaders, including Guy de Lusignan who later helped Richard defeat Isaac, had arrived to do homage to Richard and to seek his support against the political manoeuvres of Phillip II 'Augustus' King of France. On 12 May, the king celebrated his marriage to Berengaria in the chapel of St. George in the Limassol area. The ceremony was conducted by Nicholas, Richard's chaplain, and then, Berengaria was crowned Queen of England by John Fitz, Bishop of Evreux. It is worth noting that this was the first and last time (to date) that a queen has been crowned away from Britain.

By the end of May, Isaac capitulated after suffering a humiliating defeat at Tremethousa - the ancient Trimythos principal town of Mesaoria. The whole island, including the mountain fortresses of Buffavento, Kantara, Kyrenia and St. Hilarion (called "Dieu d'Amour" or "Castle of Love", by the Franks), and Isaac's stronghold (Kolossi Castle) were now in the hands of the English King.

Richard imposed a capital levy of 50% on the inhabitants and the government was then put in the hands of two Englishmen, Richard of Canville and Stephen of Turnham, who were instructed to send regular supplies of Cyprian wine, barley, wheat etc, to the Holy Land. The traditional laws and customs of the island were confirmed but as a sign of the new order all loyal 'Griffons' were required to shave off their beards ensuring that they looked like westerners. The booty extracted from Cyprus was vast and amongst the horses taken was *'Fauvel'* - Isaac's unmatched steed. On his return to England, it may be added, Richard dedicated Isaac's imperial standard to the memory of St. Edmond - Suffolk's martyr prince.

Our story soon takes a further twist. In early June, Richard sailed from Famagusta en route to Palestine. However, a revolt was brewing in the island and a relative of Isaac's, a monk, was being put up as the new *'emperor'*. Stephen of Turnham crushed this so-called rising and hanged the *'emperor'*. Some time after he reached Palestine, Richard, once more in need of money sold Cyprus to the Order of the **Knights Templars** for 100,000 byzants (or besants, the great gold currency of Europe in the Middle Ages), of which 40,000 was to be paid at once and the remainder by instalments.

The Templars however, soon found their new burden a heavy one. The war with Saladin was already absorbing all their energies in Syria and the small garrison they were able to maintain in Cyprus could barely cope with the impoverished Cypriots. Accordingly, in May 1192 (following the Easter massacre in Cyprus), they begged Richard to buy back the island on the same terms as he had sold it but the King, who was not prepared to lose the cash he had received, induced **Guy de Lusignan** to acquire it as some compensation for the loss of his Kingdom of Jerusalem. He took possession of his realm towards the end of May and for 297 years Cyprus became a **Frankish Kingdom**. Around 300 French noblemen, a personal guard of 200 and many soldiers accompanied Guy and settled in Cyprus - mainly in or around Nicosia.

Before we proceed with a brief discussion of the next epoch it must be emphasised that it had always been the fate of the island to be governed by a succession of rulers who were, generally speaking, different in race and religion from the bulk of the inhabitants. Taking the year 1192 (the beginning of the Frankish dynasty) as an illustration we find the following: by far the largest racial and religious element which went to make up the population of Cyprus was of course the Graeco-Cypriot; the Arabs in spite of their frequent incursions, did not settle in any great number (Arabic place-names are Kantara and Komi Kebir); the Syrians, were entirely fused with the Greeks (Syrianochori near Morphou bears witness to their presence even though it may have been an agricultural settlement); the Armenians, to this date, have never lost their national identity; the Maronites are still present in Cyprus; the Jacobites, Nestorians and Jews were also of some importance. Thus many races and languages were represented in the island. It has been said that *"the tongues of every nation under heaven are heard, read and talked and are taught in special schools"*.

*Above:* View of Kolossi Castle, Limassol.

*Left:* The Lusignan coat of arms seen on the eastern side of the castle. The centre shield depicts the emblems of the Kingdoms of Jerusalem, Cyprus and Armenia.

In economic terms the Cypriots, like the rest of Europe's peasantry, were harshly taxed and the peasants were not allowed to leave the land on which they worked. They were simply neglected by their imperial masters. Some managed to keep their land while others prospered as craftsmen, doctors or men of commerce. The majority toiled in the fields for long hours - they simply existed for there was no *'life'* for them. Politically, the situation was very much the same: only the rich and the professionals had any say in the running of the country and even then only on a local level. However, at least up to 1250, these were few and far between.

The Lusignans ruled the island on a feudal system - all privileges belonged to the nobles, with the masses reduced to serfdom. There were three main classes of landless native Cypriots:

(a) The lowest was that of the *'paroikoi'* who usually paid an annual tax and rendered the corvee (angaria) of two days' labour a week to their lords, who also took one third (triton) of their produce (excluding the seed) of the fields.

(b) Slightly higher in status were the *'perperiarii'* who were originally 'paroikoi' but had since become freemen. They also paid a similar tribute - a "landshare".

(c) At the apex were the *'lefteri'* (freedmen) or *'francomati'* who had been emancipated either on a lump payment to their lord or by his mere grace. Their lands and crops were free save for a small proportion, varying from 1/5 to 1/10, which was taken by their master.

Two other classes but in a different category to the three mentioned above were the *'White Venetians'* and the *'White Genoese'*. They were usually of Greek, Italian or Syrian origin who enjoyed the fruits of their labours and who usually paid only an annual tax to the island's overlord.

Another tax that should be pointed out is the *'stratia'* or hearth-tax. Although inherited by the Lusignans it was kept by them even though they suppressed the *'stratiotai'* (soldiers) for whose payment it was originally established.

It appears therefore that in the post-1192 years, the Cypriots were even worse off than before. The land was distributed among the barons and the knights to whom most of the Cypriots were attached as serfs. In the words of Porcacchi, a Venetian historian *"the tyranny of the masters grew so fiercely insolent that some bartered their slaves unblushingly for dogs and other animals"*. Harsh words! Objective historical evidence does not however support such a contention.

Ecclesiastically, the policy of the Franks was to effect the subordination of the autocephalus Orthodox Church of the people to the Church of the ruling race. Roman Catholic sees were endowed with the property taken from the Orthodox bishoprics and a series of acts of oppression culminated in 1260 (3 July), in the issue by Pope Alexander IV of the famous *'Constitutio Cypria'* or *'Bulla Cypria'*, whereby the Latin Archbishop was made the supreme ecclesiastic, chief of Latins and Orthodox alike. The Latins therefore persecuted the already established Greek Orthodox Church of the island, robbing it of its revenues, controlling its ordinations and 'burning' its bishops as heretics. Hence in 1231, thirteen Greek monks were condemned to death at Kantara because they refused to accept certain Catholic beliefs. Yet, the Orthodox Church thrived under persecution and its monasteries, particularly those in remote mountain ranges, where the painted churches may still be seen today, continued to prosper. The Church had undoubtedly become a

*Left*: The Lusignan Coat of Arms

*Above*: Henry II, a Lusignan King, 1285-1324. Silver coin showing the king enthroned and on the reverse, the Lion of the Kingdom.

focus for the islander's obstinate sense of Greekness in an alien Latin world.

To summarise the above, it may be said that in 1192 Cyprus commenced nearly 400 years of western but independent rule which saw the introduction of western feudalism into a land which had hitherto been Greek in its institutions and Orthodox in its religious beliefs. At every level Cyprus was horizontally divided into two separate and distinct sections. At the apex was the feudal class, mostly of French origin and the foreign merchants (the vast majority being Venetian and Genoese) who resided in the island (especially in Famagusta and Paphos), and at the bottom were the local Greek inhabitants who were serfs and labourers. The ruling class belonged to the Catholic church and the Greeks to the Orthodox one. The elite spoke mostly French and the masses spoke Greek.

Nevertheless, the lot of the Orthodox Cypriot was improved in the 15th century by the passionately Orthodox queen of John II, **Helen Paleologa**. Helen was the daughter of Theodore II Paleologus, ruler of the Morea. Her daughter Carlotta also followed a pro-Hellenic policy. Furthermore, rulers such as Hugh II and Hugh III (called 'the Great') in the 13th century, Hugh IV and Peter I in the 14th. century, contributed immensely towards the stability and financial prosperity of the island. In fact, Peter I, a benevolent monarch, attracted scores of Egyptian Jewish traders to the island by promising equal treatment to all minorities. However, rivalries, claims and counter-claims, feudal disputes and the inefficiency of other rulers, disturbed the island's growth.

And, there was worse to come. During the reign of Peter I (1359-69), Turkish vessels twice attacked the island. Taking advantage of the seriousness of the plague (the so called 'Black Death' of 1347-49 took the lives of something between 1/4 and 1/3 of the inhabitants), and of the king's absence in France, these vessels landed near Pentayia and then near Rizokarpaso. Looting and senseless destruction followed. The Cypriots retaliated and pursued their attackers across the seas to Anemouri. The place, directly to the north of Kyrenia, was pillaged and many hostages were taken, just as the Turks had done earlier.

Another significant event occurred in 1374. Following a quarrel dating from 1364, Famagusta, one of the richest and most cosmopolitan cities of the Mediterranean, was taken by the Genoese from Peter II. The *'emporium of the near east'* continued to be a colony of that commercial republic until 29 August 1464, when it was reconquered by James II, the illegitimate son of John II.

Further disasters were to follow in the 15th century. It was ravaged successively by plagues (the one of June 1438 resulted in many deaths and lasted for 17 months), locusts and droughts. In the midst of such misfortunes the Sultan of Egypt (the 'Mamelukes'), accusing the Cypriots of allowing the roaming Christian pirates to pillage the Saracens and then buying the booty declared war and invaded the island in 1426. The Cypriot forces were defeated at Khirokitia (7 July 1426); King Janus was taken prisoner and carried to Cairo. He obtained his freedom by consenting to a ransom plus an annual tribute of 5,000 ducats to the Sultan. To this day the site of the battle can be seen. It is called '*Kremmos tous Frangous*' - the cliff of the Franks. The island was then overrun by Egyptian troops; Nicosia, the capital was occupied, its fortifications destroyed and its palaces almost reduced to ruins. The churches, monasteries and houses of the Christians were pillaged and many of them were taken prisoner by the Saracens. All this was followed by the so-called *'peasants insurrection'* when many rose in rebellion; there was further misery for the inhabitants and much damage to Latin property. Leontios Machairas, secretary to King Janus, gave an excellent account in his 'Chronicle of Cyprus' of the fortunes of the Lusignans from 1359 to 1432. He wrote that "*they did many ill deeds which God would not endure*". 'The Chronicle of George Boustronios 1456-1489' (translated by R.M. Dawkins) distinctly shows the jealousies, petty rivalries, plots and counter-plots which existed at the time.

The apparent negative aspects of Frankish rule, which were in essence the norm for those years, were on the whole outweighed by the positive elements of that regime. To say that the period 1192 to 1489 was the most brilliant epoch of Cyprus' varied history is not very far from the truth. Sir Harry Luke in his remarkable study of 'Cyprus under the Turks' explains that in every aspect of medieval civilization the tiny island of

Cyprus played a distinguished part - its remarkable achievements in every domain of human activity invested it with an importance among the nations of Europe wholly out of proportion to its small size and population. For example:

(a)  its constitution was the model of that of a medieval feudal state;

(b)  the great legislative monument, the 'Assizes of Jerusalem', drawn up for Cyprus set the standard of medieval jurisprudence;

(c)  its men of letters, like Philippe de Novara and Philippe de Mezieres, were real pillars in the realm of literature;

(d)  in King Peter I (1359-69) Cyprus possessed one of the greatest crusader warriors the world has ever seen and in his Order of the Sword the most perfect expression of chivalrous ideals;

(e)  works were dedicated to its kings by writers such as Thomas Aquinas and Boccaccio. Moreover, there was a parallel literary beginning, albeit on a small scale, by the island's Greek inhabitants;

(f)  after the fall of Acre in 1291, Cyprus became the outpost of Latin Christendom in the east;

(g)  in the realm of commerce, Famagusta vied in importance with cities such as Venice;

(h)  the wealth and luxury of its inhabitants, especially in the 14th century, was the envy of all other peoples; and

(i)  Cyprus abounds in western medieval architecture - thanks to the Lusignans. The impressive Bellapais Abbey, the cathedrals of Nicosia and Famagusta and the castles of St. Hilarion, Buffavento and Kantara are excellent examples of Gothic architecture. However, it is a curious irony of history that nearly all such monuments are situated in what is, since 1974, the Turkish occupied northern zone.

The **Venetians** were the next masters of Cyprus. The island became first a *'protectorate'* in 1473 and then it passed into direct rule from 1489 to 1571. How did the 'protectorate' come about?

By a stroke of diplomatic craft the Venetians succeeded in inducing James II to marry **Katherine Cornaro**, daughter of the Venetian patrician Mark Cornaro. James did not long survive his marriage. After his death, which was attributed to poisoning, the republic managed to place Queen Katherine under a most humiliating tutelage. Furthermore, the crafty senators did not limit their acts to this unjustifiable interference. In 1489, having poisoned her son James III, they compelled Katherine to yield to them the kingdom of Cyprus.

The Abbey of Bellapais - founded in the 12th century by the Lusignans.

Especially in the early years, Venetian rule was characterised by total disinterestedness. The island's treasury was in a chronic state of depletion. This meant that all sorts of devices were used to 'ease' the situation. Thus serfs could purchase their freedom if the price was right and whole villages belonging to the royal domain were sold to private persons. These practices were also true of earlier administrations. Both instances gave ample opportunities for corrupt dealings by officials. With the exception of an ill-timed abortive rising in 1546, of which very little has been recorded and of another one in 1562, which was taking shape and was to be led by Diassorinos (O Didascalos - the Teacher), the history of Venetian rule was, in general terms, a mere chronicle of neglect. Perhaps the threat of war dented their appetite for any reforms. Droughts, locusts, floods and earthquakes added to the distress caused by misgovernment.

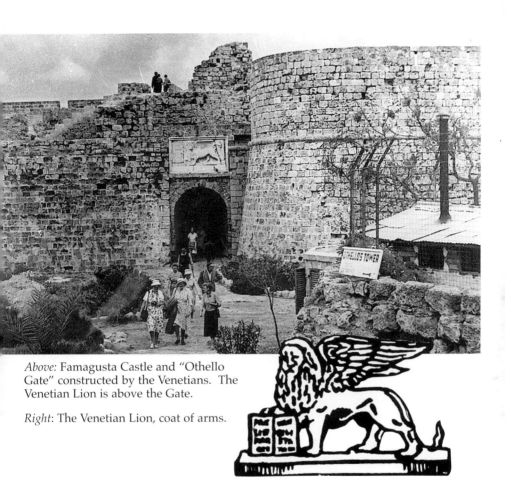

*Above:* Famagusta Castle and "Othello Gate" constructed by the Venetians. The Venetian Lion is above the Gate.

*Right:* The Venetian Lion, coat of arms.

Trade languished, manufactures practically ceased and all who could afford to do so emigrated. By the turn of the century there was a fall of around 15% in the island's population. Martin von Baumgarten, returning from his pilgrimage to the Holy Land and Mount Sinai, visited Cyprus from 8 February to 28 March 1508, and wrote rather harshly that *"all the inhabitants are slaves to the Venetians".* The persecution of the Orthodox Church was intensified and culture on the island sank to very low depths. According to a rather bitter statement by a Christian abbot, *"the Cypriots escaped from the grasp of the dog to fall into that of a lion".*

Towards the end of the Venetian era the administration became benign and tolerant. Population figures confirm that by 1570 the estimated number of inhabitants was 150,000. It must also be noted that since Cyprus was regarded primarily as a military post the Venetians built

A portrait of Queen Katherine Cornaro, the last Queen of Cyprus, believed to be a copy of a lost original Titian. Cyprus Museum

magnificent fortifications at Nicosia, Famagusta and elsewhere. They also added to the island's architectural heritage - built in 1530, the monastery at Ayia Napa is dedicated to the '*Holy Veil of Santa Veronica*'. It is believed that the original church, cut into a rock and partly underground, dates from the 8th or 9th centuries. A noble octagonal marble fountain surmounted by a dome, beside a sycamore, occupies the middle of the courtyard.

A balanced and carefully considered evaluation of the 82-year Venetian epoch shows that the island was seen primarily as a military outpost against the rising Ottomans[9], and that the new rulers made no real effort to help conciliate the inhabitants to whose welfare it was virtually indifferent. The Venetians who obtained the island mainly by extortion, shamefully lost it by their negligence, jealously and cursed pride of those to whom the preservation of it had been entrusted. One in particular, Sir Eugene Sinclitico (Count of Roucha and probably a westernised Hellene), commanding the land forces, was described by Alexander Drummond (a British diplomat) as "*a brave but empty madman*".

---

(9) The capture of Constantinople in 1453, which signalled the end of the Byzantine Empire, sent cold shivers across Christian states.

*Above:* Medieval map of Cyprus.

*Left:* Medieval map of Cyprus and surrounding area

A map of the walled city of Nicosia dated to around 1574. River Pedieos runs through the city.

# Chapter TWO

---

# THE ARRIVAL OF THE OTTOMANS

## 1570 – 1878

The Ottoman Empire under Suleiman I (1520-1566), its benevolent and far-sighted ruler, justifiably called *'The Great'* and *'The Magnificent'*, had reached the summit of its power and splendour.[1] He was however succeeded by a prince to whom his own national historians have given the epithets *'Selim the Sallow'* (Sari Selim) and *'Selim the Drunkard'* (Sarhos Selim). To western historians he is known as *'Selim the Sot'*. Selim II the eleventh Sultan of Turkey (1566-74) coveted Cyprus while he was the governor of Kutahya[2] in his father's lifetime. It seems he found the attraction of Cyprus' wines and liqueurs irresistible. He was consumed therefore with a feverish desire for the possession of the island; a feat which he accomplished in 1570-71.

The causes of the so-called 'Cyprus War' need no thorough examination here. Suffice to say that amongst these were the Turco-Venetian relations which showed a turn for the worse; palace friction at the Porte between the hawks (e.g. Joseph Nasi, a Jew who held in fief the island of Naxos and hoped for the investiture of Cyprus) and the doves (e.g. Mahomet Sokolli, the Grand Vizier); and economic issues etc. In February-March 1570, an emissary from the Porte arrived in Venice and threatened that if the island of Cyprus was not voluntarily surrendered it would be seized by force. The Venetians replied on 25 March that they were firmly resolved to defend their legitimate possessions and trusted in the *'justice of God'*.

By late May 1570 the Ottomans carefully prepared a well-equipped fleet at Constantinople. Under the command of **Mustapha Pasha** (*'Lala'* or *'Tutor'*), with Piale Pasha as admiral of the fleet, the Turkish invading force, consisting of well over 220 long vessels of which 160 were galleys, the rest galliots and about 80 ships of burthen of various kinds, set sail on 27 June. By 1 July 1570, Turkish troops began to disembark in Cyprus. The port of Limassol was soon overrun and on 9 September, after a siege of some 48 days, the island's capital was captured. A large number of Nicosia's inhabitants were put to the sword. In Famagusta, **Marco Antonio Bragadino** (1523-71) the town's leader and governor-general, led a desperate resistance against overwhelming odds. The city did not capitulate until nearly a year later, on 1 August 1571, after a blockade of ten months.

The peace terms appeared to be generous. All Italians were to be allowed to embark, with colours flying, for Crete together with any

---

(1) In brief, Constantinople was captured in 1453 (the siege lasted from 6 April to 29 May), Syria in 1516, Egypt in 1517 and Rhodes in 1522.

(2) Anatolian province in northwest Turkey - west of Ankara and south of Constantinople.

Map engraving showing the Ottoman naval blockade of Cyprus

Greeks, Albanians or others who wished to accompany them. Greeks who elected to stay behind would be guaranteed their personal liberty and property and would be given two years in which to decide whether they would remain permanently or not; those who then decided to leave would be given safe conduct to the country of their choice. The document, setting out these terms, was signed by Lala Mustapha Pasha and authenticated with the Sultan's seal. It was then returned to Bragadino and Baglioni, the two heroic leaders of the ten-month resistance, with a short note complimenting them on their courage and on their magnificent defence of the city. On 5 August, Bragadino sent word to Mustapha proposing to call and formally to present him with the keys of Famagusta. The Turkish leader replied that he would be delighted to receive him - and so he did! Suddenly however, his face clouded and his manner changed. In a mounting fury, he began hurling baseless allegations at the Christians accusing them of murdering Turkish prisoners, of concealing munitions and of not respecting the peace terms. Bragadino's lieutenants (Baglioni, Martinengo and Quirini) were executed in his presence but the treatment meted out to him topped all atrocities. After being subjected to the most excruciating public tortures, which he bore with great fortitude (Mustapha three times made him hold out his neck under the axe; he cut off his nose and ears, stretched him on the ground and trampled on him using all kinds of insults), he was flayed alive: his skin was stuffed with straw and suspended from the yard-arm of a vessel which was sent to Constantinople. His skin was then exposed in the prison in which the Christian prisoners and slaves were confined. It remained there for some years until redeemed by his brother Antony and his three sons, Mark, Hermolaus and Antony, for a great price and laid at the Church of St. Gregorio from where it was transferred in 1596 to its present resting place in the Church of Saints John and Paul in Venice.

Now that the killing had begun it was very hard to stop it. The island was sacked and plundered. The Italian historian, Paulo Paruta (1540-98), in his most lucid account of the sieges of Nicosia and Famagusta, recorded that the Turks destroyed whole villages and hamlets, churches and monasteries and committed other bestial and cruel acts - even against the dead![3] The undisciplined soldiery (at times on their own initiative) were spurred on to even greater atrocities because the siege of Famagusta was unpredictably costly;[4] amongst those killed were many prominent nobles and commanders.

It is worth noting that even though the whole island was henceforth under Turkish control, the Ottoman navy suffered a crushing defeat at Lepanto[5] on Sunday 7 October 1571, from the united fleet of the League - Venice, Spain, the Papacy and several smaller associated states. Don John of Austria (not yet 25 years of age), commanded the Christian fleet which overran the enemy in one of the greatest naval battles since Roman times. The legend of Ottoman invincibility at sea was shattered once and for all. Worse still, it had become clear that Sultan Selim had failed as leader of Islam against the *'unbelievers'*. Cut off by the Shiite schism from its Persian and Central Asian religious and cultural roots, the Ottoman Islamic empire, with its universalist claims was becoming a limited Turkish empire - no more than one of the several great military powers in Europe and Asia.

The League however secured a moral rather than a material victory in 1571. Following the abortive campaign by the Christian armada (a light-hearted and disjointed effort to reverse the Ottoman advance) in 1572, a treaty was signed at Constantinople on 7 March 1573. Besides paying a large indemnity and making various miscellaneous concessions, Venice ceded the island of Cyprus. Consequently only Crete, Paros and

---

(3) See C.D. Cobham 'Excerpta Cypria' 1908. Pages 107-19

(4) Venetian, other Christian and Islamic sources differ greatly over the number of men lost. It has been said that the Turks lost around 50,000. What is not disputed is that the death toll, on both sides, was very high.

(5) Now known as Navpaktos in the Corinthian Gulf.

*Above:* The siege of Nicosia by the invading Ottoman forces.

*Below:* An engraving depicting the torture and humiliation of Marco Antonio Bragadino, the heroic defender of Famagusta the Ionian islands remained in Venetian hands. The Cyprus war of 1570-73 was over. The Ottomans had lost a battle (Lepanto) but they had won the peace.

Cyprus remained in Turkish hands until 1878 - it was then conditionally ceded to Great Britain. For 307 years the Cypriot masses, once again, fared badly under their new rulers. Yet for a substantial section of the upper or ruling classes (especially those who acquiesced with the new administration) and of the higher clergy there were benefits (especially after 1660, as we shall see below) beyond their wildest expectations. Those who collaborated with the new regime (often called cryptochristians or '*linobambakoi*') were duly rewarded - some retained their land, others made successful false claims to land and property and others were simply '*moslemised*'.

What were the effects of conquest and settlement? We have already seen that a cross-section of Cypriot society either co-operated with the new regime or simply accepted it as a necessity which they hoped might have resulted in an improvement in their overall standard of living. Such hopes rarely materialised. We have also seen that the upper echelons (or 'archons') of Frankish, Italian and Greek society not only co-operated but were kept in their positions by the Turks in order to establish and solidify their rule. Secondly, and often forgotten, is the following: the ruin precipitated on some Venetian families was frightening. The Turkish war which consumed much Venetian wealth, underlined the hazards of engaging in trade in the Levant which was close to enemy territory. Some patricians (e.g. the large Cornaro, Pesaro and Giustinian families), experienced not only grave financial losses, but also the indignities of enslavement and they were forced to cut into their surviving resources by ransoming themselves and their families. Those who did not have the financial resources (just like a lot of Greeks) were reduced to extreme poverty and had to make a living as muleteers or pedlars.[6]

The third and vital issue concerns the demography of the island. Following the conquest, Cyprus' population showed a marked decline. Many were put to the sword and entire villages and hamlets were wiped out. Moreover, the Turks forced a large number of Greeks to resettle in Anatolia - mainly near Antalya. These were considered as hostages for the good behaviour of their compatriots. Other Greeks, rich enough to afford it and lucky enough to escape, fled to France and Italy. As though this was not enough the Turks carried out their plan of transplanting the island's population a step further.

---

(6) Sir G. Hill: A History of Cyprus (4 volumes). Volume 4. 1952. Page 1.

The Porte issued a decree on 9 April 1571 aimed at sending mainland Turks to Cyprus. The system applied was styled '*surgun*' (exile) but this population transfer was not generally speaking, imposed by force; in reality, it was effected by selecting those willing to be transplanted. Other documents also speak of such movements. According to the '*tahrir*' (census) of 1572, the new settlers numbered around 20,000. This included the permanent garrison - infantry (*janissaries*) and cavalry (*spahis*) - which numbered approximately 3,780. Bernard Lewis[7] a prominent historian, stresses that Ottoman records for the period immediately following the conquest contained several 'deportation' orders for the transfer of populations to Cyprus. They included Turkish peasants so that the countryside should not be exclusively Greek and Christian but partly Turkish and Muslim. There were also orders to transfer Turcoman tribes (Turkish pastoral nomads) from Anatolia, so that stock-raising and the supply of animals for food and transport should be safely in Muslim hands.

The Turks proceeded to institute a policy which directly created the so-called '*Cyprus Problem*'. It was very similar to that which the English government was pursuing, about the same time, in Ireland and it had similar results. This was the policy of '*transplantation*' - importing Moslem Turks, speaking a foreign language and practising a different religion, to form an ascendancy and help keep the native Greeks - the majority - under control. And, from about 1576 onward we find orders to send Jews to Cyprus - presumably in order to restore the commercial prosperity of the island following the departure of the Venetians. In reality, the purpose was mainly to consolidate Turkish rule by counterbalancing the Christian element in the island's population.

In addition, the Moslem population of Cyprus originated from the Franks and to a smaller extent from the Greeks who, in order to escape the ensuing massacre or enslavement, adopted Islam in order to enjoy greater quiet but continued secretly to observe the numerous customs of the Greek Orthodox Church. They were called renegades, cryptochristians or simply '*linobambakoi*' (linen-cotters). Niven Kerr, the British consul in Cyprus, observed in a letter dated 4 June 1844, to Sir Stratford Canning (a prominent British politician), that there were several villages whose inhabitants, although professedly mussulman, secretly embraced the Greek religion and attended the services of that Church. In fairness to the island's new rulers it must be emphasised that the Ottomans instituted their well-documented policy of '*istimalet*' i.e. leniency aimed at winning the hearts of the peasants. In so doing, an obedient tax-paying populace was normally the outcome.

---

(7) The Jews of Islam. 1984. Page 123

*Above:* Janissaries - infantry, constituting the Sultan's guard and the crack troops of the army. Formed originally from renegade prisoners and children taken from Christian subjects. The system was extended in parts of Cyprus.

*Left:* This stamp illustrates Bairakdar Mosque, built on the Constanzo Bastion around 1820 to commemorate the standard-bearer who fell on the spot during the capture of Nicosia, in 1570-71.

What of the island's form of administration? Cyprus was divided into 17 cadelisks or administrative districts (reduced to 6 during the 19th century), each having its *agha* or governor and *cadi* or minister of justice. Turkish administration and personnel varied tremendously over the years. Favouritism and corruption, the twin cankers of Ottoman rule, determined the choice of the highest officers in the state. At the top, the administration of the island was, generally speaking, in the hands of the governor (*Mutassurif*), assisted by a council over which he presided. It was composed of the *Mufti*, or highest mussulman religious authority, the Greek Archbishop and or Dragoman (or interpreter, especially in the post 1660 period), the *Evcaf-Nazir*, or administrator of mussulman religious property, three mussulmans and two christian notables. The council usually met once a week and its decisions were embodied in documents called '*musbatas*', which were signed by all the members present. From its membership it can be seen that all initiative came from the muslim majority.

The fifth issue that needs brief comment is the following: Serfdom[8] disappeared and after the expulsion of the Latin priests the Greek Orthodox Church was restored. The island's Greeks were henceforth recognised as a '*millet*' or nation under the leadership of the Church of Cyprus and its Archbishop who was, especially after 1660, the '*millet bashi*' or ethnarch. The Church in fact, was the upholder and protagonist of the continuous existence of a well-defined Greek Cypriot national community. Moreover, for many years of Turkish rule (especially from the 1660s to 1821) a certain measure of 'autonomy' was granted to the Christian population - the non-moslem element, often called '*dimmis*' (tolerated infidels) who were virtually guaranteed their lives, liberty, property and religion.

Another point that needs elucidation is the institution of the office of the '*dragoman*'[9] During times that were very difficult for the local population this practice, which provided the link between state and people, took on great importance both economically and politically. The relevant Porte decree in the middle of the 18th century reinforced this tradition. Moreover, it gave the Archbishop, together with the bishops and the dragoman, the authority to apportion and collect taxes. This meant that the dragoman, who could communicate directly with the Sultan, achieved the second highest political position in the island after the Pasha or Governor. At the same time it made him a target for the

---

(8) Human beings 'attached to the soil' like chattels or other goods.

(9) Dragomans were usually chosen by the bishops or by the notables and their election was confirmed by the Sultan. The first dragoman was probably Piero Guneme (1608). He came from a noble Latin Cypriote family.

schemes of the Turkish administrators who wanted a free hand to amass a fortune, at the expense of the people. The most famous dragoman was perhaps **Hadjigeorgakis Kornesios** (born in Kritou-Terra Paphos around the middle of the 18th century), who married the niece of Archbishop Chrysanthos and who for a time (c. 1780 - 1805) became the most important person in Cyprus.

*Left:* The House of Hadjigeorgakis Kornesios has been restored and is now a museum in Nicosia.

*Above:* A portrait of the most famous Dragoman - Kornesios.

The problems and hardships associated with an alien regime and its strange governmental institutions were further accentuated by natural disasters. Thus, the pestilence of 1624 was so severe that the number of villages and hamlets were reduced by one third. The plague of 1691-92 was responsible for the death of around 30% of the island's population. As if these disasters were not enough the economy and general well-being of the inhabitants were further paralysed by unjust taxes. Successive changes in the administration meant that the people were harassed with exactions of all kinds, enough to reimburse its rulers after one year in office. Both mussulmans, christians and other ethnic minorities had equal cause to be dissatisfied with the maladministration that continued unhindered. Insurrections and mass protests were therefore joint affairs.

The rebellions prior to 1680 were minor events yet were highly significant with long-term effects. Those of 1578, 1580 and 1593 about which we know very little were instigated by the surviving members of the old ruling class[10], who tried to incite the masses against the existing regime. A considerable number perished. In 1617 the flag of revolt was raised by one called Vittorio Zebeto. This was another failure.[11] What were the effects? These defeats led to a superficial moslemisation of many rural families especially in the northern parts of the island. Extreme poverty was also a significant factor in the acceptance of a new religion. Also important is the fact that the activities of the crypto-christians led to a Cypriot mentality which may be termed 'tolerant and hesitant'. Tolerant because they accepted, at least in practice, the new regime and hesitant because by accepting it their Greekness was dampened and hence they were less eager to participate in rebellious activities. They were also suspected on many occasions as being spies and informants. Another study perhaps, can prove or disprove this allegation.

There were other mass protests or rebellions which were much more serious. The first uprising occurred in 1680 under the leadership of **Mehmed Agha Boyadji-Oghlu** and lasted for 7 whole years. It was a mass protest against harsh taxes and maladministration. It was a protest brought about by petty rivalries and jealousies amongst the various lords of the land. After some difficulty the rebellion was crushed and Oghlu, together with some of his closest followers, was executed. After this insurrection the island became for some time the personal possession of the Grand Vizier. This led in turn to further exactions and then in 1712 a band of armed men from the Turkish fleet attempted to usurp the authority of the existing administrators. They stated that they were acting on direct orders from the Sultan; they were soon found out and executed.

Another protest in 1745 was easily dealt with. However, the revolt of 1765-66, had wider repercussions. As soon as **Chil Osman** had entered his post as agha in July 1764, he issued an order compelling the payment by each christian subject of $44^1/_2$ piastres and by each moslem of about 22 piastres. Within a few months he had managed to extort 350,000 piastres over and above the legal assessment. A special mission to Constantinople, believed to have been led by Hadji-Vasilis of Mia Milia, was successful in persuading the Sultan to order Osman not to demand the half of what was collected. A special envoy was also sent to the island to see that the order was enforced. The bishops and around 300 other leading personages

---

(10) Usually aided and abetted by western powers and by the so-called "stateless adventurers."

(11) Also a failure was the earlier one of 1607-08 which was to be led by the notorious Norman corsair Jacques Pierre, known for his great experience as 'the Captain'.

arrived at Osman's palace on 25 October 1764 to hear the order read. The assembled crowds suspected that Osman was plotting to kill all the notables in his own residence and when part of the floor actually collapsed they rushed the palace. Osman and about 18 others were murdered. The incident was patched up but a commission was sent by the Porte to inquire into the events that led up to it.

A considerable amount of money was thus required to cover the expenses of the commissioners, compensation for the victims, the rebuilding of the Saray, thefts from the treasury and other demands. Hafiz Efendi was left behind to arrange for the entire settlement. Because of his greed however, the expenses were overestimated. This placed the tax collectors in an unenviable position and when they visited the Mesaoria villages they were forced to run for their lives. The exactions were however pressed and open rebellion ensued. Events moved at a steady pace: On Easter Tuesday, April 1765, around 300 Turks from the Mesaoria and Famagusta districts seized Kythrea with its water mills and thus cut-off the capital from its supply of flour. Concessions were granted but the tax continued to be collected. Some months later, at a fair (panigyris) in Myrtou, **Khalil Agha**, commandant of the fortress of Kyrenia, was chosen to lead the rebellion against tax injustices. All religious and socio-economic strata of Cypriot society supported Khalil and by August over 3,000 armed men were under his orders. The government completely lost control of the situation but Archbishop Paisios and the bishops of Paphos and Kyrenia escaped to Constantinople to plead for help.

Khalil withdrew to Kyrenia. The authorities then promised that excessive taxes would not be levied and that all the insurgents would be pardoned. But, it was not long before Hafiz decided once more to collect the taxes. Khalil reacted by making attempts to dislodge the administration at both Famagusta and Nicosia. The men under his command grew and grew and it appeared that the island was within his grasp. Perhaps if he had been a more decisive person that would have been the result!

Meanwhile, the Porte dispatched Ibrahim Bey to Cyprus to deal with the rebellion. In June 1766 Kior Ahmed was also sent to the island this time with a far superior force (2,000 troops, 500 horse and 16 ships), and Kyrenia was blockaded. After a three-week siege Khalil surrendered and by August the revolt was over. Khalil was garroted; his lieutenant Emir Ahmed was impaled and around 200 were beheaded. According to custom their heads were sent to the Sultan.

The cost to the islanders was crippling. Half a million piastres fell on the heads of around 15,000 tax payers. More was to follow. In 1771, one named **Hadji Baki**, believed to be a native Turkish peasant, managed to get himself appointed as chief of the treasury. Four years later he poisoned the new Turkish governor, Hadji Ali Agha, and several others including the governor's deputy. By 1777, this quite illiterate woodcutter who was banished from the island in 1767[12] was appointed governor calling himself Hadji Abdul Baki Agha.

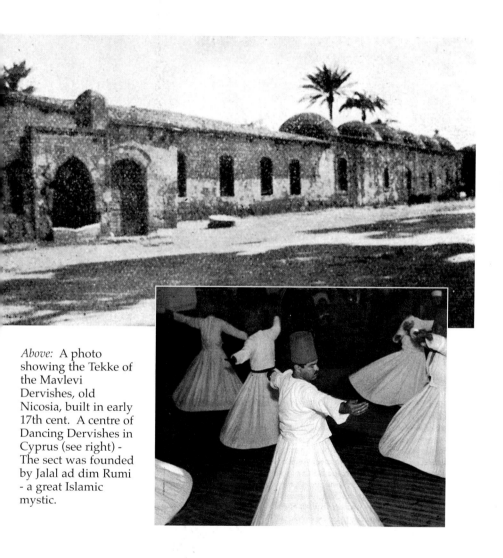

*Above:* A photo showing the Tekke of the Mavlevi Dervishes, old Nicosia, built in early 17th cent. A centre of Dancing Dervishes in Cyprus (see right) - The sect was founded by Jalal ad dim Rumi - a great Islamic mystic.

(12) On charges of trickery, deceit, treachery and many others.

The same story is repeated many times in the annals of Turkish rule over Cyprus. Even Turkish troops mutinied in 1799 but in 1804 the results were very serious. Stirred by rumours of a shortage of foodstuffs, the troops together with the Turkish civilian population of Nicosia, raised the flag of revolt against the governor, the Archbishop and the dragoman (Hadjigeorgakis), who was at the time perhaps the wealthiest person in the island. The insurgents gained possession of Nicosia but following the dragoman's appeal to the Porte, the revolt was suppressed. The Turks however resented the powers of the dragoman and in 1806 enlisted the help of Altiparnak ('six fingers') a colonel at Tarsus, to champion their cause. Christian life and property suffered greatly. However Altiparnak was soon taken prisoner and flayed alive. In 1809 and 1810 Cyprus was to lose two intellectual and cultural benefactors. Hadjigeorgakis was executed in Constantinople on charges of corrupt behaviour and in 1810 Archbishop Chrysanthos was exiled to Euboea.

A brief summary of events in the 19th century is not out of place: Despite the protests and revolts outlined above it must be emphasised that Turkish rule, thanks to the co-operation of large sections of Cypriot society, was firmly entrenched. Taxes raised crippled the inhabitants; apart form the 'garrison tax' and 'produce tax' raised by the Sultan there were taxes raised by the governor-general and local governors. And there were taxes collected by the Greek bishops - a responsibility entrusted to them in 1660. This practice was in accordance with the customary procedure of the Porte in using the leaders of a country's majority to act as tax collectors and thereby keeping the displeasure of the people in manageable bounds. Despite their enhanced and omnipotent position, the status of the church leaders was difficult and delicate. They often became victims of intrigue, plots and rebellions. The events of the 19th century were indicative of that trend.

Another characteristic of the Turkish administration which brought much controversy was the creation of the position of dragoman. With the dragoman directly in control of affairs and the archbishop enjoying immense prestige, the Greek population became, in effect for many years 'self-governing'. This was a unique experience for the islanders.

As if these anomalies were not enough the inhabitants were further 'punished' by acts of nature. A severe pestilence in 1624 resulted in many deaths and the plague of 1691-92 wiped out a large proportion of the population. The two earthquakes of 1741 and 1756 (the former damaged the cathedral of Saint Sophia), brought great material destruction. The dearth of 1757-58, being the outcome of the drought and locusts, meant that a slice of the island's population fled to Syria and Asia Minor. The year 1768 was also one of famine. To those misfortunes was added the stark reality that the mohammedan lords, who possessed considerable areas of land, seldom engaged in farming but simply drew what they

Selimieh Mosque - the original Latin Medieval Cathedral of Ayia Sophia Nicosia, then turned into a mosque.

*Above:* An old external view from the east

*Left:* The interior of the mosque - an impressive structure.

*Below:* Old stamp illustrating Buyuk Khan in old Nicosia, built by Muzaffer Pasha in 1571 after the occupation as a house for "the benefit of all foreigners".

could from the impoverished Cypriot. The island's peasants were further tested by the greedy, senseless and self-motivated activities of the newly-rich mohammedan and other lords[13] like Hadji Baki who 'fought' to control larger and larger areas. More and more exactions were therefore added to the already long and multi-form tax list.

We may also add that the widely expected collapse of the decadent Ottoman empire never materialised. It succeeded in crushing every revolt against its authority. Hence for the Cypriot and other middle eastern and Balkan nationalities the dream of an Ottoman breakdown never really came about.

*The 19th century was dominated by five major events:*

1. Cyprus benefited slightly from the reforms promulgated by Sultans Selim III and Mahmoud II. The two liberalising charters, Hati-Sherif of 1839 and Hati-Humayun of 1856, which applied to all their dependencies, were practically meaningless albeit, a step in the right direction.

   As regards Cyprus the annual tribute was finally fixed and the practice of leasing the island to the highest bidder was abolished. Moreover, a salaried governor was appointed and was to be helped by a council known as the *'divan'*. Thus relative prosperity showed mild signs of emerging and a sizeable increase in the population[14] was the outcome. Also the liberalising governorship between 1868 and 1871 was a great bonus to the inhabitants.

2. The disturbances of the 1820s associated with the Greek rising. On a charge of conspiring with the insurgents in Greece, the Turks on 9 July 1821 hanged Archbishop **Kyprianos** and **Meletios**, his archdeacon, beheaded three bishops (**Meletios** of Kition, **Chrysanthos** of Paphos and **Lavrentios** of Kyrenia) and many laymen. It is worth noting that the archbishop issued an encyclical on 16 May 1821 advising his flock to remain calm. Even though revolt in the island never materialised in any form or shape, a number of Cypriots were members of the **'Philike Hetairia'**, the Hellenic revolutionary society and fought at Messolonghi, Roumeli and the Morea. Several hundreds 'escaped' from the island to join the revolutionary forces. Cyprus, it may be added was known to Hetairia members by the secret code number of 13.

---

(13) Often referred to as 'Ayans' or 'Ayianides'. The 18th and early 19th centuries bear witness to their detrimental and 'peasant bashing' activities.

(14) From around 105,000 in the 1820s it increased to 125,000 inhabitants in the 1850s

Archbishop Kyprianos who was killed during the Turkish purge of 1821, was named by the people - 'Ethnomartiras Kyprianos' (the Martyr of the Nation)

What exactly led to the killings? The Porte was in great disarray at the time and did not approve of **Kutchuk Mehmed's** (the island's governor) intentions of putting to the sword leaders of the so-called *'Greek insurrection'*. It finally sanctioned the killings and the seizure of property belonging to the accused.  G.I. Kepiades, in his 'Reminiscences of 1821 in Cyprus' described the massacre (followed by looting, rape and other atrocities) as *"the most monstrous spectacle ever seen"*.  Vasilis Michaelides, perhaps the finest of the Cypriot dialect poets, described the events in his magnificent 560-verse narrative poem *'The Ninth of July 1821'*.  The common grave/monument  erected at Phaneromeni church in Nicosia in 1872-73 honoured the victims (believed to be 486) of the purge.  The killings did not stop with prominent people: monks, priests, young and old, innocent peasants and other laymen did not escape the sword.  Those able to flee the island disguised themselves and embarked for Genoa, Marseilles and elsewhere.

There were other atrocities.  Scores of villages and hamlets (mainly) had entirely disappeared.  Many churches had been turned into mosques and a few into stables.  General Thomas Gordon, a British historian of some repute, wrote in 1832 that *"the whole of Cyprus was converted into a theatre of rapine and bloodshed"*.  This, undoubtedly, is an extremely harsh statement which should be viewed with scepticism.

3. The revolts of the early 1830s[15] were protests not only against maladministration and unjust taxes but the two Greek-led ones had enosist aspirations. Following the success of the Greek insurrection, **Count Capodistria** who had come into power in 1828, immediately expressed a desire for the union of Cyprus with the new state. The rising led by **Nicholas Theseus** (nephew of Archbishop Kyprianos) was easily put down. The *'Ides of March'*, as one writer commented, were fatal for the Cypriots. Theseus with the help of Bottu, the French consul, managed to escape on board a Greek ship to Rhodes. The renowned French poet Lamartine, who spoke of Theseus as being "good-mannered and intelligent" took him to Constantinople to plead his case. Having failed in his mission he left the Ottoman dominions. In 1839 he returned to Greece and was appointed consul in Beirut - a post which he held for a few years.

The second revolt of 1833 was led by **Giaur Imam**, a well-to-do Turk of Tremithousa (situated around 10 miles southeast of Polis in the Paphos district). It was a massive protest against the payment of unjust and exorbitant taxes. For a time he managed to *'rule'* Paphos and made plans to attack Limassol and Larnaca. After several months of highly successful disobedience the revolt was crushed around July.[16]

The third rising of 1833 (July) had a much stronger enosist element than the one led by Theseus. At its head was **Ioannikios**, a fiery monk born at Ayios Elias and said to have fought in the Greek War of Independence. From rather patchy historical evidence we find that *'o kalogeros'* was encouraged by leading Cypriots, by several European consuls in the island and helped by Albanian troops to whom he promised lavish prizes. He proceeded to raise the insurgent's flag at Trikomo but the revolt fizzled out and was crushed within four days. The defeated received no mercy. Many were hanged, others tortured and the countryside was devastated. The impoverished peasant was left to foot the tax bill. The three rebellions were costly.

4. The fourth major event of the 19th. century was the so-called *'archaeological sin'* which was committed at the expense of the island's heritage. In Cyprus, as elsewhere, mischievous digging (tomb-robbing) had a venerable history. The widely-travelled Edward

---

(15) One in 1830 was easily erased from human memory. However, the three protests in 1833 were rather different. Those led by Theseus and Ioannikios were motivated by the Greek Cypriot aspiration for union with motherland Greece.

(16) The governor's troops freed after crushing the Karpass revolt (led by Ioannikios), moved on Giaur and defeated him. He managed to escape on board a Greek schooner bound for Alexandria.

Daniel Clarke who visited Cyprus in 1801 refers to the English consul, an Italian called Signor Peristiani, digging up statues and figurines in Larnaca and to goldsmiths of the island who traded in antiquities. He is certainly backed-up by other writers and travellers. Under the Ottoman domination, chance discoveries by Cypriot peasants were exploited by officials who followed up reports of finds by their own investigations and simply carried away the results. However, this regular and profitable activity was apparently far from being on the scale which it attained in the 19th century.

Since the 1850s but especially between 1865 and 1875 this trade of antiquities began to develop on a far larger and more damaging scale. Consuls and local administrators were among the prime movers in the unofficial and usually clandestine antiques trade. Tombs were laid bare and robbed indiscriminately; those of Idalium, Golgoi, Kourion, Kition, Amathus and Paphos were hardest hit. Messrs. T.B. Sandwith, R.H. Lang, G. Collona-Ceccaldi and Luigi Palma di Cesnola, competed fiercely and nearly always for personal gain. The latter, who was followed by his brother Major Alexander, boasted in a letter to Sir Henry Layard (Britain's Ambassador to Constantinople), that he had in his possession *"the island's whole history"*.

Thanks to the British connection a high standard of professionalism was brought to the archaeological investigations of the island. Sir **J.L. Myers**, often referred to as the *'father of Cypriot archaeology'* was aided in his task by various societies and by Max Ohnefalsh-Richter. In 1833 the Cyprus Museum was established in Nicosia. Although illegal sales were reported well into the 1880s the problem had virtually ceased to exist.

5.  For the second time in its illustrious history the island of Cyprus became a valuable possession of England. It is a significant fact because, to date, the English hold the unique distinction of being the only foreign country to hold Cyprus twice. In 1191 it was acquired by chance and recourse to war and then sold within a few months for a handsome fee. In 1878 (687 years later), it was taken over by diplomatic agency and it remained under the English Crown for 82 years. It must be noted that at least until 1914 the island remained under the sovereignty of the Sultan. To protect their commercial and strategic interests the British, according to Lord Salisbury (Foreign Secretary), saw fit to *"erect another dyke behind the shattered Turkish break-water"*. He once remarked that *"his military experts were capable of finding reasons to occupy Mars for the defence of the British Empire"*. Prime Minister Disraeli (created Lord Beaconsfield in 1876) also emphasised that Queen Victoria henceforth reigned over the *"jewel of the Mediterranean"*.

Before we move on to the next distinct phase in the development of modern Cyprus we must briefly highlight the main issues and characteristics of the years 1571-1878. It must be stressed from the outset that with the advent of the Turks, the island sank into a *"long sleep"* - from being a kingdom (true of the Lusignan dynasty), renowned throughout christendom, the island had become an obscure Ottoman dependency. Moreover, the behavioural pattern of Turkish administrators was one of unpredictability; its tax gathering[17] (the number of risings bear proof to this injustice) was crippling; its religious policy, generally speaking, was one of tolerance although as in 1821, it was punctuated by acts of sheer brutality; its administrators were self-motivated and greedy; its 'justice' was riddled by bribery and corruption; schools were few and far between (most were run by the Orthodox Church) and hence literacy levels were extremely low; the medical well-being of the people was very poor; public works were non-existent and Cyprus' heritage was left to rot or, as in the case of tomb-digging, exploited. Yet the Ottomans held Cyprus for 307 years - serfdom was abolished and after the expulsion of the Latin hierarchy Greek Orthodoxy was restored.

Such were the stark realities of Cypriot life. Yet it cannot be disputed that throughout history man's way of life has changed considerably. The evolution of civilization has abolished ethics and customs that in their time were regarded as indispensable and has substituted them with others, which in their turn, also became outdated. Their impact however, on the historical events of a particular period was so great that nowadays it is necessary for us to study how people lived in those days in order to understand their acts and attitudes. What is our assessment therefore of the island's population? The Cypriot peasant, cramped in 'feudal' bonds and medieval poverty had one method to escape from his material lot - religion. He became first superstitious then God-fearing and prayed constantly for the salvation of his soul. To attend church services and functions (weddings, christenings and other festivals) were his only recreational activities.

Moreover, the social and economic gulf between the rich and the labouring masses was as wide as the Mediterranean sea itself. Although not 'tied' to the land, the peasants were 'bound' on it out of sheer necessity since there was nowhere else to go. The alternatives were either to starve or seek an existence from charity (rarely available) which was really beyond the character of the toiling, proud and respectable Cypriot. The masses were therefore either 'bound' to the land or to the mines. In such circumstances crime existed but more importantly youngsters were

---

(17) Taxes were collected for the Sultan, for the government and district administrators, for the higher clergy of the Greek Church and for the owners of farm land. In addition, there were levies on produce and following a natural disaster or a rising further exactions were imposed.

forced to work extremely long hours to supplement the meagre family income. Consequently, large families were the order of the day and survival was the ethos of the period. Such families ate and slept in one or two rooms - often adjacent to stables. Much of Cyprus even in the late 19th century was still remote and isolated. Most peasants lived and died in their village without even seeing the nearest town.[18] Even though the agricultural revolution (new methods of draining, drilling, sowing, manuring, breeding and feeding animals etc.) touched the entire European continent (some more than others), Cyprus continued to exist with outdated and primitive methods. The peasants continued to live under conditions of extreme misery and degradation.

And, what about the Cypriot diet? It was very basic and one based on vegetables such as beans, onions, chic peas, lentils, olives and supplemented by as much bread as possible. Red or white meat was rarely eaten: families often resorted to selling even home-reared fowl so that some of their other basic needs could be met. Some wine was drunk however, especially in mountainous areas where vineyards were plentiful.

The picture drawn so far is a depressing one which, it can be said, also pertained to other dependent countries. In contrast however, the professional classes (e.g. doctors and lawyers), skilled artisans and the few shopkeepers that existed evidently fared much better under such a system. Some had the opportunity to educate themselves and to travel abroad. Some were prominent in providing something for the poor; others were responsible for 'importing' new ideas from other countries.

This leads us to another very important and related point: the period under discussion was one of great cultural decline. The more educated and progressive people of the island were forced to take refuge in other countries, notably Italy, where Greek communities thrived under benevolent rule. Two writers deserve a special mention: **Neophytos Rodinos**, born around the end of the 16th century, wrote extensively in both Greek and Latin. He was a great scholar whose patriotism was beyond question. The other is **Archimandrite Kyprianos** born in the middle of the 18th century, who lived in Trieste and Venice for many years. His work *'Chronological History of the Island of Cyprus'* (Venice 1788) not only marked an important point in the history of the language but was also of historical and literary value. It may be noted that the cultural renaissance in Cyprus began in the 1870s. As soon as the British arrived, printing presses were set up, the first newspapers started to circulate and the first books were printed. Communication with Europe became easier and new ideas started to filter through to Cyprus, mainly from Athens.

---

(18) Communications were practically non-existent. Generally speaking, there were only mule and camel tracks.

Lastly, any people living under harsh conditions and denied both material and spiritual welfare, are bound to develop some defence mechanisms for protection and self-preservation. The Church, as already noted, with its privileges accorded to it by the Ottoman administrators, was a strong institution and played an important role in safeguarding the national identity of the island's Christian inhabitants. However, the largely poverty-stricken, isolated and illiterate section of the people developed under foreign rule its own folk culture (music, dance, song, tales and legends) in which it expressed itself and its spiritual world. Since this was a period when the Church played an important role, it was only natural that many of the stories were based on religious themes. Place legends and traditions also made up a large category of folk tales.

Of unique importance is the fact that peaceful co-existence and fruitful co-operation between the Greeks and Turks of Cyprus, during the long Ottoman administration, is a precise historical event and beyond any shadow of doubt. Some brief remarks will suffice:

We have already noted that the recurring mass protests and rebellions were joint affairs. Both had cause to complain against harsh taxes and maladministration.

Also noted earlier is the fact that part of the Turkish population of Cyprus originated from local or Greek-speaking inhabitants.

In the economic sector there existed complete unity and mutual dependence. There were never two separate economies in Cyprus - one Greek and one Turkish. It must be added however that certain trades, such as building and cabinet-making were practised almost exclusively by Greeks, whilst others such as midwifery, folk-medicine, quilt making and sackcloth-weaving, exclusively by Turks.

The cultural and folklore relations between the two communities are also deep and presuppose therefore a long and prolific mutual dependence. Thus the Greek folk poets in the prologue to their poems which they used to recite at fairs and other places, called upon both Greeks and Turks (and others) to listen to them because all groups used to take part in such community festivities. It is worth noting that there were also Turkish folk poets who composed in Greek in the traditional manner.

This successful co-existence and mutual influence of the two groups was shown by the fact that most Turks in Cyprus spoke Greek and in some villages Turkish school children actually performed patriotic Greek plays. Moreover, the close connection between the two languages in Cyprus added a great number of Turkish words and phrases to the Greek spoken in the island.

Three old engravings of the 17th/18th centuries: *Above top:* Kyrenia and its formidable Castle *Above:* The Larnaca Aqueduct built in 1747 by Abu Bekr Pasha *Below:* An old view of Larnaca town with Stavrovouni mountain in the distance.

Many aspects of the folklore of both Greeks and Turks have a common origin. An example is the '*Zeimbekes*'. Their fame as sailors for the Byzantines, Franks and the Ottomans and, at times as pirates, spread from coast to coast and both dances and a special costume (the '*vraka*' or baggy trousers) had their origin in these sailors. Because of these Zeimbekes, there are many similarities between Greek and Turkish dances and music.

Architecture is also a feature which is common to both groups. The railed balconies, large windows and the broken arch seen in public buildings are typical examples. A further feature which needs brief comment is the following: The narrative poems of Cyprus and especially the '*Akritica*' (border ballads), the legends about mythical persons and heroes, about old buildings and treasure, spirits and '*kalikantzari*' ( a sort of goblin or demon), exist equally between the Greeks and the Turks of Cyprus. It has in fact been shown that certain 'akritic' ballads exist in fuller versions among the Turks of Karpasia and Paphos than among the Greeks.

Finally, the customs and traditions of the two groups are almost the same except that the Greeks call upon the Christian God and the Turks upon Allah. Thus, both have the same traditions about predicting the sex of a baby, about spells and nostrums, about votive offerings, about preparations for a wedding, about funerals and about the life of farmers and shepherds. Thus, like his Greek counterpart, the Turkish farmer puts a pomegranate among his seed and turns towards the east before planting it. Similarly, a clay vessel is broken over the grave of both Turk and Greek. Such examples can be multiplied. Suffice to say that these features are clear evidence of a long period of peaceful co-existence and harmonious contact between the two communities in Cyprus.

Two contrasting images of life in Cyprus around the mid and latter part of the 19th century.

*Above Left:* a peasant woman breastfeeding her baby and looking after her goat.
*Right:* Two affluent women relaxing.

A young couple dressed for a local religious feast.

Hoisting the British flag in Nicosia, 1878.

# Chapter THREE

## THE BRITISH CONNECTION

### 1878 – 1960

# (i) Years of Uncertainty 1978-1914

In the 1870s, the fortunes of the Ottoman Empire assumed a new dimension. Its demise after nearly 400 years on the ascendancy, the fear of a Russian advance into the Balkans and the Mediterranean, the development of a new European order based on the emergence of new nations which resulted in a shift in the fragile European balance of power and the surge for new markets and territories by the established and emerging industrialised nations meant that the "*rosy realm of Venus*" became a prized possession. Amid some intra-governmental debate, the secret convention between Britain and Turkey, dated 4 June 1878 and called the '*The Cyprus Convention*', transferred the island to the British Crown. The Convention was later sanctioned by the Berlin Congress of June-July 1878. An annex signed on 1 July, a supplementary agreement signed on 14 August and another agreement signed on 3 February 1879 solidified the British hold on the island. Queen Victoria wrote that, "*the whole country was delighted*" with such an acquisition.

The terms were simple but uncertain: In return for the 'protection' of the bankrupt Ottomans, a tribute of nearly £92,000 and, as it turned out 4,166,220 okes (or 10,865,416 lbs) of salt per annum, Britain was to administer and occupy Cyprus. Furthermore, if Russia at any time restored to Turkey her three Armenian conquests of 1877, then Cyprus was to be evacuated and returned to Turkey. This however, was a hollow provision - as was the one concerning the 'protection' of Turkey in the event of war. Thus, when Ardahan and Kars were transferred to Turkey in 1921 Cyprus was not relinquished by Britain. It was first annexed in 1914 and in 1925 it became a Crown Colony.

As to its strategic importance Cyprus directly commanded the entrance to the Suez Canal[1] the coasts of Palestine and Syria and the southern provinces of Asia Minor. With Gibraltar in the west of the Mediterranean, Malta in the centre and now Cyprus, the process of converting it into a distant '**British Lake**' was complete. Disraeli had earlier described the island to Queen Victoria (5 May 1878) as "*the key to western Asia*". And, with Britain henceforth the chief adviser and comforter to the Porte, its moral influence among all the nations of the east, and especially the people of India, was considerably increased. Economically and commercially, Cyprus once more brought many advantages to its new occupier. For 82 years this "*rosy realm of Venus*" remained one of the most valuable possessions of the British Crown.

---

(1) The British government in November 1875 became the owner of around $1/2$ of the Suez Canal Company stock (shares). When the British occupied Egypt in 1882, Cyprus reverted to the role of a 'somnolent resort'

Hoisting of the British flag in Nicosia – 1878 engraving

Vice-Admiral Lord **John Hay**, the island's temporary guardian arrived at the bay of Larnaca on 4 July 1878. However, Cyprus and its inhabitants were an unknown quantity to both Hay and to his crew.

Captain Harry Rawson was sent on shore on the 8th and 9th to test the situation. He was well briefed by Watkins, the British consul (appointed to reside in Larnaca on 13 February 1877) and following his second visit he laid an informative but short report before Hay. He described the townsfolk as *"quiet and sociable, very lazy and given to pleasures of every sort"*. He went on to say that *"since they were not fanatical they would not fight"* and though *"robberies, assassinations and brigandage were nearly unknown, drunkenness was not uncommon"*.

However, the inhabitants of Nicosia, being chiefly Turkish, were described as *"fanatical, men devoted to their religion and faithful to their caliph; in other words, men who might possibly turn out to fight"*. Such fears did not materialise. Driving in a wagonette with no military guard, Hay entered Nicosia by the Famagusta gate at 11.30 a.m. on 12 July. As it was Friday and the hour of prayer at the Saray (the Turkish governor's official residence) nothing could be done until later. The firman was then read

*Above:* The British High Commissioner and Greek Orthodox priests blessing the British Flag at Kykko Metochi.

*Below:* The first British forces land in Larnaca.

Both engravings from 1878.

and Hay was handed the reins of the administration. In his brief address Hay explained that as a result of the convention that had been concluded between HM Queen Victoria and the Sultan and enforced now by an imperial firman, he was commanded by HMG[2] to occupy the island in the name of the Queen and to assume its temporary administration until a governor was appointed. He went on to promise justice, progress and equality to all the inhabitants. This very plain and businesslike address, spoken in English, was of course not understood[3] by those present. Only the words *'Queen Victoria'* were comprehended and were soon echoed by the crowd amidst tumultuous cheering. All this took place within the saray and when Hay and his officers emerged on their way to the flagstaff they were followed by large crowds. The marines were drawn up and Captain Rawson hoisted the Union Jack, which was then saluted. As soon as this brief ceremony was over, Hay formally announced to the people that HM Queen Victoria now reigned over Cyprus. The crowds once more applauded enthusiastically. Hay was then followed to the rostrum by George Kepiades, a prominent Greek and the historian of the purges of 1821, who expressed the joy of the Cypriots and their hopes for the prosperity and full political liberty.

At 7.30 a.m. on 22 July Sir **Garnet Wolseley** arrived in HMS Himalaya, landing at Larnaca at around 6.00 p.m. and accompanied by some 1,500 troops. He then issued a proclamation (in English, Greek and Turkish), in which he gave assurances of the Queen's wishes for the prosperity of the island and her desire to take measures for the promotion and development of commerce and agriculture and to endow the people with the benefits of liberty, justice and security. Everyone welcomed the British occupation as a break in Cypriot affairs; in fact, the substitution of a christian empire for a mohammedan one was seen as the golden bridge for even greater achievements.

The period between 1878 and 1914 (from occupation to outright cession) was dominated by five major issues:

1. Problems of settlement;

2. The Hellenic ideal or Meghali Idhea (Great Idea);

3. The emergence of the Constitution;

4. The Tribute and the Economic Situation; and

5. Church disputation.

---

(2) Her Majesty's Government. A British consular agent was originally established in Cyprus by the Levant Company in 1796.

(3) There were of course some who could read and understand English - some even spoke French.

Captain Swaine and his escort enter Lefkoniko village triumphantly – 1878 engraving.

## Problems of Settlement

In 1907 Winston Churchill[4] stressed that Cyprus in 1878 came under British rule *"ruined and prostrate from centuries of horrible ill-usage"*. Consequently, the problems encountered must have been many. Those associated with the Sultan's lands were troublesome since the departing Turkish administration claimed more or less all the land for which the inhabitants showed no title. In the end large areas were ceded by the Turks and a settlement, which took several years to finalise, was reached. Then there were tax problems but more serious was the issue of the tribute.

The process of clearing up the accounts of the administration was complicated by the endeavours of the Turks to present as large a balance as possible in the treasury. It was in their interests to do so, since the annual tribute (as per the Cyprus Convention) was to be based on the average surplus of the last five years. Moreover, to meet the expenses of the Russo-Turkish War of 1876-77, taxes had been doubled. This created further problems for the tax collectors, who had the unenviable task of

---

(4) 1874-1965  He was then Parliamentary Under-Secretary of State for the Colonies

extracting more and more from Cypriot peasants who could hardly make ends meet.

Law and Order was another thorny issue. Wolseley asserted that impartial justice was his motto and mentioned as illustration the fact that he had in his first three months in office, imprisoned one tax collector for robbery, one Greek churchman for refusing to pay tithes and one Maltese antiquity hunter for breaking the law. He also insisted on the immediate deportation of around 314 Turkish convicts whose presence on the island was as undesirable as it was dangerous. Under Turkish rule[5] it may be noted, the island was made the receptacle for the worst criminals in the Sultan's empire. Wolseley was also convinced that Turkish *'cadis'* should instantly be removed from their posts as judges although he believed that they should be retained as expounders of existing law while verdicts should be delivered by a British judge or commissioner. He further emphasised that if they were kept the Greeks - the mass of the population - would never feel satisfied that justice had been done to them.

. The question of privilege, which caused a lot of recrimination, was also a matter for deep consideration. While the peasantry were quite satisfied with the way things were going in the early years of the new administration, the privileged classes - those who had exemptions from taxation - lost all tax gathering rights[6] and hence a new grievance was born. This played a major role in increased agitation for union with Greece. The clergy were the biggest losers but other wealthy classes such as lawyers, merchants and bankers also lost out.

The problem of corrupt office holders (allied to the one of law and order) was perhaps at the root of many problems which faced the island. Nepotism, bribery and corruption had been allowed to grow and flourish without check. Officials once appointed became untrustworthy, dishonest, greedy and arrogant. Wolseley was convinced that radical changes were needed to stir the island's energies and set forward her welfare. However, following a strong hint from the government in Westminster, he set about purifying rather than abolishing the decadent Turkish institutions. One of his first acts therefore was to nominate 6 British officers - of whom the first was Colonel **Robert Biddulph** (eventually his successor) - to take the place of the *'kaimakans'* who had administered the six districts into which the island had been divided. The British excuse (for keeping things more or less as they were) of course was uncertainty of settlement.

---

(5) The Roman and Byzantine Emperors also carried out the same policy. The banishment of undesirables to Cyprus was therefore not new.

(6) In 1878-79. Wolseley often described the bishops as "cunning, deceitful and essentially untruthful."

*Above:* Two images from the occupation of Cyprus, sketches of the times – 1878 engraving.
*Below:* Another engraving shows the headquarters of Sir Garnet Wolseley at Kykko Metochi near Nicosia, with the church of St. Prokopios in the distance.

Health was another issue which had to be tackled by the new administration. Obviously acts of nature such as earthquakes could not be prevented but the poor health of the inhabitants and afflictions such as cattle disease (an outbreak occurred in 1879/80) and destruction of crops by locusts (to prevent which a considerable amount of money was spent between 1881 and 1885) could, with the right men and resources, be alleviated.

Education and language were also major problems. Illiteracy and therefore apathy were the rule rather than the exception. Schools were few and far between (most were run by the Orthodox Church) and towards the end of the 1870s there were around 150 in the entire island of which most were small and inadequate. The language problem meant slower progress within government circles. Thus, at the first, and quite successful meeting of the legislative council which met on 9 December, the languages spoken were English, French, Greek and Turkish.

These and many other problems faced Wolseley, in addition to the usual difficulties which always face an incoming administration. It must be said however, that one of the outstanding successes of the British occupation was the elimination of corruption from all branches of the island's government.

## The Hellenic Dream

The ideal of having a greater Hellas encompassing all Greeks who were under the domination of foreign states, was centuries old. In the case of Cyprus it was much older than the British occupation. Attempts were made by the island's Greeks, usually at the instigation of friendly nations, to free themselves and hence decide their own destiny. In the 16th and 17th centuries such appeals or attempts proved abortive.

During the 18th. century the same story is repeated. Yet there was a difference. Following the Russo-Turkish war of 1769-70, two important events for Hellenism took place. First, Cyprus showed some signs of recovery both economically and politically and second, the concept of Hellenism found political expression in the 'Philike Hetairia' founded by Constantine Rhigas in Bucharest in the early 1780s. Although the movement received a check with the execution of Rhigas and his 7 associates (including the 31 year-old Cypriot Ioannis Karadjas) in 1798, it was revived and expanded in Odessa by Tsakalov, Skoufas and Xanthos in 1814. From 1818 onwards several Hetairia emissaries visited the island (known by the secret code number of 13) and the part of Cyprus in the coming struggle was determined. The events of 1821 and the two enosist rebellions of 1833 in Cyprus have already been discussed in the previous chapter.

The movement for union with Greece, therefore, had begun before the British occupation. Furthermore, the provisional character of the Cyprus Convention and the precedent of the Ionian Islands[7] fostered the belief that it was only a matter of time before a similar gesture would be made over Cyprus. Resolutions, memoranda, deputations, protests and riots in favour of union with Greece are to be found with great frequency in the annals of Cypriot history after 1878.

For over 3000 years the '**Greekness**' of Cyprus was beyond doubt - at all times Greeks were in the majority. Thus the struggle to unite Cyprus with the Greek mainland was from the outset a Greek-Cypriot affair. Only certain elements of the Turkish minority[8], as we shall see in later chapters, objected. Contrary to what has been written elsewhere, the vast majority of the Turkish population did not support the repressive measures imposed by the British to check the agitation for enosis.

Enosist aspirations were expressed in many ways and forms: In 1880, a wave of enthusiasm swept Cyprus as Greece mobilized for war against Turkey. Scores of volunteers and 107 mules were the Cypriot contribution. King George I praised the islanders and in a sincere letter to the Archbishop, dated 2 December, he re-iterated that this was clear proof of the true strength of Greek feeling - Hellenism - an indissoluble bond based on descent, religion and tradition.

Public statements by English politicians, like W.E. Gladstone (the great Liberal leader and four times Prime Minister of G.B. between 1868 and 1894) and Sir Charles Dilke, another leading parliamentarian, in favour of either enosis, cession, or retrocession, were seized upon by the Cypriots. It is to be noted that in July 1881 Queen Victoria made it known that she would not "consent" to give up Cyprus.

In 1897, once more, the Christian element of Cyprus demonstrated yet again their Hellenic feelings by sending an estimated 760 volunteers to fight in the so-called '*Thirty Days War*' between Greece and Turkey. They were commended for their heroism, especially at Velestino. Sir Walter Sendall pointed out to his superiors in Whitehall that the chief aider and abettor was the recently appointed Greek consul named **Philemon**. He was regularly greeted by the Greek inhabitants as the representative of "*our king*" but paradoxically enough he was regarded by the authorities in Cyprus as a '*sincere gentleman*' who was '*especially friendly to England and the English.*'

---

(7) Britain took them from the French during the Napoleonic Wars of the early 19th century and following enosist unrest in 1849, ceded them to Greece in 1864.

(8) The biggest minority (around 18%); mainly descendants of the Ottomans who ruled Cyprus from 1571 to 1878.

A Greek Cypriot volunteer in
the wars of mainland Greece's
liberation struggle.
End of 19th century

Nevertheless, the High Commissioner issued a proclamation on 23
April calling on all the inhabitants to abstain from acts likely to cause
disturbances. He then informed the Colonial Office that the anxiety that
still existed arose partly from the composition of the police force. He was
of course referring to the loyalties of Christian and Moslem policemen in
the event of clashes between the two communities. By 6 May the most
perfect tranquillity prevailed everywhere. Yet two notable incidents
during the Greek Easter celebrations (24/25 April 1897) which very nearly
set the patriotic embers of the two sides alight, are worth recalling. The
first incident occurred at a Famagusta church where an explosion injured
35 people and killed a child and an old man. Although several moslems
were arrested, the motives, if any, of this reckless act were not established
by the authorities.

The second episode took place in a Limassol church and it nearly
provoked communal violence. As in the above case, during the ceremony
of the 'Judas Bonfire' (lit in the precincts of the churches on Easter eve), a

native Turkish police officer was seen to enter the church smoking a pipe. Once more the moderating influences prevailed and there was no trouble. In fact, communal violence was a rarity in the island.

The Greek-speaking, Greek-thinking, Greek-feeling Cypriots continued their agitation for enosis by all available means. It was consequently no surprise when a Greek cadet training ship 'Admiral Miaoulis' visiting Limassol in 1906 occasioned fervent enosist demonstrations.

Further outbursts resulted from the visit of Winston Churchill in 1907 - he arrived in the morning of Wednesday 9 October and departed on the evening of Sunday the 13th. Churchill received all local dignatories. A memorandum from the Greek elected members of the legislative council emphasized the three cardinal issues: union with Greece, abolition of the tribute and wider political liberties for the people's elected representatives. Concerning enosis, the memorialists pointed out that *"such a desirable consummation will doubtless be fulfilled in the plenitude of time and that in the meantime, the people of Cyprus will be content to remain under the British flag"*.

In his reply[9] to the Greek elected members he stressed that it was only natural that the Cypriot people who were of Greek descent should regard their incorporation with what may be called their mother country as an ideal to be earnestly, devoutly and fervently cherished. To Churchill such a feeling was an example of the patriotic devotion which so nobly characterized the Greek nation. His government however had to consider also the views of the island's Moslems and the fact that the British occupation of Cyprus should not lead to the dismemberment of the Ottoman Empire. Furthermore, as to the alleged precedent of the Ionian Islands, they had actually been in the possession of the British government and Cyprus was not. So ended Churchill's reply.

The Greeks however persisted with further protests, letters, telegrams and deputations. Members of the Royal family, senior ecclesiastics and parliamentarians were targets for telegrams and memorials. All moves expressed the steadfast desire of the Greeks for national restoration. And, on 28 April 1912, approval was given by the members of the legislative council, who had resigned *en masse* on 17 April, to the formation of a central committee under the presidency of the archbishop, for carrying on the national struggle. The resolution adopted declared that no power in the world, no oppression could alter the national sentiment and will to be annexed to Greece.

---

(9) CMD (Command Papers) 3996. 1907-08. Volume 71, Page 985

*Above:* A group of local Cypriots, both Greek and Turkish, in the Troodos area.

*Right:* Local villagers with traditional holiday dress

The Turco-Italian War of 1911-12, which brought a Turkish defeat, caused some excitement in certain towns of Cyprus. The disturbances in Nicosia and elsewhere were not at all serious but the '*jamouda*' (little mosque) incident in Limassol on the night of 27 May 1912 caused some concern.

A synopsis of the events is as follows: some Greeks stoned two carriages full of Turks coming from the village of Malia. At once one of the Turks drew a knife and stabbed two Greeks. The bells of the Katholidgi church began ringing and the Greeks, sensing trouble, arrived in large numbers. A brawl developed but when the police opened fire the crowds dispersed.

On 15 June a three-man mixed commission was appointed to carry out a full enquiry into all matters relating to the riots. The commission was unable to come to a unanimous conclusion as to the actual cause of the disturbances (the British and Greek members stated that the riot was not premeditated, whilst the Turkish member insisted that it was) but they were all of the opinion that the local police commander was justified in firing on the rioters. The casualties reported by the commission were as follows:

3 killed and 100 hundred wounded, caused by the rioters to civilians;
1 officer and 14 men wounded, caused by rioters to police;
2 killed and 9 wounded, caused by rifle fire of the police.

Furthermore, at least 18 persons were sentenced, using the outdated Ottoman penal code, to imprisonment ranging from 9 months to 15 years. These sentences were reduced considerably in June 1913. Disturbances of this nature were rare and caused by certain irresponsible elements, both Greek and Turk, usually flaring up on the spur of the moment. A typical example occurred in 1909 when, following some excitement caused by several meetings of Greeks, around 700 Turks assembled in one corner of Nicosia and armed themselves with swords and knives; nothing happened.

Further delegations and memorials (and sometimes counter-memorials) fill the annals of Cypriot history right up to the advent of the First World War - and beyond. Language, tradition, race and religion prompted the Greeks of Cyprus to struggle for union with Greece. Such feelings, beliefs and attachment was only natural. There was however, another factor that kept this desire alive - the voice of the clergy and of the educated professional classes - i.e., the apostles of the **meghali idhea** (great idea). For years the Greeks had been dreaming of a Greater Hellas in which all Greeks, especially those living under foreign governments, would unite under one flag. No Greek thought however of bringing his compatriots in Egypt, the United States or Britain into this Hellenic fold but nearly every Greek thought in terms of rescuing his enslaved brothers from Turkish rule. The most concern was shown for those in the Smyrna district, the Bulgarian littoral, Macedonia, Epirus, the Dodecanese Islands and Cyprus.

This Great Idea, the hope for a greater Greece, was a national ideal that transcended party lines. Hence the desire to expand, to liberate more and more Greeks from Turkish rule became the motivating force of Greek foreign policy. Indeed, since independence, the Greek people were passionately attached to a foreign policy inspired by the meghali idhea.

Greece obtained the Ionian Islands in 1864; Thessaly and one district of Epirus in 1881; Crete, southern Epirus, a large portion of Macedonia

Sir Garnet Wolseley, the British High Commissioner receives a Turkish delegation of notables on the occasion of Bairam – 1878 engraving.

and most of the Aegean Islands came to her as a result of the Balkan Wars of 1912-13. Greece as a result increased its territory by 68% and its population from approximately 2,700,000 to around 4,800,000. This was a powerful incentive for other Greeks to aspire to join the motherland, aspirations which were greatly encouraged by President Woodrow Wilson's[10] plea for government with the consent of the governed. All subject peoples took new hope. Greeks were duly convinced that Cyprus should be Greek and as King Henry V had once said 'they' have a *"just quarrel"*.

# The emergence of the Constitution

Less than two months after the arrival of Wolseley, an Order in Council[11] dated 14 September 1878, established a legislative council and an executive council to run the affairs of the island. The latter was constituted as might be directed by instructions addressed from time to time to the island's administrators by Whitehall.

(10) 1856-1924. The 28th President of the United States; led that country from 1912 to 1920

(11) Together with proclamations, writs and ordinances, orders in council are prerogative powers of legislation which are still important in the armed forces, civil service and the colonial empire. They provide a convenient mechanism for implementing important governmental decisions.

The legislative council consisted of the High Commissioner and not less than 4 and not more than 8 other members - half being officials and others unofficial. At its first meeting on 9 December 1878 it was composed of 4 English, an Italian, a Greek Cypriot and a Turkish Cypriot. It is important to recall that at its third meeting on 19 December, it took into consideration a proposed ordinance regarding the sale of land to subjects of foreign countries. The three non-British members objected but it was finally passed. Hence, the freedom which Britain promised the Cypriots turned out to be the autocratic ('*monokratoria*') rule of the High Commissioner who possessed practically unlimited powers.

Protests began to pour in - those of 1881 being particularly effective. Soon the British government contemplated changes; moreover, Cyprus was transferred on 6 December 1880 from the Foreign Office to the Colonial Office. An Order in Council dated 30 November 1882 modified the existing form of administration.

The subsequent elections however brought out certain long-standing divisions in the island. For instance, the so-called '*Old Turkish Party*' objected at first believing that the elections and the formation of the legislative council would stabilize the British regime thereby giving the non-Moslem majority a chance to impose its will on them  Yet on most issues in the 1880s and 1890s the elected Cypriot councillors were in complete agreement.

The '*new*' legislative council[12] assembled on Thursday 21 June 1883 and those present were the High Commissioner and 6 British official members, 8 Greeks (one was absent) and 3 Turks. This undemocratic form of colonial administration (communal representation was first formulated in Cyprus) meant that those areas of business not decided solely by the High Commissioner were handed to the legislative council. This however, worked on the principle that the British and Turkish members at least equalled or exceeded by one, the number of Greek members with the High Commissioner having the  casting vote. An Anglo-Turkish combination, therefore, could carry any measure against the united opposition of the Greeks representing around 80% of the island's population. Although some form of representative government was given there was no provision for majority rule and the constitution was attacked as a "*sham gift*"[13]. This system was maintained, especially after Cyprus became a Crown Colony (1925) through a process of privileges for the Turkish members, antagonizing the Greek Cypriots and providing therefore the basis for '*divide and rule*'. Indeed, the policy of the

---

(12) Western traditions of political representation were therefore introduced in the very early years of British rule

(13)  The Edinburgh Review. Volume 173 (1891) pages 453-4.

*Above:* The newly formed legislative council. Early 1880s.

*Below:* The British district commissioner "Kaimakan" and local representatives judging an assault case at Eptakomi near Nicosia.

*Above Top:* Larnaca waterfront with its increased trade.
*Above:* A party of British government officials leaving Nicosia.
*Below:* Limassol waterfront with the new pier. All 1878 engravings.

colonial administration tended almost always towards enhancing separation between Greek and Turk. In brief, the legislative council after 1882 consisted of the High Commissioner and 18 members of whom 12 were to be elected (3 by mohametan voters and 9 by non-mohametan electors) and 6 were non-elective. Changes were few and far between although non-mohametan (the term favoured by the colonial administration) representation was increased to 12 in 1925.

# The Economic situation

The Cypriots were assured in 1878 that measures would be taken to promote and develop commerce and industry. The inhabitants were given to understand that half a century's peace and good management would push the island to as high a position as it had occupied in the time of its greatest glory. As The Times commented on 22 July 1878 *"Englishmen will not prove inadequate to the island's development"*. Once more, however, man and nature combined to inflict severe blows on the already retarded Cypriot economy. In 1877-78 there was a drought, a plague in 1880 and bad harvests in 1877 and 1889. In 1880 and 1882, two floods in Limassol caused nearly 30 deaths and unquantifiable damage.

The inhabitants were asking for material help to provide for schools of agriculture, an agricultural bank, irrigation works, replantation of trees in the forests and the introduction of new seeds etc. They were also insisting that the tithe (a tax on produce and stock) and the tribute should be abolished.

A Greek Cypriot deputation, led by the archbishop, arrived in England in 1889 to plead in person for some remission of the fiscal burdens facing the inhabitants. The archbishop was received by Queen Victoria and was created Doctor of Divinity by the University of Oxford. The deputation however received no encouragement from the Conservative government of Lord Salisbury.

The tribute was perhaps the most important factor in the fortunes of Cyprus. Britain, in return for the occupation of the island, undertook to make good to Turkey the average difference between the island's revenue and expenditure in its last 5 years as an Ottoman province. Since Turkey had spent nothing on the island but had, on the contrary, taken what it could get out of it, the difference worked out at £92,799. 11s. 3d a year, a sum which was debited annually from its revenue. Usually, British governments had voted a grant-in-aid of a fluctuating amount, which in 1910 was fixed at £50,000 a year. The tribute was abolished in 1927.

Kitchener (seated) and his team in 1883

ROAD NETWORK
IN **1881**

RIZOKARPASO
KYRENIA
LAPITHOS
TRICOMO
KARAVOSTASI   NICOSIA
FAMAGUSTA
PERISTERONA
POLIS   TROODOS
PLATRES
MATIATI
LARNACA
**PAPHOS**
ZYGI
LIMASSOL
——— Constructed and improved
    since 1878
----- Roads Proposed
······· Military Roads

ROAD NETWORK
IN 1904

RIZOKARPASO
AKANTHOU
LAPITHOS   KYRENIA
LEONARISSO
MYRTOU
LEFKONIKO
TRICOMO
MORPHOU
NICOSIA
KAMBOS
KLIROU
ATHIENOU
FAMAGUSTA
POLIS   TROODOS
AGROS
PLATRES
LARNACA
ORA
PAPHOS
ZYGI   Open up to 1904
LIMASSOL   ----- Under Construction

Horatio Herbert Kitchener who
undertook to survey the island

This payment retarded growth. The Cypriots kept on protesting by all means available to them: press, pulpit, delegations, memorials, deputations etc. They soon found an influential ally. Winston Churchill insisted that all taxation raised should be used for the benefit of the island's inhabitants. Following his first visit to the island in 1907, he reported to the Cabinet on the condition of Cyprus. He stressed that the payment of the tribute was an *"iniquitous and immoral arrangement... and a blemish upon Imperial policy....."*[14]

Some reforms were certainly passed but Churchill quite rightly stressed that an improvement upon Turkish standards was not a sufficient or suitable defence for British policy.

*Above:* Weaving loom and accessories (wood engraving)

*Right:* A group of local weavers

(14) Colonial Office (CO.) 67/241/4139 H. At the time, Churchill was Under-Secretary of State for the Colonies

Britain justified the poor economic progress of Cyprus using the argument that the island was held in trust and indeed the only British possession in the strange position of not being either inside or outside the British empire. Or was Cyprus simply side-tracked and therefore neglected due to the fact that Britain secured Egypt in 1882?[15] Or can we say that the British authorities lacked the foresight and the willingness to develop the island? To sum up, the economic story of the island can be described as one of great expectations but small beginnings.

## Church Disputation

Another issue which helped to raise Greek passions was the so-called *"squalid schism"* within the Church between 1900 and 1910, brought about by the death of Archbishop Sofronios II on 22 May 1900. Epifanios, the Bishop of Paphos who had precedence over the bishops of Kition and Kyrenia, had died on 5 February 1899 and so the contest was taken up by the two surviving clerics.

The election, organised by the Holy Synod of Cyprus, took place in September 1900 but its validity was disputed and the tranquillity of the island was disturbed by disputes between the highest functionaries of the Christian Church. Attempts to resolve the dispute were made - even by the Oecumenical Patriarch - but to no avail. The contest involved the whole Greek population, with charges and counter-charges put forward by the supporters and opponents of the two candidates, declarations of support and so forth. At one stage in 1903 charges were brought by 600 persons against the Bishop of Kition for alleged ecclesiastical offences.

Demonstrations and riots were also common with the early months of 1908 being particularly eventful. The High Commissioner, alarmed at the disturbed state of public feeling in Nicosia, requested troops to be sent from Limassol. That was in March. The riots of April were even more serious and evidence exists showing that they were not spontaneous. During the night of 9 April, the disorder culminated in a serious riot, in the course of which firearms were freely used. On the following day the High Commissioner issued a proclamation that in order to put an end to the disorder, Nicosia would be occupied by the police and attempts to disturb the peace would be forcibly suppressed. He warned peaceable people to avoid scenes of disturbance. Although considerable damage was done to property and some serious injury inflicted on individuals, it appears that there was no loss of life.

---

(15) In that year G.B. occupied Egypt. Consequently its trading routes to India and the Near and Far East went via Gibraltar, Malta and the Suez Canal. Cyprus was downgraded and sentenced to some 32 years *'imprisonment"*.

In April 1909 the Bishop of Kition was elected archbishop under the Archiepiscopal Election Law, although the Bishop of Kyrenia was appointed archbishop by the church of Constantinople. However, in early 1910 the Bishop of Kyrenia at last consented to recognize his opponent as archbishop and resumed his see with the title 'His Beatitude the President of Kyrenia'.

The dispute was finally resolved in April 1910 following the elections to the sees of Paphos and Kition. Moreover in 1914 the Holy Synod drew up a constitutional charter for the Church of Cyprus, regulating its administration on the basis of the sacred canons and prevailing practice, thus preventing the recurrence of any similar conflicts. It provided for an electoral body of 66 elected general representatives (22 clerical and 44 lay), voting jointly with the Synod which was reinforced at archiepiscopal elections by 7 abbots and certain other dignitaries. The total was to be 77 members. Thus when Kyrillos II died in 1916 he was peacefully succeeded by his opponent Kyrillos III who led the church until 1933.

Archbishop Sophronios (1865–1900) lying in state

# (ii)  From Annexation to the First Major Popular Protest 1914-1931

**Complacency and near total disinterestedness** - this must surely be our verdict of the years of uncertainty.[1] Yes, Britain was faced with an awesome task but it was a task she did not attempt to fulfil. Churchill's memorandum to the Cabinet in 1907 categorically asserted that *'an improvement upon Turkish standards is not a sufficient or suitable defence for British policy'* - this is certainly the crux of the matter: **Cyprus had been simply neglected.**

Following the Annexation Order of 5 November 1914, Cyprus formed part, both de facto and de jure, of His Majesty's Dominions. British citizenship for the inhabitants was finally settled in November 1917 and in 1925 Cyprus was proclaimed a **Crown Colony**. An Order of the King in Council (6. 2. 1925) reconstituted the legislative council; the Royal Letters Patent and Royal Instructions (10. 3. 1925) which were published in a special issue of the Cyprus Gazette (1. 5. 1925) regulated the affairs and administration of Cyprus.

Very briefly, the relevant sections and effect on Cyprus of the two European treaties must be mentioned here. The Treaty of Sevres (near Paris), which developed from the San Remo Treaty of the same year, was signed on 10 August 1920. The three articles concerning Cyprus are numbers 115, 116 and 117. Article 115 states that the High Contracting Parties recognize the annexation of Cyprus proclaimed by HMG on 5 November 1914; the next article states that Turkey renounces all rights and titles to Cyprus, including the right to the tribute formerly 'paid' to the Sultan; lastly, Article 117 says that Turkish nationals born or resident in Cyprus will acquire British nationality and lose their Turkish nationality, subject to the conditions laid down in local law.

The second agreement of 1923 deserves a closer examination. The Conference of Lausanne which met (not continuously) from November 1922 to July 1923, was one of the most important diplomatic gatherings after the First World War. Even the US sent Senator Hamilton Levy to salvage something for the American oil companies  Thus a Foreign Office minute dated 25 July records that *'the Americans want to keep Ismet at Lausanne negotiating a separate treaty with them by which they shall obtain more favourable terms than we have been able to get.'* The treaty was signed on 24 July and contained 143 articles of which four will be mentioned:

---

(1)  1878-1914: From Occupation to Annexation.

*Above:* The official declaration proclaiming Cyprus a British Crown Colony in a ceremony in old Nicosia on 1 May 1925.
*Right:* Silver coin of King George V commemorating the declaration

### Article 15

Turkey renounces in favour of Italy all rights and titles over the Dodecanese.

### Article 16

Turkey hereby renounces all rights and titles whatsoever over or respecting the territories situated outside the frontiers laid down in the present Treaty and the islands other than those for which her sovereignty is recognized by the said Treaty.

### Article 20

Turkey hereby recognizes the annexation of Cyprus proclaimed by the British Government on 5 November 1914.

## Article 21

Turkish nationals ordinarily resident in Cyprus on 5 November 1914 will acquire British nationality subject to the conditions laid down in local law and will thereupon lose their Turkish nationality. They will, however, have the right to opt for Turkish nationality within two years from the coming into force of the present Treaty, provided that they leave Cyprus within twelve months after having so opted.

Hence, by article 16, Turkey surrendered all titles and claims over Cyprus. Likewise, by accepting the agreements Greece endorsed and put her name to the cession of Cyprus to Great Britain. Article 20 gave no veto to either Turkey, Greece or to any other country over the disposal of Cyprus by HMG. The Turks however reserved the right to receive into Turkey, during the following two years, any Cypriot Turk who wished to retain Turkish nationality. In the period up to 1925 only a small percentage of those living on the island were attracted to Asia Minor by the promise of grants of land. In June of that year, Turkey opened a consulate in Larnaca in order to assist any movement of Turkish Cypriots. In fact by 21 October 1927 only some 2,500 to 3,000 out of the 9,000 or so persons who opted for Turkish nationality had actually left Cyprus to 'return' to Turkish territory. There was therefore, as the Foreign Office observed, '*a Turkish colony of some five to six thousand people in the island, who for this and the succeeding generation may be a source of anxiety to the authorities*'. Yet the presence of the Turkish community in Cyprus was also described on many occasions by leading British officials as '*an asset from a political standpoint.*' The British ploy of playing the two communities, with their distinct religious beliefs, against each other was seen as a way of perpetuating British rule in Cyprus.

Greek nationalism was betrayed by Article 15, which gave the Dodecanese to Italy (this was acknowledged by Venizelos in his pact with Mussolini in 1928) and by Article 20, which gave Cyprus to Britain. One may ask what happened to the spirit of nationalism created by Versailles in 1919? Both the Dodecanese and Cyprus were assigned to foreign powers without even being asked.

Lausanne was important for three other reasons. First, it marked the definite triumph of Turkish nationalism under Mustafa Kemal Pasha (Ataturk, or Father of the Turks, born in Salonica in 1881). His chief military collaborator was Ismet Pasha (later Inonu), a fellow officer from the days of the First World War and a true Ottoman, who in his own way had perhaps become as westernised as Mustafa Kemal. Ismet headed the Turkish delegation at Lausanne; Turkey's search for a western European identity was at last a reality.

The Ottoman empire had ceased to be but a new national state of Turkey had arisen in Anatolia under the guiding hand of Ataturk, who

*Above:* A military parade by the walls and moat, Nicosia. Such a show of strength was a regular event.

*Right:* Mounted policeman of the late 1920s.

*Below:* A stamp showing the badge of the new colony.

*Above and left:*
Views of police officers of
the period.

directed its destiny along the path of modernization. The new Turkey was
liberated from antiquated financial and economic bondage and was ready
to begin life anew in a revived and independent spirit. The long struggle
of the Turks for national independence is one of the great epics of recent
world history. That independence, won on the battlefields of Asia Minor,
was to be finally achieved by no less notable victories in diplomacy at
Lausanne. Ismet ominously intimated that Turkey would 'never' accept a
Greek Aegean or a Greek Cyprus.

Second, Lausanne marked the disastrous defeat of Greece and the
end of the Hellenic dream in Asia Minor. It was humbled beyond all
expectations. Lausanne formally registered the triumph of Turkish aims
and the failure of the Allied powers to maintain their original peace
settlement. The expulsion of the Greeks from Asia Minor resulted in the
death of some 15 per cent of the Greek population and the permanent
absorption of another 1 1/2 million Greek refugees whose arrival
increased the mainland population by 30 per cent.

Lausanne was called by Lloyd George in his book *The Truth about the
Peace Treaties* as an *'abject, cowardly and infamous surrender'*. It recovered
for Turkey practically all the territory which had been taken away at
Sevres for the benefit of Greece and Armenia.

Third it signified a victory of French over British policy in the Near East. The French sphere of political and economic influence in the region was not only consolidated but expanded. For Cyprus the treaties had a twofold importance: first, Turkey renounced all rights to the island. Hence not even a whisper was raised when Cyprus later became a Crown Colony (1925). Second, the Greeks of the island believed that the British would sooner or later grant them their ultimate wish since Turkey was now definitely out of the way. Britain's uncertainty of tenure, especially between 1878 and 1914, was often cited as a reason for not granting union with Greece and for not carrying out economic, social,constitutional and other reforms.

Once more a long list of customary problems needed to be tackled. In addition, other issues also dominated Cypriot politics.

## *The Economic issue:*

It is beyond doubt that under British rule Cyprus fared better than under its earlier rulers. Cyprus was handed over to Britain by Turkey in a thoroughly exhausted and ruined condition. Communications were practically non-existent;[2] post offices, hospitals, printing presses and schools were hardly in evidence. By the early 1920s however we find fairly good roads and bridges and a railway which ran from Famagusta to Nicosia; over 70 post offices with around 200 rural mail stations dealing with over 3 million letters, cards, newspapers, books and parcels; hospitals were found in all the districts; around 15 newspapers were published - showing eloquently the material and educational advancement of the Cypriots; also we find 764 schools with well-trained teachers. This was labelled *'unexampled prosperity'*.

Yet, there were many negative aspects and complaints were regularly included in the memoranda sent to the governing authorities. Cyprus was predominantly an agricultural country and it was here that least progress had been made. Furthermore the people suffered high levels of taxation; the tribute and the Imperial Defence Tax were imposed over and above the usual taxes. Living standards were low, and poverty, accentuated by the malpractices of the money-lending few over the ignorant and uneducated, was widespread. There was a mass exodus from the villages to the towns, children worked long hours under intolerable conditions[3] and wages were generally low.

---

(2) Sir Samuel and Lady Baker, during their travels in Cyprus in the early months of 1879, explained that they were "stuck continuously by the mud" and that only "animal tracks existed in some places".

(3) It seemed as though the Britain of the 17th and 18th centuries was 'transplanted' onto 20th century Cyprus.

Much can be learnt about the island's economic ills if we simply summarise the contents of a letter dated 17 September 1917 sent by A.J. Cunningham[4] to the Colonial Office. He was at pains to stress that Cyprus was being exploited by a handful of *'bloodsucking advocates'* or *'legalized spiders'* and several wholesale merchants, who not only controlled the legislative council but in practice also governed ecclesiastical decisions, school and village councils. Amongst other things he suggested the opening of an agricultural bank to make advances to villagers at low rates of interest. Cunningham saw the current socio-economic condition of the island as an affront to human existence and dignity. His suggestions, though noted were not acted upon. However, in 1925 the tithe was abolished and in 1927 the tribute also received the same fate. In July King George V also expressed the hope that the government *"must see its way and abolish"* the tribute. Moreover, co-operative credit societies increased in number from 28 in 1925 to 236 in 1930, catering for about 2/3 of the villages. Also, an Agricultural Bank was established in June 1925 under the joint auspices of the government and the Ottoman Bank.

No one however can shy away from the facts: According to the Survey of Rural Life in Cyprus,[5] conditions of living were roughly equivalent to those which prevailed in England during the 15th and 16th centuries. The rural population as stated by the Survey constituted 80.5% of the total yet only around 3/5 of the land was under cultivation, the rest being held by the government and the Greek and Turkish institutions. The Survey, which fixed a very conservative minimum level of subsistence, found that over 25% of the rural population lived below that level, some 50% around that scale and the rest above it. Most peasants were illiterate and over 70% were chronically indebted to usurers and merchants whose actions for recovery afforded lucrative employment for numerous advocates. Forced sales of property which numbered 959 in 1920 increased to 2916 in 1926 - in fact an increase of 304%. Sir Ronald Storrs explained that when he assumed the governorship in 1926 he found on the legislative council 8 advocates three of whom were money-lenders; one landowner who was also a money-lender; one bishop of the Orthodox Church; one merchant and one farmer. He went on to say that even though the real interests of Cyprus were those of the peasant producer, the interests represented in the council were exclusively those of the *"numerically insignificant class of parasites who made a living out of him"*.[6]

---

(4) He was for some time the Assistant Island Postmaster. His paper was entitled 'England's Duty to Cyprus'. See CO 67/187/46085. Pages 589-600.

(5) Prepared in 1927-28 on the instigation of Sir Ronald Storrs, the Governor. Its findings were published in booklet form in 1930.

(6) Orientations. 1937. Page 570

Two contrasting views of the economic and social divide of the period.
*Above:* Women and children of the 'Elite Aristocracy' of Nicosia.
*Below:* Poor conditions of a pottery workshop in Nicosia.

*Above Left:* Typical family from Pano
Lefkara – 1921
*Above right:* Local Cypriot "Vrakas"
*Right:* Britons tasting wine at the turn of
the century
*Below:* Rural scene after the harvest

The Cypriots also suffered from that monstrosity of feudal and manorial domination - forced labour.[7]  Hence, what the heroic French revolutionaries fought - in the name of liberty, equality and fraternity - to abolish in 1789 still persisted in Cyprus 142 years later.  Legislation was enacted in 1931 to put an end to compulsory labour.

The island's inhabitants therefore had to endure excessive and unfair taxation, forced labour, exploitation, court actions and the world economic slump especially of the late 1920s; additionally, they suffered an unworkable constitution and political persecution.  The above issues, needless to say, give weight to the criticism that Cyprus was merely occupied rather that administered or developed.  They also illustrate the fact that the island, not being on the direct route to India (Britain, Gibraltar, Malta and Suez), was slowly acquiring the status of a second class colony; hence, the government was not particularly interested in its development.  The British failure to cure the evident economic grievances of the island was continually attacked by the press - a medium which assumed great significance in Cypriot politics.  Economic and political unrest was rife in the 1920s.  The political outlook of the people was undergoing change and the labour movement was beginning to make its voice heard.  The formation of trade unions added a further dimension to the island's history - stoppages and strikes were henceforth better organized and well supported.

## *The Constitution:*

The annexation of the island on 5 November 1914 was not accompanied by any change in the constitution; in fact, the demand for wider political representation continued unabated.  However, an Order in Council dated 6 February 1925 increased the membership of the legislative council.  It was to consist of the Governor, 9 official and 15 elected members of which three were to be elected by mohametan voters and twelve by non-mohametan voters.  From the brief table below it can be seen that an Anglo-Turkish combination could carry any measure against the united opposition of the Greeks who represented around 80% of the island's total population:

|  | 1882 | 1925 |
|---|---|---|
| High Commissioner (Governor) | 1 | 1 |
| British non-elective members | 6 | 9 |
| Mohametan elective members | 3 | 3 |
| Non-mohametan elective members | 9 | 12 |
| **Total** | **19** | **25** |

---

(7)  Mainly for village road construction.

The elections of October 1925 duly provided a legislative council with 15 elected members and the reconstituted chamber met for the first time on 6 November. However, in addition to the increase in the size of the council, a unique restriction was imposed on its powers. The provision, which was contrary to the Colonial Laws Validity Act of 1865, stated that the council, despite its representative character, might make no law to alter the constitution. In fact, these so-called *'new arrangements'* were no different from those which already existed - the debating chamber had no more power than before and the issuing of Orders in Council was often used to override its decisions. In 1927 alone, seven such orders were passed. It was therefore a non-democratic form of colonial rule since only those areas of business not decided solely by the Governor were handed to the legislative council and even then, there was the threat of passing laws by the use of prerogative powers.

## Political issues:

*Enosis* agitation, the offers and promises made by Britain to give up the island and Cyprus' contribution to the war effort of the allies (1914-18) will be dealt with in this section.

Firstly, a few words about the so-called *'offers and promises'* between 1912 and 1919 and Cyprus' war effort on the side of Britain and her Allies. Amongst several more general pronouncements, there were two *offers* in 1912 and 1915 and two *promises* in 1919. After the first phase of the Balkan Wars the combatants met in London (from 16 December 1912 to 6 January 1913), to discuss peace terms. At the head of the Greek delegation was the *'maker of modern Greece'* , **Eleftherios Venizelos**, who holds the distinction of being the first Greek Prime Minister to raise the question of Cyprus in an international gathering. Lloyd George, an influential political figure who was at the time Chancellor of the Exchequer and who had intimated on several occasions that Greece should be given Cyprus, asked Venizelos whether Britain could use the naval facilities provided at Argostoli (Cephalonia) in return for Cyprus. This unofficial request and offer was accepted in principle by Venizelos, yet neither Athens nor London pursued the proposal to any sort of conclusion in 1912 or 1913. In Cyprus however, the archbishop, who chaired a meeting of notables and provincial delegates on 7 January 1913, *'proclaimed'* the union of the island with Greece. On 18 January, *Eleftheria,* a Greek Cypriot newspaper, published an article to the effect that Cyprus was shortly to be handed over to Greece and that Constantinos Papamichalopoulos had been designated by the Hellenic government as its first governor of Cyprus. The Turkish Cypriots were alarmed but the High Commissioner assured them that their interests would be safeguarded if and when such a change occurred.

# Cyprus Police Force under the British administration:
Various uniforms and ranks of officers

| **Rural Constable** with Badge and Staff | **Private** Summer Uniform (Khaki) | **Private** Winter Uniform (Blue Serge) | **District Sergt-Major** Summer Uniform (Khaki) |

| **Turkish Inspector** Winter Uniform (Undress) | **Turkish Inspector** Summer Uniform (Full Dress) | **Turkish Inspector** Winter Uniform (Full Dress) | **Local Commandant** Winter Uniform (Undress) |

Further offers of territory were transmitted to Greece in 1914 and 1915 - in return for immediate participation in the war effort on the side of the allies. Offers of territory were also made in November 1914 and January 1915. In October 1915 Cyprus was the '*bait*', in addition to other concessions in western Thrace and Asia Minor - both it may be noted inhabited mainly by Turks and not British sovereign territories. Furthermore, there was no mention of naval facilities nor any talk of the Turkish minority in Cyprus being an obstacle. In Athens the pro-German establishment was adamant. The opportunity of acquiring Cyprus was lost. Greece eventually entered the war on the side of the allies but by 1917 they were already on the road to victory and there was no reason to change the island's administration.[8]

Nevertheless in 1919 Cyprus was again '*promised*' to Greece. A record of a conversation on 13 May, during a Council of Four (Britain, US, France and Italy) meeting between Lloyd George (Prime Minister of Great Britain) and Woodrow Wilson (President of the US) went like this:

LG  –  *It is my intention to give Cyprus to Greece.*

WW – *Excellent idea.*

LG  –  *(referring to the Turks). They have no right in a country which they had converted to mere desert.*

Amongst the various reasons as to why this '*promise*' was not kept was the one put forward by military tacticians who argued, very forcibly, that there were strong strategic reasons for not giving up the island. The second '*promise*' was made by Ramsay McDonald, the leader of the Labour Party, in February 1919. Speaking at the Socialist International Conference (held at Berne, Switzerland), he emphasised that his party supported Cypriot self-determination and that, if he ever came to power, he would do everything possible to carry out this commitment. McDonald however, who led the short-lived Labour government of 1924 (22 January to 3 November), failed to honour his pledge. It is important to note that in October 1919 Walter Long (First Lord of the Admiralty) submitted a memorandum to the War Council outlining proposals to cede Cyprus to Greece. Another '*promise*' in 1930 also came to nothing.

Within the context of such offers and promises we must pinpoint Cyprus' overall contribution to the allied war effort - for so small an island it was simply phenomenal. Approximately 13,000 men, between the ages of 18 and 41 were recruited as muleteers for the British Salonica Force; approximately 47,000 animals (goats, mules, donkeys and horses); around £9,000 was raised for the British and Belgian Red Cross Funds; (nearly one million in today's terms) large quantities of foodstuffs and timber were

---

(8) There is a plethora of official documentation on this issue. See FO 371/9897 and CAB 41/36/2, amongst others.

Members of the Paphos Law Court in the late 1920s.

exported for the use of the expeditionary forces. Moreover, the island was used as a place of detention for prisoners of war and a convalescent depot. Cyprus' contribution was certainly massive. As a result the resources of the island were being strained to the utmost. It may be added that the Cypriots acquitted themselves well on many fronts and were commended highly for their heroism and work-rate under difficult conditions.

With such a favourable atmosphere (the euphoria created by these offers and promises and the island's massive and highly successful involvement during the course of the hostilities), the educated proponents of the *meghali idhea* intensified their efforts to achieve national self-realization. They were also spurred on by the Cretan example, especially of 1913. In that year Crete proclaimed its union with the mainland - an action which was legalized when Turkey abandoned her suzerain rights in a clause of the 1913 Treaty of London. In fact, the political consciousness of the inhabitants had been awakened and had expressed itself in a growing desire of the Christian majority to realise its nationality. They also believed that the Muslim preference for the status quo and antipathy to union should not prove permanent; they pointed out that in Thrace, amongst other places, the Turkish minority lived happily within a Greek majority. Memoranda, petitions and deputations, once more, fill the annals of Cypriot history. The effects of the 1918 deputation deserve some comment.

On 5 December, a deputation consisting of the archbishop and the eight Greek members of the legislative council left for London to press their demands on HMG. After meeting Venizelos in Paris the deputation arrived in London on 3 January 1919. They were then received by Viscount Milner, the Secretary of State for the Colonies, on 3 February. Milner listened carefully; even though he appreciated and respected the aspirations of the memorialists he was not prepared to give a definite reply. The Christian delegation on 5 May also appealed to parliament, church, press and the nation at large. For nearly two years the Cyprus delegation laboured in London without success. The message from Downing Street on 7 November 1919 was that the uncertainty of the international situation in the Middle East precluded a *"definite reply"* to the deputation's petition.[9]

What were the results of this initiative and consequent failure? *Firstly*, memorials by the Moslem population of Cyprus recorded the customary protests. They pleaded against such a union and prayed for the continuance of British rule. More importantly however, there were signs of unrest among the Moslems of Nicosia. In 1919 a small party [10] advocating the return of the island to Turkey was formed. It was led by Dr. Mehmed Essad and Dr. Hussein Behije. Sir Malcolm Stevenson, at the time he was the officer administering the government of Cyprus but was later appointed High Commissioner, described Assad, who had arrived in Cyprus as a refugee in November 1914, as one of the leaders of the *"anti-Greek section"* and Behije *"a local practitioner who was generally drunk"*. Associated with Essad and Behije was Hasan Karabardak, a *"rowdy individual and leader of the hamals"* (local porters), who took a leading part in the disturbances of 1912. Soon however, the symptoms of the unease had disappeared.

*Secondly*, the failure of the delegation to London, led to bitterness, resentment and frustration. A new dimension was added to the Cyprus problem. Events moved very fast. There were public meetings and protests and on 8 December 1920, the Christian members of the legislative council resigned en masse and unanimously decided to initiate new forms of struggle. The year 1921 was not only the centenary of Greek independence but the year in which a new political organisation was set up to direct the enosis struggle. It also witnessed disturbances in Nicosia, the imposition of martial law and the deportation of **Catalanos**.

---

(9)  See CO 537/696

(10)  It had very limited support and was called the "Union with Turkey Party".

On 6 and 7 April, Greek Independence Day was the occasion for a disturbance in Nicosia which the police succeeded in putting down with difficulty . Fresh disorders were feared during the Greek Easter - with the prospect of racial riots. The enlistment of 90 ex-policemen and the call for troop reinforcements by the island's authorities were in the end not needed. Further festivities which may have culminated in riots were abandoned by the organisers.

Meanwhile the colonial administration imposed martial law and tightened internal security. On 24 April the deportation of Nicolas Catalanos was ordered by the High Commissioner. It was alleged that he addressed an inflammatory speech to a number of persons at the New Hellenic Club. The charge was denied and his banishment provoked numerous protests.

Soon a new organisation was set up to direct the enosis struggle . On Sunday 23 October, a meeting of representatives, known as the **National Assembly** was held in Nicosia under the presidency of the archbishop. Further meetings took place on 4 and 5 December and on the latter date a new political organisation, known as the **National Council**, was set up. It replaced the Central Committee of the National Cause and was to be responsible to the National Assembly and thence to the people for its actions. Petition followed upon petition - *enosis and only enosis* - was the motto. Yet one failure followed another failure. Moreover, the tightening of internal security resulted also in the deportation of **Filios Zannetos** in December 1922.

Zannetos was the Mayor of Larnaca, for many years a member of the legislative council and a doctor much loved for his philanthropic activities. On the day he left Larnaca a very mixed crowd openly wept for *'their'* doctor. He left them with chants of *'union and only union'* ringing invitingly in his ears.

It may be added that if this action by the authorities was designed to repress national sentiment then it had precisely the opposite effect. The Greeks vowed to continue the struggle for enosis - using all the available means at their disposal. The coming to power of the second British Labour government on 5 June 1929 prompted the delivery of a long memorandum on 20 July. Several months later a three-man deputation led by Bishop Nicodemos[11] arrived in London to put their case direct to HMG. Amongst other meetings and contacts, on 25 October they had an hour-long interview with Lord Passfield, Secretary of State for the Colonies. The essence of the Minister's reply was that what Cyprus needed was less scope for political discussion and more opportunities for

---

(11) The bishop possessed a strong personality and remarkable abilities as a church man, scholar and parliamentarian

constructive work. '*Nothing doing*' was the polite government response. Protests and counter-protests were triggered by this response. New forms of political expression were discussed. A decisive step was taken in Nicosia on 26 January 1930, when the Pan-Cypriot National Assembly voted for the establishment of a '**National Organisation**' the object of which was to promote the cause of enosis. Good use was made of the press in Cyprus, Greece the US and Britain. Letters and articles appeared regularly and the movement seemed to be gaining ground.

Cyprus however, was already in very deep waters: on 24 November 1926 the elected members of the legislative council threw out (this was not the first occasion) the Appropriation Bill[12] by a unanimous vote of 13 to 9 and ipso facto the Colonial Estimates for 1927. On 7 February 1927 the estimates etc. were passed by Orders in Council, numbers 176 and 177. The same method was repeated in 1928. Such action by the authorities caused widespread disapproval and consequently unrest.

**Education** was also brought into the arena of controversy. For years Greek schools were dominated by the Church and its unionist supporters. The Elementary Education Bill of 1929 stated that the control over the appointment, promotion, transfer, dismissal and discipline of elementary teachers of all communities should pass from the '*political*' committees to the government. Even though the Annual Report for 1928 stated that education was functioning satisfactorily, within a year it was '*found*' that schools were inefficient and functioned only for the purpose of glorifying Greek and Turkish ideals!

The crisis sunk even further. We have already discussed the negative attitude and declaration of Lord Passfield in 1929. Now it was the turn of Philip Snowden to cause further dissatisfaction. The Chancellor of the Exchequer informed the House of Commons on 8 July 1931 that the tribute surplus was henceforth disposed of. It had, of course, already been abolished in 1927. The Cypriots consequently expected taxation to be reduced; instead, the governor proposed increases. Meanwhile, the world economic blizzard of the late 1920s and early 1930s was causing new problems. Because of the general fall in commodity prices the customs tariff was in need of readjustment and revision in order to safeguard the island's revenue. A seven man committee, composed of 3 British officials, 3 Greeks and 1 Turk, proposed a temporary levy of 50% on official salaries over £100 a year and the substitution of specific[13] for ad valorum[14] customs duties. These recommendations were unanimous and were duly

---

(12) See despatch by the elected members of the legislative council to the governor dated 28 December 1926. CO 67/220/3. Pages 37-38

(13) Duties based on the quantity purchased.

(14) Duties in proportion to the value of goods purchased.

accepted by the governor who proceeded to introduce a bill in the legislative council. The elected members however, refused to agree to any legislative measure involving fresh taxation.

The governor knew that as long as the three Turkish members remained loyal to him the wishes of the Greek majority could be overridden. But the activities of Assaf Bey, the Turkish Consul, the anti-colonial mood that prevailed in the island and perhaps more importantly, the formation of labour organisations for all peasants and workers ensured the election of **Misirlizade Nejati Bey**, who could not be counted upon to support the government. When the vote for the revised tariff was taken in the legislative council the Greeks solidly opposed it and Nejati Bey voted with them. He was called '*the 13th Greek*' and the '*little Turk*' and in effect possessed the casting vote in the debating chamber. The measure was thrown out but the governor imposed it by an Order in Council. The already creaking constitutional machinery now threatened to break down completely. The governor informed his superiors in Whitehall on 4 June 1931 that the loyal Turkish community which had always been regarded as a useful safeguard in troubled times '*cannot at present be guaranteed*'.

The British '*trump card*' had finally lost its value. Moreover, there were other issues which helped to bring the embittered Cypriots and the colonial administration towards the confrontation arena. One such issue was the formation of political groupings like the National Council or National Assembly[15] in 1921-22 and the KKK (the Communist Party of Cyprus) in 1925. We have already discussed the activities of the former. The latter, which was succeeded in 1941 by AKEL (the Progressive Party of the Working People), aimed its work at solving the problems of the working class and impoverished peasants; it also called on all the inhabitants to fight for the island's self-determination. The authorities were alarmed and they proceeded to ban many (mainly leftist) publications. In 1928 internal security was tightened even further and on 1 January 1929 the KKK went underground; its newspaper *Neos Anthropos* (New Man) was forced to close down only to be replaced by a bi-weekly one called *O Neos Ergatis* (The New Worker). Court actions were also brought against leading leftists.

---

(15) It was eventually succeeded by the National Organisation in 1930. Another unionist organ was EREK (Ethniki Rizospastiki Enosis Kyprion - the Cyprus National Redicalist Union), which was set up in 1929 as a secret organisation but officially formed on 18 October 1931. Its organ was the newspaper Irreconcilable (Adiallaktos). Its reputed membership was 1200 of which 500 belonged to its political wing. Political parties were declared unlawful in late 1931.

The aggrieved and *"humorous Cypriots"* (Sir Ronald Storr's favourite description) were now in the mood to see the introduction of radical changes. On 12 September 1931, three days after the publication of the Order in Council which introduced a new customs tariff, the Greek elected members of the legislative council were summoned by the Bishop of Kition (cousin of Archbishop Kyrillos) to a meeting at Saitta (a summer resort near Troodos) to decide on future policy. There were further meetings on 3rd, 10th, 11th and 17th October. Agreement however, on a common front eluded the participants. Yet, at the last meeting the Bishop of Kition, **Nicodemus Mylonas**, read a manifesto which advocated resistance to colonial rule and demanded its immediate overthrow.

The bishop was now at the centre of a crisis as his advocacy of illegal measures was hailed by the extremist elements. On the 18th he addressed a crowd at Larnaca, advising them not to be afraid of Britain's fleet and not to obey the laws, for in the quest for union *'blood should flow if necessary'*. Two days later the bishop arrived in Limassol and raised what is now customarily called the *'fiery cross'*. He addressed a crowd of over 3,000 at the sports ground and he declared the union of Cyprus with Greece - he proceeded to do the same at the enosis club. At the stadium similar appeals were addressed to the people by **N.K. Lanitis** and **Zenon Rossides**.

Despite the polemical speeches, the crowd dispersed quietly. Nicosia was henceforth to be the focal point of discontent. The secretary of the National Organisation received a telegram from Lanitis which concluded that *"never before has there been a more panegyric approval"* of the bishop's activities. The effects of the telegram were instantaneous. The events of **21 October** sparked the first outbreak of major violence in the island. Politicians and leading enosists spoke for union and only union; the members of the legislative chamber resigned en masse; the church bells began ringing to summon the people and shopkeepers were told to shut their shops. The assembled crowd repeatedly shouted *'to Government House'*.

At that juncture **Dionysios Kykkotis**, chief priest of Phaneromeni, the most important church in Nicosia, stepped forward and declared revolution. A Greek flag was handed to him and he abjured the people to defend it. One more speech was made, the speaker kissed the flag and the cry *'to Government House'* was renewed with frenzy. The leaders seized the flag and at around 6.45 pm began to move on the half mile trek to their declared destination. Passing the government timber yard, the crowd which was composed mainly of youths, helped themselves to sticks of various sizes and by 7.45 pm the *'exit'* gate was reached. By 8.00 pm the crowd broke the police cordon at the exit gate and moved into the grounds and within a stone's throw of the wooden building. At around 11.00 pm Government House, an inflammable mid-Victorian military bungalow, was set on fire.

Three views of the destruction and burning of Government House in Nicosia during the disturbances of October 21, 1931.

# The Cyprus Gazette
## (Extraordinary)
### Published by Authority

**No. 871.**

THE DEFENCE (CERTAIN BRITISH POSSESSIONS) ORDER IN COUNCIL, 1928.

REGULATIONS.

RONALD STORRS,
Governor.

In exercise of the powers vested in him by the Defence (Certain British Possessions) Order in Council, 1928, His Excellency the Governor has been pleased to make and hereby makes the following Regulations :—

1. These Regulations may be cited as the Defence of Cyprus (No. 2) Regulations, 1931, and shall be read as one with the Defence of Cyprus Regulations, 1931 (hereinafter referred to as the principal Regulations), and the principal Regulations may together be cited as the Defence of Cyprus Regulations, 1931, to (No. 2) 1931.

2. These Regulations shall come into operation on and from the date of their publication in the *Cyprus Gazette.*

3. The following Regulations shall be inserted in the principal Regulations :—

" 12. No meeting or assembly of more than five persons shall be held in any place or building without the permission in writing of the Commissioner of the District first obtained :

Provided that nothing in this Regulation contained shall be deemed to apply to any persons being members of the same household.

" 13. Any person who takes part in any meeting or assembly held in contravention of Regulation 12 hereof shall be deemed to have acted in contravention of these Regulations.

" 14. All officers of the Cyprus Military Police and all officers of His Majesty's Naval, Military or Air Forces and all other persons acting in their behalf or under their instructions shall have power to disperse by force any meeting or assembly held in contravention of Regulation 12 hereof and shall not be liable in any criminal or civil proceedings for having by the use of such force caused harm or death to any person.

" 15. No person coming from outside the Colony of Cyprus shall land in the Colony of Cyprus without the previous permission in writing of the harbour or port authorities of the District in which such person intends to land or disembark.

" 16. No person shall print, exhibit or circulate any pamphlet or notice of any kind without the permission in writing of the Commissioner of the District first obtained."

Dated the 24th day of October, 1931.

(M.P. 1529/27.)

---

**No. 872.**        **Telegraphic use of Codes.**

With reference to the Order of the Governor in Council No. 1444 of the 3rd day of October, 1931, published under Notification No. 870 in the *Cyprus Gazette* of the 23rd October, 1931, His Excellency directs it to be notified for general information that the use of the following codes is permitted in telegrams :

A.B.C., 5th and 6th Editions.
Bentley's Complete Phrase.
Bentley's Second Phrase.

Messages in private or any other code not recognised will be stopped. In every case the name of the code used must be indicated on the form ; no charge will be made for transmission of the name of the code.        (M.P. 829/23.)

By His Excellency's Command,

A. B. WRIGHT.
*Acting Colonial Secretary.*

An official record of the post 1931 restrictive measures

By the end of the evening 15 civilians were injured of whom an 18 year old youth, Onoufrios A. Clerides, died shortly afterwards. The excitement caused by the Nicosia disturbances spread to the other parts of the island. In Limassol, the commissioner's house was burnt down; in Famagusta, police and troops from HMS Colombo (arrived on 25 October and landed 30 marines), opened fire and Haralambos Fili, an 18 year old from Lefkoniko was killed; in Paphos and Larnaca demonstrations took place mainly outside police compounds. It must be noted that apart from HMS Colombo, two cruisers (HMS London and Shropshire) and two destroyers (HMS Achates and Acasta) had also arrived on 23 October.

Though towns, especially Nicosia, were the main centres of discontent scores of villages were also active. W. Lunn MP, addressing the House of Commons on 22 April 1932 correctly pointed out that conditions of extreme poverty will ferment disturbances in any community and Cyprus was no exception. Yet, within a week of the *'first outbreak of violence'*, order, with the exception of certain minor disturbances in a few villages, was restored.

# (iii) The 1930s: Repression and Consolidation.

Before we discuss the Cypriot scene of the 1930s certain misconceptions should be cleared up.

*Firstly,* there is no evidence to suggest that the October outbreak was in any way deliberate or prearranged. It is however probable that the outbreak would not have taken the form it did but for the enosis agitation. The ground for the disturbances was prepared by the extreme leaders of the union movement in the hope that the occurrence of general demonstrations would advance the cause of union. Conclusively, it can be asserted that the *'revolt'* was simply a vast popular protest and not a premeditated uprising. The people in fact demonstrated with sticks since they did not plan serious trouble nor did they possess any firearms. Moreover the majority were youngsters who were simply out for an evening stroll and some fun.

*Secondly,* attempts had been made to lay the blame on Greece for the disturbances. The hellenic government had nothing to do with it - its motto was *'strict impartiality'*. In spite of the great pressure brought to bear on Venizelos by the press and organised supporters of the unionist movement, he had flatly refused to give any encouragement to the Cypriot leaders or their sympathizers in Greece. The Premier had clearly done his best to act with propriety and with regard to the obligations arising out of the friendship between Greece and Britain. The agitation however was not obliterated. A manifesto in sympathy with the Cypriot cause, signed by 45 prominent Greeks and headed by Admiral **Paul Koundouriotis**[1], was published in all the Athenian newspapers on 31 October. The Holy Synod of the Church of Greece issued a statement in the same sense and the archbishop of Athens telegraphed to his British counterpart. Church masses were held in many districts and at Amarousion, eight miles outside of Athens, some 3,000 people attended. Armistice Day (11 November) was celebrated in Athens as '*Cyprus Day*' and a secret committee was formed in Piraeus to equip 1,000 volunteers ('*comitajis*') for Cyprus. In addition to the campaign in the press, practically all the municipalities, chambers of commerce, leagues and local societies passed resolutions in sympathy. Student disturbances at both Athens and Salonica had to be suppressed.

The *third* misunderstanding concerns the **Koundouriotis Circular**. This directive regarding the uprising of the Cypriots and its suppression was received by British MPs and newspapers in the early spring of 1932. It contained allegations of mass killings, maltreatment of innocent civilians, the employment of brutal methods by the security forces firstly to extract the information needed and then to pacify the inhabitants, injuries amounting to thousands (mostly minor) and the confiscation of property belonging to deportees.

The authorities, both in Nicosia and in London, dismissed it as being utterly false and baseless in almost every particular. Although there were exaggerations it must surely be correct to say, after scrutinising the various reports and documents of the colonial and foreign offices, that some events were certainly sidestepped or misrepresented by the colonial administration. Two Colonial Office minutes in January 1932 certainly give credence to the above assertion.

*Fourthly*, and contrary to reports by certain uninformed and biased quarters, the use of violence was condemned by all although some speakers both before and during the riots freely mentioned the need for sacrifices and possible bloodshed. In his encyclical of 2 November 1931 the archbishop excluded violence as being one of the ways in furthering and promoting their national aspirations and, in his letter to the governor on 19 November he expressed the deep grief of the Greeks at what had

---

(1) Often called '*the grand old man of the Greek political world*'. He was appointed Regent on 18 December 1923 and first President of the Greek Republic on 25 March 1924.

*Above:* Police militia on parade

*Right:* A local police officer with a cafe owner *('kafedjis')*

Dervis, the Mayor of Nicosia, together with Sir Richmond Palmer inspect a local police guard of honour.

taken place. Furthermore, the Greek members of the Nicosia municipal corporation, headed by Dervis, its mayor, expressed regret at the burning of Government House[2] in a letter addressed to the officer in command of the military forces and dated 26 November.

The *fifth* misconception relates to the activities of the Turkish inhabitants. It must be emphasised from the outset that the goodwill of the Muslim population and of other minorities towards the government never wavered throughout the disturbances. However, during the whole period of the disorders there was not the least exhibition of anti-Greek feeling or any single instance of betrayal by anyone to the authorities of those who had compromised themselves in the disturbances. On the contrary, **Netaji Bey**, issued a manifesto during the disturbances calling upon his fellow co-religionists to remain quiet *"because our Greek brethren are only demanding what is their right"*. It is also significant to point out that the heartiness and co-operation between Cyprus' two religious entities had of late been strengthened by the complete reconciliation brought about in the early 1930s between Greece and Turkey which had probably convinced the island's Moslems that the union of their island with Greece would ensure the same absolute equality of political rights with the

---

(2) The burnt wooden bungalow was replaced by a stone building of outstanding beauty designed by Maurice Webb in a blend of the island's traditional styles.

Greeks as enjoyed by their co-religionists of western Thrace. Articles in Turkish newspapers also expressed sympathy with the Greeks. This state of affairs alarmed Whitehall's policy -makers.

The *sixth* issue that needs brief comment is the so-called *'non-Cypriot determinant'*. The October outbreak coincided with the world's greatest social catastrophe of recent memory - the unmanageable economic depression which caused the ruin of millions. Economies were shattered, food prices rose, industrial depression multiplied unemployment and the masses of the urban labouring poor were deprived of their modest income at the very moment when the cost of living rocketed. The Cypriot not only faced this economic cataclysm but also had to endure martial law. This led to dissatisfaction, underground activity, a consolidation of political groupings and finally a further eruption. On the economic front it led to strikes and in the 1940s violence.

Some statistics of the events are well worth recording: In the four months following 21 October the number of trials and convictions were -

Persons tried.......................2,952

Persons convicted...............2,679

Successful appeals.....................0

Unsuccessful appeals..............22

Appeals pending.......................7

Persons still on remand........304

The major offence was stealing salt: in some districts this misdemeanour accounted for 90% of all trials. Salt was stolen because it was very expensive owing to the tax on it and an alleged shortage and because the government was stock-piling it to push the price even higher; moreover, government stores were easy to break into since they were generally unguarded. The next major infringement was the theft of firewood from the forest. Very minor crimes included the possession of firearms and entering police stations.

The official casualty figures, which are open to question, show that **30 were wounded** and **6 were killed** during the disturbances. There were also many minor injuries most of which were not even reported. Altogether 10 **Greeks were deported**. The deportation orders were issued under the Defence (Certain British Possessions) Order in Council 1928 and the Defence of Cyprus Regulations 1931. The deportees were:

Nicodemos – *Bishop of Kition* ............................................................ Clergyman

Makarios – *Bishop of Kyrenia*............................................................ Clergyman

Dionysos Kykkotis –
*chief priest of Phaneromeni Church, Nicosia*............................................. Clergyman

Theophanis Tsangarides – *Influential Radical Union Member*.. Merchant

Theodoros Kolokasides –                              "                    ................. Dentist

Savvas Loizides –                              "                    ................. Advocate

George Hadjipavlou –
*ex-member of the legislative council* ......................................................... Advocate

Theophanis Theodotou –
*ex-member of the legislative council* ......................................................... Advocate

Haralambos Vatiliotis – ('Vatis')
*Communist Party, prominent member* ..................................................... Clerk

Costas Skeleas (alias Aristidou)
*Communist Party, prominent member*...................................................... Printer

By 6 November all had left the island on board the steamers *'Franscesco Papale', 'Thurso'* and *'Sicilian Prince'*. The list was later extended to another 16 including Christodoulos Christodoulides, Evdoros Ioannides, N. Yerolakides and E. Nicolaides, who were living abroad but were henceforth barred from entering the island. They were declared *'prohibited immigrants'*.

Instead of examining the causes of the mass protest and applying suitable remedies the authorities chose the easy way out - i.e., repression. A stern Defence of the Realm Act (D.O.R.A.) was imposed. The legislative council was abolished - a move that was contrary to the Colonial Laws Validity Act of 1865. It should not be forgotten that the British had been on the lookout for some opportunity to get away from the old 1882 system. The press was placed under harsh censorship; in essence newspapers could publish nothing about local conditions except what the government handed out. Moreover, between 1927 and 1933, some 36 publications were prohibited.

Political parties were dissolved and on 15 August 1933, the criminal code was amended with the main object of enabling the authorities to deal effectively with the communists and with all other undesired associations. On the following day the KKK and eight other communist front organisations, including the Cyprus Relief Workers Association, were proscribed.

Trade Unions were forbidden and their members victimized. Meetings of more than five people were also prohibited. Municipal elections were abolished and it was only in March 1943 that the first such elections were allowed to take place.

Every form of national manifestation was persecuted and other laws even restricted further the liberties of the people. Thus, a law passed in 1939 gave unlimited authority to the police "to place under arrest or banish any person who works, or is likely to work, in such a way, or who might use his relative freedom of movement, for the propagation of ideas detrimental to the defence of the state".

Finally, someone had to pay for the damage caused to government property. The Reparations Impost Law passed on 21 December 1931 implemented the decision that destroyed property estimated at just over £34,000 (around £6,000 was levied on villages) should be duly replaced and repaired. The orthodox community immediately paid up - a tax on land easily recouped the amount demanded. The verdict of HMG, eight months after the events of 1931, was that the *'insurrection'* was probably the best thing that happened to the island during the governorship of Sir Robert Storrs. The above concluded that, "the boil which has been troubling Cyprus for years had come to a head and burst; the correct local treatment has been applied and a future diet has been prescribed which should prevent a recurrence of the trouble." [3]

Briefly, these restrictive measures - the famous 27 *'illiberal laws'* enacted between 1931 and 1937 - did not crush but on the contrary exacerbated the feelings of the inhabitants. Political activity which was driven underground was canalised into a multitude of forms, such as professional and cultural bodies, literary and scientific societies, sports organisations, peasants, workers and producers associations.

The Cypriot scene of the 1930s was without doubt dominated by six main issues:

**1)** A milder enosis agitation fortified by the extension of cultural, social and academic activities. Open agitation for union gradually died down but it was kept alive more by persons and organisations outside the island than from within. In Greece, the *Cyprus Central Committee*, the *Cypriot Students' Brotherhood* and other bodies were working very hard for the enosists' cause. In the US the *Pan-Cypriot Brotherhood of America*, often protested against the suspension of human rights and liberties and demanded amongst other things the abolition of the penal code, the defence and education laws and an end to press censorship. Of particular

---

(3) CO 67/247/9. The minute by the Colonial Office was dated 21 June 1932

importance were the activities of Cypriots living in London. The *London Cypriot Committee* formed in 1932 was broadened and renamed the *Committee for Cyprus Autonomy* in 1936; it finally became known as the *Cyprus Affairs Committee* in 1943. It centred its activities on the labour movement and the House of Commons. It dealt not only with the national issue, enosis or self-government but with economic problems and with questions concerning civil rights and liberties.

The press outside Cyprus was also vociferous on the side of the islanders and their quest for a more liberal and just regime. Articles in British journals such as the *Economist* and the *New Statesman and Nation* not only urged the initiation and passage of reforms but also the cession of Cyprus to Greece. *The Times Educational Supplement* of 20 August 1932 and another article in *The 19th Century and After* in 1934, were also pro-Hellenic and pro-reform. The latter in fact, advocated inter alia the exchange of Argostoli (Argostolion, Cephalonia) for Cyprus.

In the island itself the general lull was broken on several occasions by a variety of events and by the activities of certain individuals. Heading the list was **Leontios Leontiou**, Bishop of Paphos, who throughout his career and especially as locum tenens during the vacancy of the archiepiscopal see (1933-1947), was the most persistent and irrepressible of all unionists and a man who threw himself heart and soul into his work. He did not follow the other bishops into exile because at the time of the October *'rising'* he was Archbishop Lang's guest in London. He was not allowed to land in Limassol on 13 November 1931 and he proceeded instead to Constantinople. Yet, he was promised a safe return on the condition that he signed an undertaking to abstain from political activities. The bishop refused to bind himself in such a way but pursuant to the government's decision to treat agitation for union with Greece as sedition, he was allowed to return. Following the warm welcome given to Leontios on his arrival in June 1932, he plunged into his self-appointed role as leader and demanded union and only union. His actions caused the authorities to retaliate and court prosecutions were served with great rapidity.

The activities of Leontios had attracted the attention of the Athenian press - also that of London and the US. In Greece all forms of national manifestation were seized upon and discussed in great detail. However, the imposition of a dictatorship in 1936 by General John Metaxas resulted in much less publicity and projection of the unionist cause.

There were also the customary delegations to London. The one of 1937 consisting of D.N. Demetriou OBE, for many years a member of the executive council and mayor of Larnaca, G.S. Vasiliades, member of the advisory council and deputy mayor of Larnaca and John Clerides, a lawyer of considerable reputation, returned to Cyprus empty-handed and proceeded to explain their actions in the newspaper 'Eleftheria'. Its issue of 19 September also included other articles on the same question. As a result the proprietor's permit was suspended for three months.

In 1938 Whitehall received another prominent Cypriot - Dr. Themistoclis Dervis OBE, mayor of Nicosia, who had an interview with J.B. Williams, a senior Colonial Office official, on 19 October. In addition to the more usual demands, Dervis pleaded for the introduction of more representative institutions and also that clemency should be granted to Theodotou, one of the deportees who was 78 years of age and suffering from arteriosclerosis. In fact, Theodotou was allowed to return on 31 December 1939.

Delegations, petitions and other forms of expression had a three-fold target: a commission of some repute to investigate British misgovernment; the restoration of constitutional liberties and ultimately enosis and an improvement in the economic position of the impoverished inhabitants.

2) The economic situation created a lot of ill-feeling between different sections of the island's socio-economic stratum and between the entire population and the government. Very briefly, according to the official statistics of the Land Registration Department (covering the interwar period) 18,000 mortgaged properties were sold and 19,500 judgements were given for the forced sale of property which was not mortgaged. The owners consequently remained landless and were obliged to become mineworkers at ridiculous wages, to emigrate or simply to starve.

High taxes were still the rule and had resulted in a serious reduction in the purchasing power of the people. Moreover, the bulk of this enormous taxation fell on the poorer classes, since around 4/5 was indirect (on goods purchased) and only 1/5 direct (on income). This anomaly and excessive taxation in general was regularly pinpointed as being unjust and immoral. With the world slump of the late 1920s early 1930s adding further distress, workers were forced to go on strike for long periods to defend their rights. In the first six months of 1939 a cross-section of employees ranging from blacksmiths to carpenters, tailors and bakers in Nicosia, Limassol and Famagusta districts went on strike. Some demands were met others were not. The Cypriot working class was ready to explode. Sir Ronald Storrs aptly remarked that *"economic duress is the agitator's meat and the peasant's poison...."*[4] The government was simply reluctant to promote the welfare of its subjects. However, of great importance to the island's workforce was the emergence, following pressure from Britain (not from the government, of course), of trade

---

(4) Orientations. 1945. Page 503

*Above:* A group from the Nicosia Society during a trip to Troodos.

*Below:* A local rural festival of pony competitions at Pissouri Fair, 1936

*Above and Below:* Two local pre-war scenes in Nicosia. The one above shows a scene at the Square of the Central Courts. The one below is by the entrance of Ledra Street unions. Legislation permitting the formation of unions was enacted in 1932 by which such bodies, if accepted, could register with the newly created office of the Register of Trade Unions. This and other laws passed in 1941 were largely based on British trade union legislation. Such growth, as seen from the table below, was bound to be reflected in a much greater economic involvement. And so it was.

| | Members | Number of Unions |
|---|---|---|
| 1932 | 84 | 1 |
| 1940 | 3,389 | 62 |

**3)** The lack of representative institutions was another issue which caused trouble for the authorities. Following the abolition of the legislative council the governor proceeded to set up an advisory body in October 1933. It was established on an informal basis *"to enable the government to keep itself informed of the views and feelings of the community"*. Five prominent Cypriots of whom four were Greeks (three were merchants and landowners and the other a leading advocate) and one, a Turkish doctor, were invited to form this council. However, it must be said that due to its composition and limited terms of reference it was highly ineffective. The governor, once more, was omnipotent. The feelings or views of the community were totally disregarded. This was a grievance of the greatest magnitude that needed to be tackled. Storrs once more remarked that *"alien rule is not easy to bear, save by the lowest savages...."* [5] Other high ranking officials, both in London and in Nicosia repeatedly expressed their misgivings and even disgust at such a state of affairs.

**4)** Another prominent issue of the 1930s was the archiepiscopal question. We have already noted the fundamental change in the relationship between the autocephalus Greek Orthodox Church of Cyprus and the state as a result of the British occupation of 1878. Similarly, the crisis in the Church between 1900 and 1910 has already been documented earlier. In the 1930s there was another crisis.

The death from pleurisy at the age of 74 of the peace-loving **Kyrillos III** on 16 November 1933, left Cyprus once more without an archbishop. Leontios Leontiou, the bishop of Paphos was unable, owing to the absence from the island of the other two bishops (exiled in 1931), to proceed to the election of a successor. Consequently Leontios, as locum tenens, became the de facto head of the Church of Cyprus. However, when the bishop of Kition died in Jerusalem on 13 September 1937, a renewed agitation developed in the press and elsewhere about the vacant archiepiscopal see.

---

(5) Ibid. Page 477.

*Above and below:* Two views of the Cyprus Railway which for years was running a service from the Port of Famagusta to the copper–pyrites region of Karavostasi (Bay of Morphou) and further to the ore deposits of Evrykhou and Mavrovouni. This service covered 71 miles and that of the mining corporation some 9.5 miles. The railway ceased functioning in 1951.

The government hurriedly passed four laws in 1937 which attempted to deal with this problem.[6] In essence they struck at the very roots of Cypriot orthodoxy and independence and alienated the clergy even further. The approved laws (forming part of the 27 '*illiberal*' laws passed between 1931 and 1937) dealt a heavy blow to the Church. Furthermore,

---

(6) They dealt with the investigation of the affairs and auditing of accounts of churches and monasteries in certain cases; elections to the archiepiscopal see; control of the actual election and acceptance of the person elected as archbishop.

they provoked the resentment even of those Cypriots who were normally little endeared towards their church. Plans for an election were shelved in 1939 with the outbreak of the Second World War. Eventually, the above laws were repealed in 1946 and the first elections since 1916 were held in 1947. The winner was Leontios Leontiou who became archbishop on 20 June. Being a chronic diabetic he died of typhus on 26 July and Makarios II, Myriantheus, succeeded him.

**5)** The behaviour of the Turkish element also deserves some comment. As already observed and apart from isolated minor clashes, relations between the two communities were very cordial. Even when Greece and Turkey were at loggerheads on several occasions after 1878, the two sides in Cyprus behaved well towards each other. During the First World War when Turkey was not on the side of the allies and during the Asia Minor fiasco of the early 1920s, there were no outbreaks of violence. Moreover, during the disturbances of 1931 the Moslems did not connive in any way with the authorities against the Greek demonstrators. As already observed a manifesto was issued supporting the activities of *"our Greek compatriots"*. In addition, the Graeco-Turkish reconciliation of the early 1930s greatly strengthened the goodwill and co-operation between the Greeks and Turks of Cyprus. However, the activities of extremists on both sides caused some concern and on several occasions the authorities took precautionary measures to avert possible trouble. Such fears however, never materialised.

Even so the island's deplorable economic situation in the 1930s and Turkish nationalist propaganda convinced some that Turkey held better prospects for them. Events were to prove the opposite. Those who opted for Turkish nationality and actually left the island soon found that Turkey did not prove congenial enough for them.[7] Many returned disappointed and impoverished. However, the spread of 'Kemalism' continued and it was directed in the mid-1930s by the Turkish consul in Cyprus and by certain other individuals. The governor was alarmed and he reported to London that the consul had become *"the focus of all that is disloyal amongst the younger Turks"*. Moslem leaders such as **Munir Bey** were incessantly attacked as being too pro-British.[8] Turkish nationalism, especially amongst the young, was certainly on the ascendancy by the late 1930s. For years now Turkey's rhetoric openly agitated for lands once inhabited by Turks as in a way still belonging to them. Cyprus was no exception. Like communism, 'Kemalism' was considered by the authorities as being mischievous but as yet not alarming.

---

(7) As provided by article 21 of the 1923 Treaty of Lausanne. Only around 2,500 out of the 9,000 who actually opted to move to Asia Minor, left Cyprus.

(8) Often described by Storrs as the "indispensable and permanent 'Ataturk' of Cyprus".

**6)** In 1938 the situation in Cyprus was further complicated by the spread of Italian, Jewish and German propaganda. The Italians used all means available to spread fascist influences in the island. The zionists, according to the governor, considered Cyprus as being part of the 'Land of Israel' and were constantly trying to get a footing on the island similar to that which they had already obtained in Palestine. This Jewish objective was well understood in Cyprus and viewed with concern. German propaganda was more subtle and a fair number of converts were secured. A broadcast from Paris on 5 January 1939 announced that a speech had been made in Berlin on the subject of Cyprus to the effect that Germany had realised that Cypriots were a noble and ancient people who had long desired to rejoin Greece but were being kept under harsh rule by the British government. The authorities in Cyprus clamped down hard on clear-cut adherents of the German ideology.

Following the war hysteria of 1939 all issues of the 1930s receded, albeit temporarily, into the background. World War II cast a heavy shadow on all of them. On 1 September 1939 Germany invaded Poland and two days later Britain and France declared war on Germany. The war years between 1939 and 1945, were crucial for the Cypriots and their aspirations.

Two views of rural life in the 1930s, a way of life which had continued for hundreds of years

*Left:* An outdoor cooking oven (*fournos*) used mainly for baking bread

*Below:* Crushing the wheat after the harvest

# (iv) The War Years 1939-1945

Twenty one years after the end of one major confrontation Europe was embroiled into yet another - more brutal, more devastating and with much wider repercussions. The strategic value of the island and therefore the strength of the British garrison, the overall contribution of Cypriots to the war effort of the Allies and enemy attacks on Cyprus are all issues that need some comment.

From the word go the French were anxious to use Cyprus as an advance base for aircraft on seaward patrols, especially towards the Italian-held Dodecanese Islands and for giving depth to the air defences of Beirut. The British, on the other hand, did not wish Cyprus to grow into a defensive commitment involving forces that could ill be spared. They agreed, however, that the airfields of Nicosia and Larnaca should be improved and that refuelling and rearming facilities should be installed and made available to the French. Moreover, the British garrison had been increased from one company to one battalion and permission was granted to the French to send a contingent to the island. The 50th British Division worked on the island's fortifications and stayed until October 1941 when it was replaced by the 5th Indian Division which had been in Iraq. The British presence was lessened in 1942 because it was deduced that the chances of being attacked by the enemy were substantially reduced. Such reasoning was calculatively simple - Cyprus should be denied to the enemy although greater troop emphasis should be given to holding the northern flank i.e. Syria. Winston Churchill, in a personal telegram to Menzies, the Australian Prime Minister, dated 9 June 1941, confirmed[1] that it was not possible to hold Cyprus without having control of the Syrian airfields. In fact, in October 1943 the army personnel in the island totalled 10,500 of which 1.500 were British, 6,000 Indian and 3,000 Cypriot.

What about the enlistment of Cypriots and their contribution to the war effort of the Allies? Cypriot applications to join the British army and Royal Navy in 1938-39 were refused due to *'regulations'* but approval was given on 2 September 1939 for the formation of a Cyprus Regiment. Recruitment proceeded briskly and the first 250 recruits were sent direct to Egypt to be equipped, clothed and trained as motor transport drivers. To meet an urgent demand for mule transport and, in view of the good work done by Cypriot civilian muleteers during the First World War, it was decided to form two Pack Transport Companies from the next 700 men enlisted.

---

(1) PREM 3/113. Page 42. See also CO537/2487. Folio 86.

The Cyprus Regiment in North Africa – the 1010 company

To December 1945 the Cypriot contribution (in manpower) was as follows:

Cyprus Regiment (CR)................................................................12,201

Cyprus Volunteer Force (CVF) .....................................................4,431

Cypriots living in the UK, US,South Africa etc but serving
with the British Forces ..................................................................1,800

Royal Greek Forces........................................................................1,200

Greek Red Cross..............................................................................200
                                                                                                        ─────
                                                                                                        **19,832**

1. In addition: Approximately 20,000 Cypriot civilians were employed for defence works on the island.

2. Some 4,500 were employed in the civil defence services on a part-time unpaid basis. This was a compulsory service.

3. Around 4,800 were used for the Air Raid Precautions Service (ARPS). This was a compulsory service.

4. About 200 were employed on a full time basis as Local Coast Watchers and Aircraft Observers.

5. Some 200 women were members of the Auxiliary Territorial Service (ATS).

*Five further points must be noted:*

1. Enlistment for the Royal Greek Forces and for the Greek Red Cross alarmed British officials. Protests through the proper diplomatic channels ensured that by the end of February 1941 such recruitment had virtually ceased. It must be remembered that whenever Greece mobilised for war between 1821 and 1940, Cypriots of all ages and professions, be it lay or clerical, volunteered and fought with pride and distinction. Many were either lost, wounded, killed or taken prisoner.

2. Since no completed returns (final figures) are available for the number of Cypriots serving in other units of the British and Allied Forces there may be an element of error in the figure of 1,800 shown above. Some have suggested a figure as high as 5,000. Current research is inconclusive on this matter.

3. Approximately 77% of those enlisted for the CR served abroad and about 25% of those who joined the CVF. The latter was called "the Home Guard of Cyprus".

4. According to the British War Office the total Cypriot casualties from 3 September 1939 to 1 May 1945 came to 1,960 of which some 88% were lost in Greece.

5. Nearly 12% of the island's population was duly employed in the war effort of the Allies.

As in 1914, the island's total war contribution was massive. Statistics for 1942 reveal that around 10% (it rose to a maximum of 12%) of the island's population of approximately 420,000 was actively engaged in some capacity or other in the war effort. If only those between the ages of 18 and 32 are included then the percentage is well over 50% - a phenomenon beyond question. The Cypriots were the first colonial troops to take an active part in war operations against Germany and her allies and their gallantry was evident on all fronts. The Cypriot muleteers, doing much of their work by night covered country impassable by wheeled vehicles. In rugged country they stood up to discomfort and cold extremely well. The sick rate was very low and they gained a reputation for the cheerful execution of their duties under all conditions.

Cypriots took part in the historic Dunkirk evacuation of 29 May to 4 June 1940 where they were ordered to destroy their mules - an order which they very reluctantly carried out. Then they took part in the Abyssinian campaign in 1941 where the successful conclusion of the battle for Keren (situated 4,000 feet above sea level), was greatly helped by the ability of Cypriot pack transport companies to supply units under fire in the most inaccessible places. The presence of these companies shortened the siege by weeks and this campaign in itself justified the formation of the Cyprus muleteers.

# How to join the Cyprus Regiment

### If you wish to volunteer to join the Cyprus Regt. :—

1. Obtain a "Primary Medical Certificate" from the Rural or District Medical Officer.

This Certificate will be given you without charge, but it is to be understood that such examination and certificate does not necessarily mean that you will be finally accepted until passed fit after full medical examination at a later date at Nicosia or Polemidhia.

2. Report with your "Primary Medical Certificate" to the nearest Police Station and register your name and particulars.

If you have the following qualifications, you have a very good chance of being selected for the Army :—
A Cypriot British subject.
Under 35 years of age (but not younger than 20 years old).
At least 5 feet 2 inches in height (standing in bare feet).
Passed "Fit" by a Rural or District Medical Officer.
Recorded as having no "serious" crime.

3. If you are shown as "suitable" in the Register at the nearest Police Station to your home, you should obtain a Birth Certificate (or if born before 5th November, 1914, a Certificate of British Nationality or Certificate of Residence in Cyprus on 5th November, 1914). In addition, if you are married, in order to claim family allowance, you must bring your marriage certificate, which should show the day, month and year of marriage, and the Birth certificates showing the day, month and year of birth of all your legitimate children under 14.

### TRAVELLING EXPENSES
### (When you are called up)

Obtain a free bus ticket from the nearest Police Station. If rejected by the Military Authorities at Nicosia or Polemidhia you will receive a free return bus ticket to the Police Station from which you came.

### WARNING

It may be sometime before you are sent for. Do not come to Nicosia or Polemidhia unless you are given a bus ticket and Identity Card by the Police. Carry on with your normal work wherever it is. Be certain to notify the Police Station where you registered of any change of your address. Then do not report again until you are told to do so. If, when you are sent for, you change your mind, inform the Police and do not come to Nicosia or Polemidhia.

N.B.—If under 42 years of age ex-service men, ex-members of The Cyprus Police Force and specialist tradesmen may register, but must not go to Nicosia or Polemidhia unless especially told to do so.

### ADDRESS

Correspondence concerning Registration should be addressed to :—
CHIEF RECRUITING OFFICER, NICOSIA.
Nicosia, 10th April, 1940.

### GOD SAVE THE KING !

Notice encouraging locals to join the Cyprus Regiment

The Cyprus presence was also seen during the Italian campaign of 1944. They took part in the battle for Arezzo, the attack on Florence, the advance to the Arno Valley and the final capture of Faenza. Furthermore, at the battle for Monte Cassino '*the gateway to Rome*' (February to May 1944), the toughest spot and perhaps the most crucial in Italy, Cypriots once more distinguished themselves on its rugged slopes by bringing up supplies and taking down the wounded under a hail of enemy bullets and

*Above:* Victory Day – King George VI and members of the Royal Family inspect the contingent of the Cyprus Forces in England.

*Below:* The first Cypriot platoon with its British officers before departing for overseas service.

*Above:* AKEL volunteers parade in Limassol

*Right:* Anthony Eden inspects members of the Cyprus Regiment in the Middle East

*Below:* The Cyprus Regiment in North Africa ready for action shells doubled in intensity by the splintering rock. A close scrutiny of foreign and colonial office files for the period reveals that without the untiring help, hard work and devotion of these muleteers many of the operations successfully carried out in Italy would either have taken much longer or perhaps would not have been undertaken at all.

Cypriots also served in Egypt, the Sudan and under Lord Wavell in Libya and Palestine. Above all the Cyprus Regiment fought many a bloody contest with the enemy and covered itself with glory on Greek soil. In fact, of the 2,500 or so Cypriot soldiers who were in Greece and Crete some 2,000 were lost - the vast majority becoming prisoners of war. In addition, a large part of the Dodecanesian Police under British Military Administration after May 1945 were Cypriots, trained in Cyprus alongside their Egyptian-Greek colleagues. The fall of Crete in 1941 sent fears around Cyprus. It was widely believed that the island was going to be the next prey of the axis powers. Hitler's losses however were very high. The Cretan resistance upset the schedule of further offensives. It meant that the opening of the Russian front had to be set back at least another week. In view of the early Russian winter of 1941 this unplanned for delay deprived the Germans of good campaigning weather just when they needed it most. The experience in Crete made the Fuhrer super-cautious and distrustful of all future airborne operations. Consequently, when it was forcibly suggested that Cyprus should follow Crete in order to provide a jumping-off ground for an air and paratroop attack on the Suez Canal, the proposal was shelved. The Germans, although not yet on the defensive, were certainly losing the offensive.

The axis powers therefore, did not make any attempt to capture the island even though it served as an invaluable supply and relief station for the Allies. However, it was raided on numerous occasions by the Italians and by other unidentified aircraft. The axis powers were masters of camouflage and flags of all of them were seen on their aircraft by the islanders. It is highly probable that the famous German 'Junkers' (or dive bombers) with a radius of action of hundreds of miles may have been used for such attacks using the Italian-held airfields of Rhodes. The Italians probably used the twin-engined 'Savoia' bombers.

The year 1940 was relatively quiet. In July, aerial activity was on the increase but the aircraft were too high for identification. On 22 September, hostile aeroplanes raided the mining port of Xeros. Damage was slight. The attacks of 1941 were much more severe. A raid by eight Italian aircraft on 15 May gave Cyprus its first real taste of bombing. Nicosia and villages such as Dhavlos and Neokhorio were hit. There were four casualties of which three were servicemen. June was even more severe and more damaging. Paphos, Nicosia airport, Xeros and Lemba were hit. In Nicosia, one stick of bombs fell near the cookhouse of the Royal Foresters killing five men and wounding fifteen - two of which later died in hospital.

*Above:* A group of prisoners of war in Germany. Amongst them (pointed with an arrow and enlarged) is the veteran Cypriot politician Mr Glafkos Clerides who became President from February 1993 to 2003. He was then serving in the British Air Force.

*Right:* A well known Cypriot lady, who joined the RAF, Stella Souliotou who later became Attorney General of the Republic.

The attacks in July 1941 were by far the worst. Bombs were dropped at Famagusta, Wolseley Barracks in Nicosia, Larnaca, Nicosia airport and Morphou. Damage was extensive and deaths totalled around ten.

Air attacks on Cypriot landing grounds and harbours although fairly constant were on a small scale and were mainly carried out by Italian aircraft based in the Dodecanese. It must be added however, that enemy submarines were lurking around Famagusta harbour and mines were laid at its entrance. Thus, the steamtug *'Alliance'* struck a mine and sank on 29 April 1942. The captain and two of the crew were killed and five were injured.

During the last three years of the war Cyprus experienced fairly peaceful times. Although unidentified aircraft were seen over Cyprus the enemy, under the secret operational code *'Ape A'*, desisted from further attacks on the island.[2]

The threat of a serious raid or an invasion never materialised. The desire for enosis or more representative government and the state of the economy caused more trouble for the authorities. Very briefly, it must be emphasised that most of those Greek Cypriots who fought against the axis powers risked their lives in the naive view that Britain would reward them after the war by granting union with Greece - the eternal British ally. L.A. Karaphodias, a poet of some local respectability, captured quite succinctly the character of the freedom-loving islanders:

*Going to fight for the cause of freedom*
*To protect you all from our barbarian enemies*
*To victory against the wild beasts*
*To victory with Greece and Britain*

However, certain elements in the island (a tiny minority), formed in 1945 the **'Cyprus Turkish National Party'** (a loose and extremely ephemeral organisation) and showed some signs of favouring Germany. They believed that a British victory would eventually lead to enosis whereas the Germans, if victorious, would consider their own and Italian interests and would also wish to placate Turkey. Yet, Cypriots of all religious beliefs lived in the same quarters, fought side by side in many battlefields, were buried in the same cemeteries, were both mentioned in war dispatches for their gallantry and were both duly rewarded by the granting of military medals.

---

(2) There were some isolated incidents. On 16 July 1943 for example, enemy aircraft dropped bombs near the Limassol airfield.

Thus, private I. Theodoulou received the Distinguished Conduct Medal and the Military Medal was given to sergeant I. Mustafa, corporal O. Shukri and to privates P. Constantinou and T. Georgiou.

As always however, the Greekness of the Cypriots was seen and portrayed everywhere. Enosis was an idée fixe and its attainment the natural aspiration of the islanders.[3] The war years provided further opportunities to express this ideal. Petitions and memorials were once more regularly transmitted to the British authorities: wider political representation and ultimately union were always at the forefront of their demands.

During the first year of the war there appeared a new and welcome phenomenon for the unionist adherents. Following the heroic Greek resistance to Italy after October 1940, a *'Greater Greece'* movement gained ground. This was reflected in many Colonial Office minutes for 1941 and was indirectly aided by the anti-British comments of several Athenian newspapers such as the *'Proia'* and *'Hestia'*. The enosis ascendancy of 1941 was helped by several important pronouncements:

Two volunteers – *Left:* A young Turkish recruit from Uplanta, Mustapha Mehmet. *Right:* Greek flying officer S.C. Haralambides who died in action serving with the RAF

---

(3) See CO 67/327/16

1.   Winston Churchill's message[4] to the Greek Premier Emmanuel Tsouderos implied that when the war ended *'Pan-Hellenism will be at its peak'*.

2.   The *'Joint Declaration'* of President Roosevelt and Churchill known as the **Atlantic Charter** of 14 August 1941. The two world leaders announced that they desired to see no territorial changes that did not accord with the freely expressed wishes of the people concerned and that they respected the right of all peoples to choose the form of government under which they would live. The Cypriots rejoiced and, as a memorandum by the Royal Institute of International Affairs stated in 1941, *"there seems little reason to doubt that the demand for union will grow rather than diminish"*. Freedom of speech and assembly, the legalisation of political parties and economic assistance were also demanded by the impoverished islanders.

3.   On 2 June 1941 the War Cabinet discussed the future of Cyprus. Two documents, one from Lord Moyne and the other from Anthony Eden[5] were before it on that date. Eden's memorandum emphasised that *"quite apart from the necessities of the present crisis, there is a strong prima facie case for ceding Cyprus to Greece, subject to safeguards after the war"*.[6] The Royal Institute of International Affairs also stressed that Britain's interests would best be served by such a cession before the end of the war or at whatever moment promised the greatest political advantage. The War Cabinet concluded however that the island's future should be discussed with the Greek government after the war as part of the general peace settlement.

Enosist aspirations showed a fluctuating trend in 1943. On the evening of 31 January, Churchill once again arrived on the island. In his address to its leading personalities he pointed out that when the war was over the *"name of Cyprus will be included in the list of those who have deserved well..."* It was thus felt that favourable territorial readjustments were to be settled after the war. Consequently, at the municipal elections of 21 March all candidates freely gave undertakings to advance the cause of enosis and public celebrations of all kinds were taken as an excuse for demonstrations in favour of that ideal.

---

(4)  October 1941 - on the first anniversary of Italy's attack on Greece.

(5)  Respectively, Secretary of State for the Colonies and Foreign Secretary.

(6)  See FO 371/29846/198. It must be noted that at a meeting in Athens, exactly two months earlier, Korizis (President of the Council) asked Eden whether HMG could make some promise that the question of Cyprus would be settled *"according to Greek desires"*. See AIR 8/931

During a brief visit to Cyprus in 1943, Churchill was welcomed by Leontios Leontiou, the keeper of the archbishop's throne.

On 31 March however, Lord Faringdon who often spoke in glowing terms about Cyprus, suddenly expounded the theory, in a House of Lords debate, that the island was not really a part of the ancient classical Greek world and that only British mismanagement provided the strength to the movement in favour of enosis. He pleaded that Cyprus should become a self-governing colony within the British Empire. Enosist aspirations were dented even further when in the same debate, the Duke of Devonshire, Parliamentary Under-Secretary of State for the Colonies, expounded his theory of the two pitfalls. He warned the government not to be complacent and the opposition to be on their guard to avoid making the mistake of readily believing that a very limited number of agitators, not perhaps very responsible persons, really represent the aspirations of a nation rightly striving to be free.

The two speeches evoked a cascade of telegrams from Cyprus; the majority addressed to the Prime Minister. Associations and newspapers outside Cyprus were also annoyed; the American 'Atlantis' and 'National Herald' were especially vociferous. Moreover, 'The Pan-American Committee on the Cypriot National Question' was set up in New York to co-ordinate activities and to work towards achieving the ultimate Cypriot goal of enosis.

Other reports also spoke in favour of union. One in particular is worth a brief mention. A Foreign Office memorandum in 1943, deduced that there were three areas in which Greece would claim territory beyond its 1939 frontiers.[7]  In order of importance they were the Dodecanese, southern Albania (northern Epirus) and Cyprus.  The Greek claim on Cyprus it said rested on two arguments: first was the offer of 1915.  The other argument was the ethnic one that 4/5 of the population of the island was Greek.  Others argued that such a cession would be an act of generosity and wisdom.

The visit of Sir Cosmo Parkinson[8]  to Cyprus on 11 August 1944 provided another opportunity for all sections of the population to put their case to him.  He received delegations and heard all points of view. The question of enosis was at the forefront.  Yet, Sir Cosmo explained that this was a subject he was not authorised to discuss - his mission was simply to acquaint himself with local conditions and problems.

Problems on the political front were often overshadowed by economic ones.  Labour relations and the rising cost of living were thorny issues for the authorities.   Cyprus suffered considerable economic disturbance on account of the war.  The mines, for example, lost their principal market (Germany) and lack of shipping and the contraction of world outlets affected other industries.  In order to protect their rights a wide spectrum of the Cypriot working force went on strike.

On 23 February 1940, electricians and mechanics employed in the public works department workshops went on strike and demanded higher wages, shorter hours and improved conditions.  A general strike was considered but it was decided to limit it to 24 hours.

Meanwhile, on 29 February, part of the labour force engaged on relief work in Nicosia left their employment and endeavoured, early in the morning, to demonstrate at the district commissioner's office.  The police arrested 40 of whom 10 were subsequently released. The remainder were brought before the courts and cautioned as to their future conduct.

Protests, processions and demonstrations continued right through the 1940s.  In 1942 alone there were approximately 30 industrial disputes. In December, workmen employed by the government on defence and other work in Nicosia held a 10-day strike for higher pay.

---

(7)  See FO 371/37248/9151

(8)  Lately Permanent Under-Secretary of State for the Colonies.  A high ranking civil servant.

*Above:* A group of local strikers who were sentenced in April 1940 for demanding better working conditions. They were later released.

*Right:* Trade unionists parade in Nicosia on May Day, 1944.

The workers pointed out that the cost of living had risen to 246 from its August 1939 base of 100. A simple comparison will illustrate this alarming increase:

|  | 1939 |  | 1942-43 |  |
|---|---|---|---|---|
| Bread per oke (= 2 3/4 lb approx.) .... | 2 | piastres | $4^1/_2$ | piastres |
| Broad Beans per oke | $2^1/_2$-3 | " | 18 | " |
| Potatoes per oke | 1 | " | 5 | " |
| Onions per oke | $^1/_2$ | " | 8 | " |
| Eggs per dozen | $3^1/_2$ | " | 36 | " |

Nevertheless, following the strike seven trade unionists were sent to prison for having threatened the life of a blackleg.

The same pattern was repeated in 1943. The hub of the campaign and co-ordinator in-chief was PSE, the **Pan-Cyprian Trade Unions Committee**, under which the union movement was finally united in 1940. Protest strikes and processions were the rule of the day. One such manifestation occurred on 25 October when there were simultaneous processions in Nicosia, Limassol and Larnaca. Since a permit was not granted these protests were contrary to the law of 1932: 8 people were arrested in Nicosia, 16 in Larnaca and 12 in Limassol. Some were fined, cautioned or sentenced to terms of imprisonment.

Attempts by the authorities to set up cost-of-living advisory boards, composed of trade union and producers' representatives and government officials, never got off the ground. The chief problem appeared to have been their very limited terms of reference.

The year 1944 also witnessed the same pattern of strikes. On 1 March about 1,800 government labourers and craftsmen employed mainly on military projects, struck for an increase in wages. On 13 March they were joined by some 5,000 men who struck in sympathy for one day, thus bringing the military and government works almost completely to a standstill. Apart from demonstrations on 19 March in the towns of Larnaca and Famagusta, where it was necessary for the police to use batons and firehoses to disperse the crowds, there was no disorder and there were no prosecutions. However, the so-called 'labourers strike' ended on 24 May and the men returned to work promptly the next morning following an earlier assurance that the government would carry out an enquiry into the relation between wages and the cost of living and would take into account all available evidence, including the figures which had recently been communicated to the authorities by the trade unions.

The government it may be noted, were arguing that conditions and wages were fair and that strikes during the war, in public works, were simply *'immoral'*. Employers and the right echoed the governments thinking and were saying that strikes in wartime were not only *'wicked'* but highly *'undesirable'*. A deep-set rift between the left and right, employers often *'assisted'* by the government, and employees, was beginning to show its ugly face. The beating-up of strike-breakers and the use of hand grenades and other offensive weapons were now in evidence. The unrest that existed was clear for everyone to see.

Even so measures to alleviate poverty were introduced by the government in the 1940s. From 1941 to March 1946 Cyprus received free grants under the Colonial Development and Welfare Act of May 1940 totalling £720,000 (approximately £20 million in today's values) to be spent mainly on agriculture and irrigation, medical and education services. Also, during many industrial disputes its conciliation measures were very successful. Backstage diplomacy also proved rewarding in settling many disputes.

A volunteer to the Cyprus Regiment in 1940 and returning to his family *(right)* after the war

# (v) 1945-1950: Old Problems, New Realities

There was great unrest in the immediate post-war years. Measures by the government to alleviate poverty were not enough. The end of the war not only brought the soldiers home but it put a halt to military employment. Thousands became unemployed and there were no unemployment benefits, old-age pensions or other welfare benefits. If no work was available then only private charity could save them from starvation. Furthermore, taxation was high and unjust and the cost of living soared. Above all, chronic indebtedness and the stranglehold of the money lender were a millstone round the farmer's neck and agriculture, the backbone of the economy, was neglected.

Education suffered the same fate. The figures below show the gravity of the situation:

|  |  | Attending |
|---|---|---|
| Number of children: elementary school age | - 77,000 | 46,926 |
| : secondary school age | - 60,000 | 4,784 |

The low attendances, 61% and 8% respectively, show that the Cypriot youngster, as in the England of Dicken's Oliver Twist, had to find work and receive next to nothing or toil in the fields for ten to fifteen hours a day to supplement the meagre family income. For most peasant families the alternative was starvation.

The figures above relate to 1938 and 1939; for several years during and after the war they were even worse, though the trend was reversed in the 1950s and 1960s.

Understandably therefore, the economic depression in Cyprus, as elsewhere throughout the world, strengthened the elements of discontent amongst the population. It is against this background that we must now examine four major incidents which took place in 1945-46.

**(i)** The **Lefkoniko incident** of 25 March 1945. The events, which occurred in the village, exacerbated the feelings of discontent even further. It may be added that the precise consequences of this sorry tale have not, as yet, been unfolded. Very briefly, a predominantly leftist procession departed from the church service where they had celebrated Greek Independence Day and proceeded towards the village club where further speeches were on the agenda. The villagers were suddenly stopped at the bridge which was directly opposite the right wing PEK (Pan-Agrarian Federation of Labour) offices and only a short distance from their ultimate destination. The jubilant villagers were then confronted by the police and, following a brief discussion as to whether a permit for the procession had been granted or not, they opened fire killing a 26 year-old man, a boy of 12, injuring three seriously, of whom a man of around 45 died on 22 May and slightly injuring at least eleven others.

The disorders as feared, did not spread to other towns or villages. Almost unanimously however, the police action was condemned; severe punishment for the culprits and repeal of legislation controlling assemblies was demanded. Although a commission of enquiry was appointed on the evening of 25 March it was decided on 31 October that the report should not be published and that the police should not be prosecuted.

Documents released in the mid-1990s in the UK show that the commission sat in public at the local court house for 15 days and examined 35 witnesses. The chairman (R.A. Godwin-Austin) and judge Melisas (a Greek) found that the police action was *"ill-considered"* and that in their opinion *"the conduct of the policemen......is a proper subject for proceedings at law"*. The third member of the commission Judge Zekia (a Turk) expressed the opinion that although extreme force was used, sergeant Patsalides *"being a firm and rational man had reasonable grounds to fear a breach of the peace"*.

The credibility of the administration suffered another setback. A minute[1] by the Colonial Office dated 6 April recorded that, *"the Lefkoniko incident has unfortunately given all parties an effective stick with which to attack the government....."* The seriousness of the situation alarmed the governor who, in a telegram to his superiors in Whitehall (dated 31 March), pleaded that all possible *"diversions"* should be created so as to concentrate the attention of the public on local affairs rather than on nationalist politics. He pleaded that all grievances which tended to unite the parties *"should be eliminated"*. A programme of economic growth and social welfare was urgently needed. The government made a start in 1946 when a ten-year programme of development was announced. The creation of a welfare state mooted in the late 1940s came to nothing.

**(ii)** Within a few hours of the above telegram a second major incident took place - the **armoury theft** of 31 March was viewed with much anxiety. On the night in question, 8 brenguns, 6 pistols, 58 rifles and some 2,300 rounds of ammunition were stolen from the armoury of a Cyprus Volunteer Force station near Nicosia.

Within weeks the arms cache was found in the garden of an AKEL member and recovered almost intact. The Colonial Office immediately explained that a new and dangerous factor had entered the Cyprus

---

(1) CO 67/327/16

situation and remarked that *"there is a risk of violence in the Palestinian sense under the leadership of AKEL"*.[2] This diagnosis proved baseless and utterly misleading. Nevertheless, those arrested were tried by the assizes: one man and one woman were acquitted; two were given 7 year sentences and one was found guilty under the Defence Regulation 34B and imprisoned for 12 years.

(iii)  The **Famagusta Transit Camp** incident of 8 October 1945 also caused a lot of concern.  On that day Indian troops were called to the camp to get two reluctant Cypriot companies, due to be taken to either Syria or Palestine, aboard a transporter.  There was absolute chaos and shots were fired killing one Cypriot sergeant, wounding six privates two of which were serious and one Indian soldier.  The death of **Takis Kythreotis** produced quite a stir in the island.  Protests flowed into the governor from all quarters and many organisations held special meetings to consider the incident and register their disapproval.  The official view that *"soft-nosed bullets"* were fired from the crowd, was repudiated.  The government refused to allow a full public enquiry into the incident although the findings as to the facts of the official Court of Inquiry were published in the local press on 17 October.  The Cypriots protested against further service abroad and demanded the expedition of demobilisation.

Archbishop
Leontios Leontiou
*(right)*

(2)  CO 67/324/5.  Minute dated 25 April.

**(iv)** The rift between the government and the governed was widened even further by the **PSE (Pan-Cyprian Trade Unions Committee)** trial of 1945-46. PSE was the highest directive body and was thus entrusted with the leadership and co-ordination of the activities of all the trade unions throughout the island. The growth of the unions can be seen from the table below.[3]

|      | Registered Unions | Branches | Membership |
|------|-------------------|----------|------------|
| 1939 | 46                | -        | 2,544      |
| 1940 | 62                | -        | 3,389      |
| 1941 | 68                | -        | 3,854      |
| 1942 | 73                | 43       | 9,991      |
| 1943 | 84                | 68       | 9,628      |
| 1944 | 122               | 71       | 11,865     |
| 1945 | 143               | 78       | 13,394 (estimated) |

Organised labour was seen as a threat by the authorities. The offices of PSE were raided and a certain amount of literature - books on marxism etc. - was seized. PSE was prosecuted and the trial began on 17 December 1945. The case was listed as Rex v Ziartides et al; in other words the government versus the entire Cyprus TUC composed of 18 persons. The Nicosia assize court was formed by three appointed judges sitting alone, since there was no provision of trial by jury. A minute by Sir S. Abrahams of the Colonial Office dated 11 March 1946 stated that *"this is the Ottoman form of judicial procedure"*; yet, this was Cyprus 67 years after its occupation/administration by Great Britain! Some of the alleged offences were:

(1) unlawfully conspiring to overthrow the island's constitution;

(2) conspiring to overthrow by violence the established government;

(3) attempting to bring into hatred the lawful government; and

(4) attempting to excite disaffection against the administration.

The defence denied all 17 charges. On 21 January 1946 the trial ended. Twelve of the accused were sentenced to 18 months imprisonment and the other six to 12 months. PSE was found to be an illegal organisation, not because it was a trade union body but because it was *"a conspiracy advocating the overthrow of the government!"* PSE was replaced by **PEO** (Pan-Cyprian Federation of Labour) in 1946.

---

(3) See CO 69/51. Due to certain variable factors, such as monthly adjustments, the official figures often portrayed a slightly different picture.

The Haganah ship 'Exodus 1947'– transporting Jewish settlers to Cyprus or Palestine

The government was denounced as fascist and anti-working class and progressive forces in both Cyprus and Britain vowed to fight for their release. Within nine months of their imprisonment they were freed. The sentencing of the accused, it may be noted, was followed by a strike on 22 January as a declaration against *'unlawful brutality'*. During the so-called *'week of protest'* (September 1946) over 700 meetings were held demanding the annulment of the harsh laws and the release of the prisoners.

In 1946 there was another disturbing factor. On 15 May it was stated in the House of Commons that Cyprus might take 13,000 of the 100,000 Jewish refugees to settle in holdings. The famous **"Palestinian Report"** was greeted with great dismay by the Cypriots. In the first place, it was felt that such an influx of refugees, if granted citizenship, would seriously weaken the island's Greek majority. Parallel to the above was the fear that the zionists, who considered Cyprus as being part of the *Land of Israel,* were constantly trying to get a footing on the island similar to that which they had already obtained in Palestine. Secondly, at a time when the economy was undergoing a very bad time, it was felt that the provisioning of thousands of Jewish immigrants would lead to acute shortages of supplies and therefore higher prices.

Nevertheless, the attitude of the island's population throughout the period (1946-48) was one of friendship and assistance. Many Cypriots helped in the escapes, giving shelter to the escapees and aiding them in reaching Palestine. In fact, some 52,000 Jewish immigrants passed through the two detention camps (**Karaolos** and **Xylotymbou**), during the 2 1/2 years of the camps' existence. Of these, 1,800 internees reached Palestine after escaping from the camps; 110 immigrants, including 49 children, died in Cyprus and were buried in the Jewish cemetery in Margo. Around 2,000 children were born in the camps.

Cyprus was henceforth entering a new and more difficult era. The government attempted to eliminate the *"authentic grievances"* which tended to unite the inhabitants. On 23 October 1946, Arthur Creech Jones, the Secretary of State for the Colonies, informed his fellow parliamentarians that the government had reviewed its policy on Cyprus. The so-called *"New Deal"* had arrived. He promised four "constructive measures":

(1) A more liberal and progressive regime would be established to run the internal affairs of the island.

(2) A vigorous programme of economic development and social welfare. The 10-year development plan estimated to cost around £6,000,000 was the government's promised messiah.

(3) Repeal of the three local laws of 1937 concerning the election of a new archbishop. The repeal was effected by Law No. 20 of 29 October 1946 and the first elections since 1916 took place in 1947.

(4) Those exiled following the disturbances of 1931 would be allowed to return.

As already mentioned in the previous section measures to alleviate poverty and to reduce rural indebtedness were introduced in the 1940s. These however were not enough. Thus the cost of living index rose by 156% between August 1939 and December 1946 and for the same period taxes collected increased by over 400%. The typical family therefore was faced with frustrated ambitions, inescapable responsibilities and the ever-growing grind of poverty. The years to 1950 therefore were dominated by bitter strikes:

The **miner's strike** at Mavrovouni-Xero in the Solea Valley district which lasted for 124 days, proved to be the most acrimonious of the three major strikes of 1948. The others being the Amiandos asbestos mines and builders' strikes. These confrontations revealed the Cypriot working class as a well-organised and militant force.

Apart from the economic issue the authorities were faced with other problems which led to recrimination and ill-feeling. Some general observations will suffice:

*Above :* The 1948 miners strike at
Mavrovouni – Xero in the Solea Valley area.

*Above:* Pantelis and
Neophytos, two of the many
who emigrated to as far away
lands as Australia, South
Africa, Canada, the US and of
course the UK in search of a
better life.

*Above:* Poverty-stricken Cypriots. The picture
shows the interior of a two-roomed village
house.

(a) The Dodecanese Islands were ceded by Italy to Greece in 1946. The island's Christian inhabitants concluded that they were next in line to join the motherland.

(b) Following the passage of the historic resolution of 28 February 1947, the Greek government had for the first time formally associated itself with the movement for union, though in terms courteous to Britain. Greece it should be noted, depended economically and militarily on Britain in the 1940s. Finding the financial strain too heavy and feeling that *"the Greeks were a very poor investment for the British tax payer"*, HMG asked the US to take over. After 1947 it became virtually an American *'protectorate'*. Such dependence necessarily impaired the sovereign actions of the Hellenic government. Economic reliance meant therefore political compliance.

(c) By 1948 many parts of the British Empire were being granted independence - Tansjordan in 1946, India and Pakistan in 1947, Burma and Ceylon (now Sri Lanka) in 1948. Cypriot hopes were raised once more.

(d) The growth of nationalism in the Middle East had slowly eroded the Anglo-French position there - new sovereign states were springing up.

(e) The Atlantic Charter of 1941 and The Universal Declaration of Human Rights approved by the United Nations General Assembly in 1948, gave new hope to subject peoples. Cypriots constantly quoted them to justify their struggle for ultimate union.

(f) After the war the Cyprus *'movement'* was firmly supported by the Greeks of the diaspora. London, Athens and America provided massive support for the islanders. In the latter country the million or so Greeks, led by **AHEPA** and other organisations, were just as anxious to see Cyprus restored to the motherland as were the Greeks in Europe or the Greek Cypriots themselves.

(g) Apart from relying on emotional factors, Cypriot politicians concentrated on economic and social problems, pointing out that they had nothing to lose materially by ending the British connection.

(h) The Ethnarchic Council was expanded in 1945 to include laymen and with archiepiscopal elections imminent, a church-dominated national delegation arrived in London at the end of December 1946 to put their case for union with Greece. They travelled by way of Athens arriving there on 16 November; they met most of the Greek political leaders and were received by the King on 4 December. The public and the mass media expressed their unanimous support for the delegations' ideals. In London they met Creech Jones on 7 February

Various rural images and views
of the late 1940s

1947.  He listened very carefully but in the end he replied that "*no change in the status of the island was contemplated*" and he implied that self-government at that juncture "*will be viewed more favourably* " by his government.

(i)  Towards the close of the 1940s the forces of the left joined in earnest the rightwing chorus for enosis and for a time took the initiative.  The left, via the National Co-operation Front, rationalised its support for union with 'monarcho-fascist' Greece by stating that this was the first step towards the liberation of the Greek people from Anglo-American imperialism.  In furtherance of its objective a memorandum was sent to the Security Council and General Assembly of the United Nations on 21 November 1949 requesting that a plebiscite should be held in Cyprus, under U.N. supervision, if there was the slightest doubt of the entire Greek population's desire for enosis.  The Mayors of Limassol, Larnaca, Famagusta and Morphou and seven leftist leaders signed the memorandum.

(j)  "*Political immaturity*", "*a weak island unity*", "*centralisation of power*", all powerful arguments put forward by the authorities against national self-determination were not present in the late 1940s to the same extent as in earlier years.  In fact, power was more fairly shared: the enlargement of the Ethnarchic Council to include laymen was well received; political parties multiplied by the late 1940s; daily and weekly newspapers in Greek, Turkish and English abounded and literary magazines also made their appearance; the most important of which was the monthly '**Kypriaka Grammata**' (Cypriot Letters).

Also of great significance was the formation of the Society of Cypriot Studies in 1936 by leading intellectual figures of the island who vowed to collect, study, preserve and publish historical and linguistic material and study popular art in all its aspects.  Its annual publication '**Kypriakai Spoudai**' (Cypriot Studies) has proved invaluable not only to students but to researchers as well.

Elementary and secondary education had also shown great strides.  According to the census of 1911 only one Cypriot in four could read and write.  By 1950 illiteracy was rare even in the remotest of villages.  According to Lord Winster, "*Cypriots, above all, had great intellectual ability*".  This and other similar statements go a long way in proving that during the entire British period the Cypriots were not given the opportunity to try their political merits and faculties.  They were certainly fully equipped to run their own affairs and decide their own future.

Enough has been said above concerning the enosis upsurge of the late 1940s. Citing six main reasons Whitehall refused to entertain such a union:

(1) Cypriots were not yet ready to run their own affairs.

(2) Greece, which was just recovering from the dual catastrophies of World War II and the Civil War, was in no position to administer fresh territories.

(3) The Greek government had not recently asked about Cyprus.

(4) Around 20% of the island's population was Turkish-speaking and their interests and wishes had to be considered.

(5) There was no other territory in the Middle East offering comparative security of tenure which was better situated than Cyprus for use as an advanced air base for the attack of vital strategic targets in southern and eastern Europe.

(6) As a matter of principle, Britain disliked giving up pieces of overseas territories. Churchill warned the House of Commons on 20 December 1946 that, *"the British Empire seems to be running off almost as fast as the American loan...."* He emphasised that *"this process of elimination had to stop"*.

The Turkish attitude over Cyprus also deserves our attention. A paper prepared by the research department of the Foreign Office and dated 3 June 1944[4] observed that since the Turkish government had evinced little interest in the Turks of Cyprus then if Britain proposed the island's cession to Greece - a friendly nation - Ankara would not object. Further references by the Foreign Office confirmed the above analysis.[5]

Nevertheless, it is correct to say that the situation in the island was complicated by the Turkish Cypriot position which showed a noticeable change in the late 1940s. Following a large Greek demonstration in Nicosia in favour of enosis and autonomy on 3 October 1948, the Cyprus Turkish National Party (the predecessor of the Cyprus is Turkish Party - Kibris Turktur Parti formed in 1955), protested and sent telegrams to Turkey expressing its annoyance. There were student riots in Ankara and the Turkish press, but not the government, warmly supported the case of their Cypriot brethren. This pleased **KATAK** (the Association of the Turkish minority in Cyprus), which strongly opposed the possible cession to Greece but demanded instead that if Britain ever decided to relinquish sovereignty the island should go back to Turkey, its previous suzerain and

---

(4) FO 371/44188/9943
(5) In both 1946 and in its survey of Turkish policy in 1949.

nearest neighbour, which was in a much better position to defend it. **KATAK** (Kibris Adasi Turk Azinligi Kurumu) was set up in April 1943. It is widely believed that it was so established as a result of encouragement by the colonial administration.

In 1949 the Turkish agitation against enosis grew even more intense and at a press conference in February 1949, J. Sadak the Minister for Foreign Affairs, declared in unequivocal terms that Britain would "*never*" cede Cyprus to Greece. Turkey in fact soon shifted from its role as an uninterested party and then observer and, with British prompting, became especially after 1955, the third interested party when the problems of the island were discussed.

The period under discussion brings out another interesting observation - the American interest and concern over he Cypriot problem. In the mid-1940s and earlier, the American administration was on the whole in favour of an early and peaceful settlement in favour of Greece. By 1950 and due to the potent and volatile forces (precarious alliances, European involvement, the communist threat, wide economic interests, the Middle Eastern situation etc.), prevailing, the Americans revised their policy to one of being '*a benevolent observer and advisor*'. By the mid-1950s the American role was that of behind-the-scenes '*arbitrator*' and finally '*director-general*' of the whole scenario. The guidelines and overall plans appeared to have been firmly drawn. The three NATO allies (Britain, Greece and Turkey) and finally the Cypriots themselves were left to bargain over the details.

Another observation of the period concerns the military value of the island. The situation, strategic importance and re-enforcement of Cyprus attracted much attention in the early 1940s and 1950s. We have to recall that as early as 1947 the US, Britain, Canada, Australia, and New Zealand formed a network, called UKUSA, for collecting and sharing intelligence information. The '*cold war*' had finally reached the island in1948. Britain was constructing air bases equipped with radar and was transferring to Cyprus from Palestine (where its mandate was due to expire on 15 May 1948) a considerable number of troops, the Middle East radio monitoring service and the Arabic broadcasting station ash-Sharq al-Adna. Thus, in October, the RAF station in Cyprus was raised to the status of Air Headquarters Middle East and there were rumours that Military Headquarters Middle East would also be established there - as it duly was in 1954. In fact, once the decision had been taken to wind up the British base at Suez, Cyprus' stock on the British strategic market rose to its original (1878-1882) value. The Cyprus problem therefore, assumed a new dimension. New realities brought fresh and more dangerous problems. The '*game*' was just beginning!

Finally we must discuss briefly the problems arising out of the constitutional proposals and municipal elections. The abolition of the legislative council in 1931 and the imposition of other restrictive measures resulted in Cyprus being ruled on an undemocratic basis which was certainly repugnant to British ideals. In October 1946, it was announced that a more liberal and progressive regime would be established.

On 9 July 1947, **Lord Winster** (created a baron in 1942 and governor of Cyprus from 1946 to 1949) sent invitations to various persons and organisations to take part in a consultative assembly which would make recommendations on the form of a constitution to be established. The right, turned down the invitation explaining that the acceptance of a constitution implied tacit renunciation of their national aims. The left, after some hesitation and a good deal of deliberation decided to accept it - explaining that through self-government the island could more easily march towards enosis.

The assembly had its inaugural session on 1 November under the chairmanship of Sir Edward Jackson but almost from the word go there were disagreements as to the interpretation of its terms of reference. Proposals for a constitution providing for self-government were ruled out. The left then submitted a statement to the Secretary of State for the Colonies on 24 November, requesting a constitution similar to those of Malta or Ceylon. Whitehall's failure to answer the memorandum prompted a leftist deputation to visit London in February 1948. Although the delegation returned empty-handed it discussed the constitutional impasse with members of the influential Fabian Colonial Bureau which incessantly attacked the inequities of British colonial administrations.

In an attempt to break the deadlock, Whitehall issued a statement in the form of a despatch to Lord Winster on 7 May 1948 making certain proposals for constitutional reform. It was made clear at the time that it was open to the constituent assembly to recommend variations in these and other details of the proposed constitution. The proposals were published on 12/13 May. A limited form of home-rule was provided and proper safeguards for Britain's strategic interests were included in the proposals.

The limitations imposed and the powers reserved for the governor were sufficient to wreck the chance of acceptance by most Cypriot politicians. Nevertheless, a wholly unrepresentative chamber was reconvened on 20 May and on the following day a motion that "*it would be in the best interests of the people of Cyprus that a constitution in the form offered by HMG should be established with the least possible delay*" was carried by 11 votes to 7. One member was absent. The minority was composed of five Greek mayors of the left and two Greek trade union representatives who then announced their intention to withdraw from the constituent assembly. When they did withdraw the assembly finally lost its representative character. The chairman adjourned it 'sine die' and the governor formally dissolved it on 12 August, stating that these or comparable constitutional proposals would be re-examined and implemented if at any time this was requested by representative leaders of the people.[6] This offer was to remain open for for the next six years until Britain announced on 28 July 1954 that a modified constitution was to be introduced. The campaign for 'self government-union' was continued with even greater vigour. Well attended demonstrations were held in many parts of the island. A peak was reached in October 1948 when an AKEL-sponsored rally attracted a crowd of 25,000 in the capital.

The results of the three municipal elections of the 1940s were significant for the future activities of the various groupings. The first elections after the disturbances of 1931 were held on 21 March 1943. A middle-class enosist mayor was returned in Nicosia whilst the left won the mayor's seat and a majority in the municipal councils in Limassol and Famagusta. The elections were significant not only because of the leftist upsurge but because undertakings were freely given by candidates to advance the cause of enosis.

The next elections were held on 26 May 1946. The swing to the left continued. AKEL not only retained its hold on Limassol and Famagusta but won Nicosia and all but two of the principal towns. The following elections were held in different municipalities on four successive Sundays between 8 and 29 May 1949. On the first Sunday AKEL won seven out of the eight seats at Morphou (the largest rural municipality), but the returns of the following three Sundays showed a swing in favour of right wing candidates. The left retained control of its strongholds (the ports of Limassol, Famagusta and Larnaca) by narrow majorities but Nicosia was lost. Dervis triumphed over Clerides amid outbreaks of violence between the two rival groups as a result of which one man was killed, several were injured and nearly 200 arrested.

The nationalist groups which polled around 60% of the total votes cast were now in control of 11 out of the 15 municipalities. The left though not routed was decisively beaten. AKEL explained that its failure was due to intimidation of the voters by the right, falsification of the electoral rolls by government officials and significantly, the action taken by the clergy and the Greek consul.[7] However, by 1949 both the nationalists and the leftists were wholly committed to enosis, and by 1950 the Cyprus problem entered a new and decisive phase.

---

(6) The Consultative Assembly had 4 meetings in 1947 (6th. 7th.13th. and 18th. November) and 2 in 1948 (20th and 21st May). Of great interest is file no. CO 537/4036

(7) CO 67/333/7. Minute by Mary Fisher dated 27 July 1949

# (vi) 1950-1955
## The Cyprus Question is Internationalised

A new development entered Cyprus politics in 1950. **A Church-organised plebiscite**, intended to give free expression to the people's wishes for the island's future, was held on 15 and 22 January. Out of the 224,747 Greek Cypriots eligible to vote, 215,108 or 95.7% signed the petition for enosis. Many Turkish, Armenian and even English names[1] could be seen alongside the Christian signatures; civil servants and government employees did not take part.

The result of the plebiscite had no effect on the British government. It accused the Church of putting pressure on the people to vote for enosis, pointing out that the archbishop on 8 December 1949 appealed for a unanimous affirmative vote. The Church countered by stating that on 12 December it had challenged the British authorities to conduct the plebiscite themselves. Moreover, leading personalities pleaded for a UN-sponsored referendum.

The archbishop officially reported the results of the plebiscite to the governor on 4 February. Replying on the 22nd, Sir Andrew B. Wright conveyed the message of his superiors that *"the question of enosis was closed"*. Still on offer however, were the Winster constitutional proposals of 1948. Delegations were hurriedly sent abroad. The first one from the Ethnarchic Council visited Greece, France and Britain and then went on to Lake Success where it established contacts with delegates to the 5th UNO Assembly. **Alexis Kyrou,** the Greek permanent representative at the UN, gave them valuable assistance. The second delegation, from the AKEL-dominated National Liberation Coalition visited Britain and France and published a pamphlet called '*Cyprus Presents its Case to the World*' in English and French, which it distributed to MPs, private individuals and organisations in both countries. Other European countries were subsequently visited.

Without any shadow of doubt the two acknowledged Greek Cypriot protagonists of enosis were Makarios and Grivas. Brief biographical notes of both are not only desirable but necessary:

**George Grivas,** born in the Nicosia hospital on 23 May 1898 (or most probably 6 June 1897, as shown by recent research), came from the village of Trikomo, around twelve miles north of Famagusta. As a youngster he

---

(1) See CO 67/370/90580/3

George Grivas
"Dighenis" leader
of the EOKA
movement

won both academic and athletic awards at the Pan-Cyprian Gymnasium. In 1916 he was admitted into the so-called '*school of the promising ones*' - the military academy of Athens - and after graduating in 1919 he took part in the ill-fated Greek campaign of Asia Minor. At the age of 26 he was promoted to captain.

During the hostilities of 1939-45, Grivas acquitted himself extremely well and for his services on the Albanian front he was promoted to lieutenant-colonel. During the German occupation of Greece, Grivas formed, in 1943, his own secret organisation of mainly royalist officers under the name of the Greek letter 'X' (*khi*).[2] Its twin aims were the return of the king and the neutralisation of the communists who controlled the chief resistance movement.

Following a short period of inactivity, the career of Grivas entered a new phase in 1951 when he failed twice to be elected as leader of his own political organisation which he founded upon 'X'. He then stood for the

---

(2) Its supporters were called '*Khites*'.

Greek Vouli as a populist candidate but though the populist party and its supporters won the election with a large majority, Grivas failed miserably. Angry and bitter, he then swore that he would give up politics for ever.

Meanwhile, his attention was also focused on Cyprus and during the late 1940s he held regular discussions with people who shared his enosist aspirations. Visiting the island in 1951 Grivas made a thorough inspection of the entire area. Two meetings chaired by Makarios were held in Athens on 2 and 21 July 1952.

The young ethnarch had no confidence in guerrilla tactics but the opposing view prevailed and at a meeting of Grivas, S. Loizides and Archbishop Spyridon of Athens on 11 September, the last declared that *"freedom is never won without bloodshed"*.

In October 1952 Grivas was back in Cyprus and when he returned to Greece on 25 February 1953 he devoted much of his time to drawing up a comprehensive guerrilla plan which he said *"with minor modifications, acted as a general guide to my operations from start to finish of the struggle"*. On 7 March 1953 a fateful meeting took place in Athens of the political and military leaders of the Cyprus struggle. Makarios, who had just returned from New York presided and he, together with 11 others, including Grivas, took an oath of secrecy and dedicated themselves to the cause (one and only) of enosis. Makarios explained that only limited sabotage and not full-out force was needed. Grivas recounts that for the rest of 1953 and during the early months of 1954 he faced opposition not only from Makarios but from the Greek government. However, in March 1954 the first caique (light sailing vessel) called the '*Serena*' arrived from the mainland with arms and ammunition and it was followed by another in October. Grivas also recalls his meeting with Makarios on 15 February 1954, in which he detected that the young ethnarch was then very nearly ready to comply with his plans which the secret liberation committee had decided on 28 January should be put into practice as soon as possible.

Yet the final decision as to what should be done and when, was not at all clear, as was shown by the October meeting in Athens between Grivas and Makarios. The former, in his so-called '*historic mission*' resolved to return to Cyprus but, he had no visa. Consequently, he left his home on 26 October 1954 and with Socrates Loizides set sail for Rhodes. Only seven people knew of their departure. His diary for the day reads: '*God help us.....I depart with faith and courage.... I shall succeed*'.

They reached Rhodes at 3.00 pm on 27 October but bad weather delayed their departure. Grivas however made full use of their 12-day stay and proceeded to organise a centre from which arms could be shipped to Cyprus and made arrangements for the next delivery there. After dark on 7 November the two men boarded a small craft at Callithea

Bay and finally set sail at 15 minutes past midnight. At around 8.00 pm on 10 November, the small craft arrived off the west coast of Cyprus at the quiet bay of Khloraka and the home of Azinas was to be Grivas' temporary headquarters. He moved to Nicosia towards the end of the month. At that juncture Grivas not only lacked the unqualified support of Makarios but also that of a proper set-up. He set about his task of forming an organisation with unrelenting zeal.

The decisive date was 11 January 1955. Makarios, who had arrived on the previous day from America, summoned Grivas to the house of the bishop of Larnaca and there informed him that he had secured the support of Papagos, the Greek premier, for their aims, which were still to be sabotage. It was at this meeting, and at Grivas' suggestion, that the new secret organisation was christened **EOKA** (**Ethniki Organosi Kyprion Agoniston** - National Organisation of Cypriot Fighters). It replaced EMAK - the Cyprus National Liberation Front. Grivas also declared that he would not lay down his arms until Makarios told him to do so. Several days later (19 January) he was extremely fortunate to meet **Gregorios Afxentiou**, who soon became his trusted principal lieutenant. In the opinion of many Afxentiou, noted for his honesty and bravery, was to become the most revered hero of the Cypriot struggle.

Grivas was of the opinion that the *'rising'* should commence around the middle of March but Makarios preferred 25 March - the day celebrated as the beginning of the 1821 Greek Revolution. The capture of the **Ayios Georgios**, bringing the third shipload of explosives into the island, meant a brief delay.[3] However, on 29 March, Makarios gave him permission to start his operations. Grivas added *'God is with us'*.

During the early hours of **1 April 1955** a series of bomb explosions wrecked government offices, police stations and military premises throughout the island. On the same day EOKA proclaimed its existence in leaflets signed *'Dighenis'*.[4] This was Grivas' *nom de guerre* ' in his capacity as leader of EOKA. In the course of the struggle he was also called *'Arkhigos'* (leader) and *'Apiastos'* (the one that could not be taken). His fighters and close associates also called him *'theios'* (uncle) and *'o gheros'* (the old man).

---

(3) It was intercepted on the night of 25-26 January by HMS Comet, a British destroyer. Socrates Loizides and 12 others were arrested. It appears that the colonial administration knew of its arrival!

(4) Dighenes was a 10th century epic hero of Byzantine Asia Minor.

So much for Grivas. **Makarios** was born Michael Christodoulos Mouskos in the Paphos village of Panayia near the monastery of Chrysorroyiatissa. The date was 13 August 1913[5] and, while disclaiming any tendency to superstition, he had always regarded 13 as his lucky number. In 1926 he entered Kykko monastery as a novice and took the name of Kykkotis. He stayed there for 12 years and also, from the age of 20, he attended the three top classes of the Pan-Cyprian Gymnasium. At the age of 26 he was ordained deacon and sent to the University of Athens on a scholarship to study theology and some law. He graduated in 1942 and entered the church of St. Irene where he was ordained as a priest on 13 January 1946. Some months later one of the ten scholarships offered by the World Council of Churches was granted to him and in September he departed for the Methodist Theological College at the University of Boston, US.

On 13 June 1948 he was consecrated Bishop of Kition and following the death of Makarios II on 28 June 1950, he was elected as **Archbishop Makarios III** on 18 October. He was destined to become internationally known for his leadership of the enosis movement. The '*union with Greece*' campaign was turned by him into a personal crusade. His total involvement was channelled into three main avenues:

(1) Extensive travel abroad. His aim was to win support from as many countries as possible. He visited Greece and other European nations, America and the Middle East and later several Afro-Asian states. Makarios always spoke of the need for world peace.

(2) Systematic preparations at home. Makarios' aim from the outset was to grasp the national liberation struggle initiative from all other groupings. In order to do so several organisations needed to be established. In 1952 **PEON** (*Pan-Cyprian Youth Organisation*) and **OHEN** (*Organisation of Orthodox Christian Youth*), were set up. Then in 1954 such rightwing associations as **PEK** (*Pan-Agrarian Union of Cyprus*) and **SEK** (*the Cyprus Worker's Confederation*) were reorganised and set on firmer foundations. Moreover, the illustrated monthly magazine, '*Greek Cyprus* ' which began publication in 1949 was under the Ethnarchy Bureau - later known as the '*Ministry of the Enlightenment*'.

(3) Conciliation. Like a true Aristotelian Makarios believed in striking a happy medium. Unlike some of his predecessors he did not neglect the sympathies of the left although in the first two years of the 1950s he failed to come to grips with the realities of the Cypriot class system. In fact when the Ethnarchic Council was widened to include laymen it did not form a cross-section of Cypriot society; it simply

---

(5) Grivas was 15/16 years his senior.

Archbishop Makarios: The First President of the Cyprus Republic.

represented the Church and the higher echelons of the island's Christian community.

Although Makarios' political thinking was still in a formative stage he came to understand that the forces of the left, on both the domestic and the international scene, should not be alienated.[6] As a result of this policy, the first open and official contact took place between the young ethnarch and **AKEL**; the date was August 1954 just twelve days before the Cypriot appeal was lodged to the UN by the Greek government. The participants exchanged views on the best way of facing the complexities of the Cypriot problem. Certainly the archbishop could not ignore such a sizeable proportion of the island's population.[7] Although AKEL did not

(6) Yet the policy of the 'national centre' (Athens) was to seek aid only from western powers.

(7) AKEL and its affiliated organisations had the solid support of around 40% of the entire Greek and Turkish electorate.

support EOKA's violent tactics, preferring decolonization and full independence to outright political confrontation and enosis, it did not betray its armed struggle for self-determination. In fact, the *'Patriotic Organisation of the Left'* (POL - Organosis Aristeron Patrioton) 'joined' EOKA's ranks. Nevertheless, the colonial administration proscribed the party in 1955.

Very briefly, the agreed strategy of the Greek Cypriots in the early 1950s was as follows:

1.  The rejection of any constitutional proposals put forward by Britain.

2.  The intensification of the campaign to inform the Greek people about the issues facing the islanders.

3.  Co-ordination with liberation organisations in Greece and the preparation for an armed struggle. EOKA's campaign eventually opened on 1 April 1955

4.  The solution of the problem by the United Nations with Greek government initiative and help. It was here that Cypriot expectations, as we shall see below, foundered.

The colonial administration celebrates an event where prominent Cypriots were invited

Points two and three require no special mention. Points one and four need some explanation:

After the turbulent experiences of the 1940s Greece had no choice but to steer a peaceful course. Hence the problem of the late 1940s and 1950s was that if the government came out openly in favour of enosis it would be accused by its western allies of seeking territorial gains regardless of the defence requirements of the Middle East. Thus the official Greek policy had been to express sympathy with such a desire but, in pressing for a solution, to demand only the human rights of the UN Charter including the right of self-determination. Therefore, the statement by Premier Tsaldaris in 1946 that *"the question of Cyprus is not a demand and it should not be posed in a vindictive manner because it only concerns Greece and her friend GB"* was supported, at least up to 1954, by successive Greek governments. In fact, no administration could ignore the Cypriot demand for enosis. Due mainly to three factors this demand was not pressed:

1. Greece wished to settle it within the framework of Anglo-Hellenic friendship.

2. American economic and military aid to Greece from 1947 to 1951 amounted to around $1,672 million. A government that depends upon such foreign bounty necessarily surrenders its freedom of action.[8]

3. From 1945 to the early 1950s Greece suffered from a succession of weak governments. The administrations of Plastiras, Voulgaris, Sophoulis and Tsaldaris soon gave way to the strong premiership of **Field-Marshall Papagos** who won convincingly in November 1952 as leader of the Greek Rally (*'Ellinikos Sinagermos'*).

Papagos was to remain PM until his death on October 1955. In 1953 he informed Sir Charles Peake (British ambassador to Athens from 1951 to 1957), that as a solution to the Cyprus problem he proposed the granting of a liberal constitution to the island, with a plebiscite to follow within two years so as to give the people an opportunity to decide their own future. He repeated the offer of bases on Greek territory and he then advised Makarios that Greece would try to solve the Cyprus problem *'within the framework of current realities'* - in essence it was a policy of firmness and compromise best calculated to serve eastern Mediterranean security and Anglo-Greek ties.

---

(8) S. Venizelos admitted to the Greek Vouli on 12 December 1958 that it was the US which prevented Greece in 1951 and 1952 from taking the Cypriot question to the United Nations.

A stamp issued in Greece in 1954 showing an ink blot on the column from Hansard that contained Britain's "NEVER" statement

However, public pressure and Cypriot insistence prompted Greece to take *'Cyprus to the UN'*. The proponents of a radical quick-fix self-determination solution triumphed over the pragmatists wait-and-see gradualist approach. On 15 April 1954 Papagos decided to go ahead with the recourse to the UN and on 3 May he committed himself publicly. On 14 May it may be added, the UK through diplomatic channels again said *'no'* and on 28 July Henry Hopkinson's[9] statement of **'never'** emphatically confirmed it in public. The Greek appeal was transmitted to the UN Secretary-General on 20 August 1954 and despite much opposition from the UK the General Committee examined the Cyprus item on 23 September. For Greece, Alexis Kyrou requested that the principle of equal rights and self-determination, as defined in Article I (2) of the Charter, should be applied to Cyprus. He declared that his government would abide by the decision taken by the island's population.

**Selwyn Lloyd**, Minister of State at the Foreign Office (October 1951-October 1954), accused Greece of seeking to annex British sovereign territory . He went on to warn of the danger of communal strife arising out of the action since such a move was opposed by the Turkish community. Cyprus moreover, was vital to the discharge of Britain's responsibilities in the Middle East and under the Atlantic Treaty: *"Leases expire, treaties are whittled away, Greek governments change hence full administrative control is necessary"*, he argued. The Cyprus item was eventually discussed at the very end of the Assembly's session in four meetings of the Political Committee on 14 and 15 December. On 17

---

(9) Minister of State for Colonial Affairs. He simply voiced in public the conservative's steadfast and so-called belief of 'redundant imperialism'.

## THE WASHINGTON DECLARATION

Issued by the President and Prime Minister from the
White House on Tuesday, June 29. 1954.

As we terminate our conversations on subjects of mutual
and world interest, we again declare that:

(1) In intimate comradeship, we will continue our united
efforts to secure world peace based upon the principles of the
Atlantic Charter, which we reaffirm.

(2) We, together and individually, continue to hold out
the hand of friendship to any and all nations, which by solemn
pledge and confirming deeds show themselves desirous of
participating in a just and fair peace.

(3) We uphold the principle of self-government and will
earnestly strive by every peaceful means to secure the independenc-
of all countries whose peoples desire and are capable of
sustaining an independent existence. We welcome the processes
of development, where still needed, that lead toward that goal.
As regards formerly sovereign states now in bondage, we will
not be a party to any arrangement or treaty which would confirm
or prolong their unwilling subordination. In the case of nations
now divided against their will, we shall continue to seek to
achieve unity through free elections supervised by the United
Nations to ensure they are conducted fairly.

(4) We believe that the cause of world peace would be
advanced by general and drastic reduction under effective
safeguards of world armaments of all classes and kinds. It
will be our persevering resolve to promote conditions in which
the prodigious nuclear forces now in human hands can be used
to enrich and not to destroy mankind.

(5) We will continue our support of the United Nations
and of existing international organizations that have been
established in the spirit of the Charter for common
protection and security. We urge the establishment and
maintenance of such associations of appropriate nations as
will best, in their respective regions, preserve the peace
and the independence of the peoples living there. When desired
by the peoples of the affected countries we are ready to render
appropriate and feasible assistance to such associations.

(6) We shall, with our friends, develop and maintain
the spiritual, economic and military strength necessary to
pursue these purposes effectively. In pursuit of this purpose
we will seek every means of promoting the fuller and freer
interchange among us of goods and services which will benefit
all participants.

(Signed) DWIGHT D. EISENHOWER.

(Signed) WINSTON S. CHURCHILL.

December the General Assembly adopted resolution 814 (IX) by 50 votes to none with 8 abstentions. The adopted resolution read:

*'The General Assembly, considering that, for the time being it does not appear appropriate to adopt a resolution on the question of Cyprus, decides not to consider further the item entitled........'*

Of vital importance were the words *'for the time being'*. The way was now open for the Cyprus question to be submitted in 1955. The annual pilgrimage to the UN had begun. The problem became an international issue and the Greeks believed that the UN could deal with it. Opposition leaders however, were of the opinion that Greece was betrayed by its allies, notably the US. There were anti-American riots in Athens on 14 December and in Salonica two days later. Although Papagos declared that Greece was let down by its friends, **King Paul** predicted Cyprus' eventual *'reunion'* with the motherland through favourable UN action on self-determination for the islanders.

The British were adamant that they foresaw no change in the island's status. Repeated public ministerial statements and behind the scenes diplomatic exchanges were instrumental in projecting the *'no change policy'*. Consequently on 28 July 1954 it was announced in the House of Commons that it was proposed to introduce a modified constitution in the island - based on the 1948 proposals. The fresh initiative was in essence intended to :

- appease but not please;
- combat the apparent emergence of communism;
- preserve Britain's strategic interests in the area; and
- emphasise once more that no change in the status of the island was contemplated.

It was also in this debate that Henry Hopkinson used the highly undiplomatic phrase "........can *never* expect to be fully independent... "[10]

The restraint shown by Athens so far was henceforth replaced by increasing antagonism. Amongst other actions a postage stamp showing an inkblot on the column from Hansard that contained Hopkinson's *'never'* statement was hurriedly printed. In Cyprus the proposals were promptly discredited as an obstacle to enosis. On 29 July, Makarios rejected them out of hand and in a message to the people warned that no one should co-operate with the authorities in this *'constitutional conspiracy'*

---

(10) 531. House of Commons . Debates. 5s. Column 508. The statement of course did not come out of the blue. Such a policy had already been agreed in advance by the Cabinet. Moreover, the declaration occurred immediately after Britain's humiliating withdrawal from Egypt and the Suez Canal zone.

which aimed at prolonging the enslavement of the Cypriot people. Athens radio called for a flat rejection of the proposed constitution. The government expressed the same view and repeated that the issue of *self-determination for the Cypriots*' would be taken to the UN.

Opposition was also registered by various non-Greek bodies and organisations. A number of British Labour MPs, seeing that the constitution would provide a legislature made up of an elected minority and a majority composed of colonial officials and appointees, criticised the scheme because, among other defects, it did not allow Cyprus to leave the British Commonwealth if its inhabitants wished it to do so. The Labour Party Conference in October adopted a resolution deploring the policy of the Conservative government and urged its MPs to oppose its Cyprus policy on all occasions. Similarly, a resolution passed by the Liberal Party Council in December also demanded the granting of a more democratic constitution.

Meanwhile in Cyprus protests flowed from all sections; in August the authorities decided to enforce the anti-sedition laws. In turn there were further protests. The government reorganised and strengthened its intelligence services and by a series of local broadcasts, pamphlets and press communiques tried to counter the enosis agitation. The two c's (confrontation and compromise) were now in direct opposition.

The decision by Greece to bring the Cyprus question before the UN meant that the problem of enosis had entered the most critical phase of its long history. Political ideology and military expediency came into sharp conflict. Even those who viewed the prospect of Greek rule with deep misgivings felt that they could not let the cause down. Thomas Anthem a distinguished commentator of the time, pointed out in 1954 that *"rightly or wrongly. whether Cypriots are misguided and foolish in desiring to exchange a rich stepfather for a poor mother of their own blood, the fact remains that Greeks everywhere, at home and abroad, are solidly behind the enosis movement"*. Sir Harold Nicolson another prominent writer, in a letter to The Times on 15 July 1954 explained that *"even though there are several arguments against the union of Cyprus with Greece, if tied tightly together they make a sorry little bundle and if taken separately they snap at once"*.

British unwillingness to discuss the Cyprus question with the Hellenic government and the eventual Greek decision to seek justice at the UN hardened Turkish opinion. The tone of the Turkish press became hostile and the dangers posed to NATO's eastern flank were widely discussed.[11] In his memoirs Eden recalled that it was *'right'* that it should

---

(11) The Protocol on the Accession in NATO was signed on 17 October 1951; both sides assumed full membership on 18 February 1952. The 1953 Treaty of Friendship and Co-operation and the 1954 Treaty of Alliance bound the two countries more firmly together.

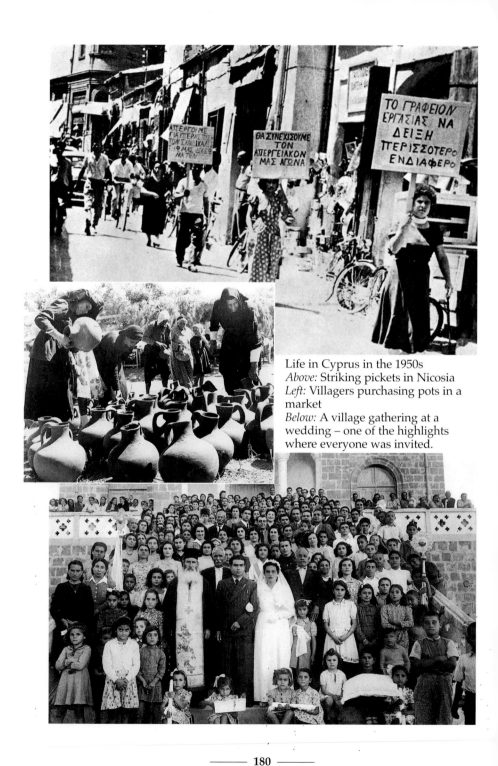

Life in Cyprus in the 1950s
*Above:* Striking pickets in Nicosia
*Left:* Villagers purchasing pots in a market
*Below:* A village gathering at a wedding – one of the highlights where everyone was invited.

speak in that way *'because it was the truth that the Turks would never let the Greeks have Cyprus'*. Eden was convinced that the problem would only be resolved between the three allies - Britain, Greece and Turkey. He suggested therefore that the Turkish press should play up the problem a bit more and thus denounce all enosis moves. In Cyprus, Turkish separatist leaders, alienated by such developments and supported by the *'mother'* country, were saying that there was *'no Cyprus question'* and that the island would *'never'* be annexed by Greece.

Even so the vast majority of the Muslim population accepted the fact that they were a minority and showed no strong reaction to the moves of their Christian counterparts. Even as late as 5 December 1955 Ian Mikardo MP informed the House of Commons that during his visit to Cyprus, the Turks put forward the same sort of views and arguments as were put forward by minority communities living in the midst of people more numerous than themselves. In a briefing paper dated 26 August 1957, Sir John Harding explained that, *"Greeks and Turks have lived together in Cyprus peacefully for many centuries"* and that, *"there is in fact much more tolerance between Greeks and Turks in Cyprus than there is for instance in many of our mixed communities between Christians and Jews, or between Roman Catholics and non-Roman Catholics and there are more historical precedents to show that the Cypriot communities can live together satisfactorily than the reverse..."*[12]

Yet, as the next section will show the harmonious relations which existed between the two communities were replaced by confrontation and finally by separation.

A building by the entrance of Ledra Street, a place of numerous political activities which was also used as a club and hostel (YMCA)

---

(12)  FO 286/1441/15118/1/57

# (vii) 1955 - 1960
## The National Liberation Struggle and the Polarization of the two Communities.

The stage was set for a confrontation. EOKA made its first appearance on the Cypriot scene with acts of sabotage in the districts of Nicosia, Larnaca and Limassol. Damage to government property for the first night's incidents (31 March to 1 April) was estimated to be around £56.000, most of which was to broadcasting equipment. Twentyone people were arrested. For over three years a fierce battle raged between EOKA and some 30,000 British soldiers for the *control* of the island.

The guerrilla movement, popularly known as '*o aghonas*' (the struggle), was seen as a chance to fight not only for national freedom but for social justice. Although EOKA was almost entirely a right-wing nationalist-led movement it had a proletarian base because it was seen to be carrying on an anti-imperialist struggle. Hence under the banner of national freedom EOKA was able to weld together vast sections of the working peasantry with the higher strata of Greek Cypriot society and the Orthodox Church in a struggle for national self-determination. The strategic requirements of the western allies, the hostage mentality in Greece, the structure of the island's class system and Turkish nationalism were however neglected. Many Greeks were under the illusion that it was not so genuine, passionate or long-standing as theirs but was expressed in the extreme politics of **Dr. Fazil Kütchük, Rauf Denktash** and a few other diehards. Turkish nationalism did exist but it was neither so active nor so well controlled as its Greek counterpart. Kutchuk was chairman of the '**Kibris Turktur Parti**' (Cyprus is Turkish Party), which propagated the theory that self-determination for Cyprus would result in the annihilation of all Turks, civil war and ultimately total unrest in the Middle East. In fact, the short-lived Turkish underground organisation called '*Kara Yilan*' (Black Snake) and predecessor to '*Volkan*' (The Volcano) was formed immediately after 1 April 1955. '*Kara Cite*' (Black Gang) was another short-lived grouping. It appears that the first Turkish Cypriot organisation (more like a protection group) was set up in 1945. It was comprised of only a few dozen members.

EOKA had no reason to attack and antagonise the Muslim inhabitants and in the summer of 1955 issued several leaflets assuring the island's Turks that it was struggling not against them but against British colonialism, that EOKA's feelings towards them were friendly and that it was expecting them to be its allies. Its fighters had specific instructions not to antagonise them; yet it was short-sighted to ignore the possibility that Britain would encourage such a reaction from Turkey.

These were the realities facing Cyprus in 1955. Alas there were no statesmen to make the proper appraisal and act accordingly. In fact the 'struggle' for supremacy and direction of the political movement among the Greek Cypriots was undoubtedly a negative factor. Competing for such dominance were the Church, the secular politicians and the urban professional business elite. In a small island however, where family plays an important role such competition often proved futile - it simply broke down. The left of course, was another dominant factor. Nevertheless, was it feasible to expect a few hundred guerrillas to defeat the west's elite force, armed with the most up-to-date and sophisticated weapons, which could have been drafted into the war zone at any time? At best the colonial forces could have been worn down and this alone would have drawn worldwide attention to the Cyprus problem.

The British continued to make half-hearted attempts to reach a political settlement while still pursuing their so-called *'primary task of restoring law and order'*. In regimental jargon, the so-called *'savage war of peace'* was in full swing. Consequently, on 15 July 1955 a Detention of Persons Law, similar to the severe British Defence Regulation 18B, was decreed. **Kurt Waldheim**, for years Secretary-General of the UN, explains the events that followed:

"To find a way out of the impasse, the British government, in June 1955, invited Greece and Turkey to discuss the future of the island. Internationalizing the problem, however, led to new complications. The Turkish government, under Prime Minister Menderes, based its claim to co-determination in Cyprus on arguments that are still present today, namely, the security of Turkey, whose coastline is scarcely sixty kilometres from Cyprus and the protection of the Turkish Cypriot community. For Menderes, there were only two possibilities: maintenance of British rule or partition of the island between Turkey and Greece...."[1]

The British invitation of 30 June was accepted by Turkey on 2 July and by Greece six days later. The projected London Conference was denounced as *"a trap"* by Makarios. Nevertheless the three countries represented by their Foreign Secretaries attended the conference which opened at Lancaster House on 29 August. Immediately the widely differing views of the three allies were brought sharply into focus. For the Greeks **Stephanos Stephanopoulos** propagated the demand for national self-determination and declared that Greece had never for a single

---

(1) The Challenge of Peace. 1980. Page 62

moment entertained the idea of a *"withdrawal from Cyprus of the British forces"*. **Harold Macmillan** explained that his government did not *"accept the principle of self-determination as one of universal application"* since, *"exceptions had to be made in view of geographical, traditional, historical and other considerations"*. For the Turks **Fatin Zorlu** insisted that his country looked upon the Cyprus question as a British domestic issue and the status quo should be maintained. The Turkish position rested on two arguments: firstly the theoretical or juridical thesis that Cyprus was given to Britain by Turkey in 1878 and hence if she wished to relinquish sovereignty the island should revert to its previous suzerein owner; secondly, the practical argument of proximity: Ankara's view being that Cyprus was in fact an extension of the Anatolian peninsula. Thus its long thin promontory which stretches to the northeast is often romantically described as *'the dagger which points at the heart of Turkey '*. The Turks borrowed a Churchillian phrase in saying that Cyprus faces their *"soft underbelly"*. In his diaries Macmillan called the conference *"abortive but by no means useless"*. In fact the conference underlined the potential Greek-Turkish antagonism over the problem - a side effect which **Anthony Eden,** the Prime Minister, had deliberately planned when calling it in an effort to disprove the thesis that the Cyprus troubles were due to old-fashioned British colonialism. Britain the sovereign over the island, was thus placed in the position of *'mediator'* in a *'dispute'* between Greece and Turkey over the future status of an island that belonged to neither of these states. The novelist **Lawrence Durrell** reflected in 1957 that, *"the key was finally turned upon Cyprus."* Gradually but surely, self-determination for the Cypriot majority has been driven beyond the realm of practical politics.

The British proposals for self-government submitted by Macmillan at the conference on 6 September, were subsequently rejected by both Athens and Ankara. Meanwhile, the news of an explosion in the grounds of the Turkish consulate at Salonica (formerly Ataturk's house), precipitated murderous anti-Greek riots in Smyrna and Istanbul on 6-7 September. This night of terror  completed the *'crucifixion of Christendom'*.[2] The official Turkish view at the time was that the riots were simply a communist plot aimed against western interests and Greco-Turkish friendship.[3] The incidents in fact were undoubtedly connived at, if not directly inspired, by the Turkish government and were aimed at putting pressure on the US to oppose the inclusion of the Cyprus item on the agenda of the 10th General Assembly. The incidents also provided useful ammunition for Zorlu in his negotiations with his British and Greek counterparts in London.

---

(2) It was estimated that capital goods valued at $150 million were destroyed.

(3) The communist party in Turkey was proscribed! The Turkish General Staff were even convinced that *"Archbishop Makarios was in the pay of the Russians"*

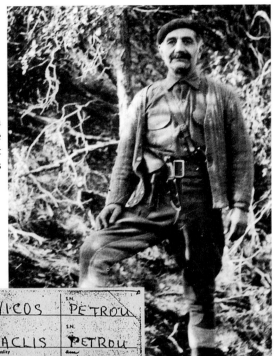

A picture of George Grivas in uniform believed to have been taken near his hideout somewhere in the mountains

One of Grivas' ID cards whilst in Cyprus.

General description of Grivas as listed on the wanted list.

Description :

Born :           1898
Height :         5'6½"
Build :          Medium, inclined to thickset.
                 Broad shoulders.
Face :           Full.
Moustache :      Small, Hitler-style.
Hair :           Chestnut, bald on top.
Eyes :           Chestnut.
Eyebrows :       Dark and bushy.
Mouth :          Wide, with firm jaw.

Action :.

(a) Whereabouts to be identified.

(b) Identification not to be disclosed

(c) Supt. SB to be advised immediately by
    telephone if whereabouts identified,
    quoting PF number and place only.

29th November, 1954.     Superintendent of Police,
                         Special Branch.

The truth however was soon to present itself. At the Yassiada trials which opened on 14 October 1960 case number two was listed as *'September 6-7 incidents'*. Ten former government officials were tried with inciting riots against the Greek population of Istanbul as a means of pressing the Turkish viewpoint on the Cyprus dispute. Evidence was given by defence witnesses that the government had been put up to staging a Cyprus demonstration by Harold Macmillan but that the rally, badly mismanaged by Menderes, had degenerated into an uncontrollable riot. The Turkish court announced its verdicts on 15 September 1961 - eleven months and one day after the trials opened. Suffice to say that Zorlu, Hasan Polatkan (Finance Minister) and Menderes were hanged in the prison island of Imrali.[4]

Back to 1955 the US was naturally alarmed by the recent tragic developments. It urged that *'quiet diplomacy'* amongst friends was the most constructive approach in settling differences. Consequently, in November 1955 Whitehall presented its **Formula for Cyprus** to the Greek and Turkish governments and to Archbishop Makarios. The formula stressed that it was not Britain's position that *'the principle of self-determination can never be applied to Cyprus'* but that account should be taken of the *'strategic position of the island'*. As for self-government, *'it is the intention of Britain to work for a solution which will satisfy the wishes of the people of Cyprus'*. Britain was assured of the US's active help over its constitutional plans and was also confident of the support of **Constantine Karamanlis**[5] over the self-determination formula. The latter's guiding principle, known as the *'policy of the national centre'*, soon became an irritant in Graeco-Cypriot relations. At the inception of this British-American concept lay the view that the alliance interests of Greece *'must'*prevail over her interests in Cyprus. The conflict between the national desire for absolute sovereignty and the pragmatic necessity of retaining powerful friends was at the root of the long-standing Greek dilemma over enosis. Professor M. Evriviades has noted that the 'burial' of enosis, if it ever happened at or a precise historical moment, took place in the summer of 1955.

Meanwhile on 3 October 1955 **Sir John Harding**, the island's new governor, arrived in Cyprus and at once Makarios expressed his willingness to meet him, hinting that a compromise was possible. Discussions between them proceeded intermittently throughout the following few months. A final meeting was held in Nicosia on 29 February

---

(4) The first two on 16 September 1961 and Menderes on the 17th. Messages from world leaders pleading for mercy failed to save the Turkish leader.

(5) Greek Premier from 5 October 1955 to June 1963. He succeeded Papagos as leader of the Greek Rally, soon to be renamed ERE (National Radical Union). He was favoured by the Greek Palace and by the US.

Sir John Harding, the hard line militarist, appointed governor of Cyprus 1955–57 failed to bring about a negotiated political settlement

1956 which was also attended by **Alan Lennox-Boyd**, the Secretary of State for the Colonies. The British assurances based on the earlier proposals were vague and ambiguous, although indirectly the principle of self-determination was recognised. A solution seemed near but differences arose apparently over amnesty, public security and the elected majority provisions. The security of the Middle East, Britain's alliance with Turkey and the irreconcilable enosist circles in Cyprus and Greece were major problems of the highest order. However HMG was not, it seems, sincere during the talks since they still insisted on having the whole of Cyprus as a base and to be in direct control of internal security, law and order etc. Harding, who was given wider powers than his predecessors in relation to security, was prompt in building up an intelligence network. After EOKA had captured a large consignment of arms transferred from Suez to Famagusta, he became personally responsible for the direction of all security operations. He requested troop reinforcements and had them trained in riot-breaking by police methods and outlying police posts were given military protection.

Road blocks and house-to-house searches were intensified. Travelling through the night without lights along narrow mountain roads, troops usually surrounded suspect villages at dawn. All males over the age of 12 were taken outside for questioning while the houses were searched in the presence of women and children. After many fruitless ventures vast quantities of arms, ammunition and army uniforms were eventually discovered and, with the help of police dogs, commandos found a network of caves in the Troodos mountains. Yet intensified

*Above:* The 'battle' at the Pancyprian Gymnasium, 28 January 1956. Arrests followed the storming of the higher education school

*Below:* Detainees behind barbed wire

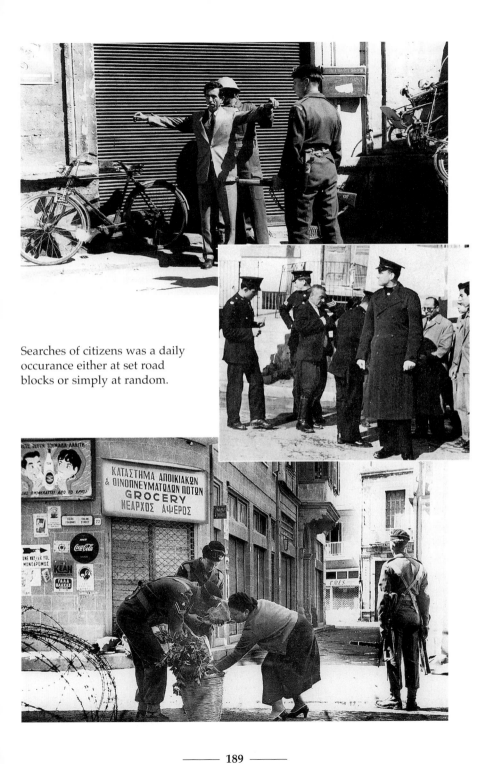

Searches of citizens was a daily occurance either at set road blocks or simply at random.

security operations brought no early results and the last week in October saw one of the worst outbreaks of disorder since the commencement of hostilities.

In November, a state of emergency was declared and under the new regulations the unauthorised possession of firearms and explosives carried a maximum penalty of death. Provision was also made for deportation, censorship, the placing of large sums of money on the heads of wanted men and collective punishment. Hence, a collective fine of £2,000 was levied on the villagers of Lefkoniko for the destruction of the local post office by fire and on the night of 13-14 December, under operation '*Lobster Pot*', security forces arrested 132 leading AKEL and PEO members and removed them to a detention camp near Larnaca. AKEL,[6] AON, EAK, PODY and four communist papers were banned under the emergency regulations as being dangerous associations whose real objectives were '*to prolong dissension and turbulence on the island*'. But PEO and other communist-oriented organisations affiliated to AKEL were not proscribed, apparently because the colonial administration wished to interfere as little as possible with the trade unions and the labour movement.

Whitehall's policy in the first 11 months of EOKA's struggle passed through several distinct and contradictory stages. It had begun with a categorical denial that the problem existed at all or at least that it involved anyone except the U.K. The Greeks had already been warned in 1954 to '*stop playing with fire*'. The next stage was the attempt to enlarge the issue by drawing in Greece and Turkey. The British '*domestic*' issue had now become an '*international*' problem. When this policy failed it was restricted to Britain and Makarios and direct negotiations followed. When these looked like being successful they were broken off because it was felt, amongst other things, that the whole structure of Middle Eastern security would be jeopardized. The unfettered use of bases in Cyprus were therefore essential. In his memoirs Eden recorded that he regarded the alliance with Turkey as '*the first consideration in our policy in that part of the world*'.

The linking of Cyprus with Turkish territorial security was a direct invitation to Turkey to enter the dispute. Another complication was added to the existing difficulties, out of which grew the demand '*ya taksim ya olum*' (partition or death) and hence more tension and bloodshed. By the second half of 1956, the US had quietly endorsed the principle of partition (as being another option) reminding everyone of other '*successful*' partitions such as Trieste. Finally, Britain became the arbiter in what was portrayed as a Greek-Turkish dispute and the protector of the West's interests in the Middle East. These shifts and turns were constantly

---

(6) The decision to proscribe the party was related to the '*abnormal*' conditions prevailing in the island. See FO 286/1302/1024/1292

Regular scenes in the streets of towns and villages with arrests of youngsters, even school kids and adults *(below)* taken for questioning attacked by the British press. The Daily Telegraph demanded on 7 June '*a genuine and positive action*'. The Spectator of the same date described the government's policy as '*silly, chaotic and barbaric*'.

Following the breakdown[7] of the Harding-Makarios talks (and there were many reasons) the next policy shift was to banish the archbishop who was henceforth seen as an obstacle to a settlement (in fact a decision had been taken months previously). According to the highly popular and distinguished diplomat Sir Evelyn Shuckburgh, Anthony Eden was "*perturbed*" and the Premier remarked that the breakdown of the talks had shown that Makarios' sole aim was "*to become King of Cyprus*". Were the talks torpedoed by EOKA? Evidence is still inconclusive on this issue.

Shuckburgh reveals further that on 5 March the Cabinet talked about Cyprus and its plans to deport Makarios and "*the other bad Bishop*". All were agreed on the deportation from Cyprus and then after a long pause Lord Salisbury suggested the Seychelles.[8] On 9 March 1956, the archbishop, who was on the point of leaving Nicosia airport for further talks in Athens was instead ordered to enter an RAF plane. He was sent to the Seychelles, arriving on Wednesday 14 March, where he was to stay for 13 months. Also exiled: **Papastavros Papagathangelou**, chief priest of Phaneromeni Church in Nicosia, **Bishop Kyprianos** of Kyrenia and **Polycarpos Ioannides**, a journalist and secretary of the latter's See. They were flown to Aden then Mombasa (Kenya) and from there HMS Loch Fada took them to their place of exile. The four deportees were lodged comfortably in the Sans Souci villa at Mahe, in the middle of the Indian Ocean. Makarios is often quoted as referring to his exile as "*a great experience and an unforgettable event*".

The deportation was criticised as being '*insane*' and '*unreasonable*'. Politically, it was a serious miscalculation. Makarios was the one true representative of the island's Greek population, who could curb acts of violence. The news of his arrest was followed by a week-long general strike. Army units cordoned-off the archbishop's palace and soldiers were posted to guard all government buildings and all the approaches to the capital. Riots also broke out in Greece and on 10 March the government, in a symbolic gesture, recalled Vasilis Mostras, its ambassador, from London.

In Cyprus meanwhile, violence grew and in April Harding undertook large-scale operations against EOKA in the Troodos

---

(7) The final meeting on 29 February 1956 was also attended by Lennox Boyd. According to N. Kranidiotis, the minister then warned the participants by saying "God save your people". See Difficult Years - Cyprus 1950-1960 (Greek edition). 1981. Page 170

(8) Descent to Suez: Diaries 1951-56. 1986. Pages 340, 343-44

*Above:* The four deportees:
*From Left to right* – Papastavros Papagathangelou; Archbishop Makarios;
Polycarpos Ioannides and Bishop Kyprianos – March 1956

*Below:* The four in a rare picture relaxing in the Seychelles mountains. Casualties were certainly far higher in the months following Makarios' banishment. Furthermore, racial strife which started mildly in January 1956 reached a climax in May. Pitched battles were fought and a barrier was set up in Nicosia to separate the two sides. The creation of an auxiliary police force manned entirely by Turks but under British officers, whose task was to control Greek riots and help the armed forces fight EOKA, served further to polarize the two communities. By February 1957, the mobile reserve of the Cyprus police consisted of 32 officers and 551 men of whom none was Greek but 560 were Turkish Cypriots. The majority of these auxiliaries were specially trained (some were even sent to Kenya for that purpose) to track down EOKA. Their connection with TMT was only too evident.

Another policy switch was then announced. On 12 July 1956, HMG appointed as constitutional commissioner the distinguished jurist **Lord Radcliffe**, who was charged with the preparation of proposals for a liberal measure of self-government for Cyprus under British sovereignty, giving the people a wide measure of control over their own affairs while at the same time safeguarding both the interests of the Turkish minority and the UK's strategic requirements. Lord Radcliffe visited Cyprus twice (14 July to 2 August and 26 September to 5 October 1956) to seek the views of the people. The Greeks demanded however that any meaningful discussions should include Makarios, their acknowledged leader. Nevertheless, his suggestions were published as a White Paper in the UK and Cyprus on 19 December 1956. The report, described as a *'statesmanlike document'* included the following propositions:

1) A legislative assembly consisting of a speaker, a deputy speaker and 36 other members of which 6 would be elected by members on a Turkish Cypriot communal roll, 24 on a general roll and 6 would be nominated by the governor.

2) A chief minister to act as head of government in self-governing matters. He would be a prominent person who commanded the largest measure of general support and be appointed by the governor.

3) A minister for Turkish Cypriot affairs would deal with issues of his community, including education. Laws affecting these affairs would require the consent of 2/3 of the assembly's elected Turkish members.

4) No bill passed by the legislative assembly should become law unless and until the governor had signified assent to it.

The proposal also described the Turkish Cypriots as a *'community'*. This was a new development. Simultaneously with their publication (19 December 1956), Whitehall announced that it had accepted Radcliffe's proposals. The Secretary of State for the Colonies (Lennox Boyd) however referred to another possible solution, that of partition.[9] The recommendations described as an *"academic exercise"* were accepted in principle by Ankara and by the Turkish Cypriot community. Athens and the island's Greek inhabitants rejected them mainly for three reasons:

a) They were neither democratic nor liberal since the elected majority principle was strangled by the almost unlimited powers of the governor.

b) They did not envisage the right of self-determination for the Cypriot people and were not therefore in accord with the fundamental principles of the UN Charter.

c) These and other deficiencies precluded therefore the solution of the Cyprus problem.

In the island, acts of violence continued unabated even though security forces scored several successes against Grivas' men. Diplomatic activity was also intensified in search of some form of compromise: at the UN a resolution by **Krishna Menon**, the powerful head of the Indian delegation, was adopted by the General Assembly on 26 February 1957 as resolution 1013 (XI). The vote was 57 in favour, none against, with one abstention. It stated that the answer to the Cyprus problem required an atmosphere of peace and freedom of expression and that a peaceful democratic and just solution would be found in accordance with the purposes and principles of the UN Charter and that negotiations will be resumed and continued to the end.

Athens was toying with a scheme for a customs union linking Greece, Turkey and Cyprus in the event of enosis.[10] Under this plan Cypriot Turks were to have dual nationality and exemption from conscription. NATO also joined the diplomatic offensive. Lord Ismay, its Secretary - General, announced on 15 March that he was prepared to offer his good offices for promoting a conciliation in the dispute in accordance with the resolution on the peaceful settlement of disputes which was adopted by NATO the previous December. Once more the Greeks were adamant that the problem was outside the competence of NATO and a matter for the UN only.

---

(9) House of Commons Debates 5s. Volume 562. Column 1268. Partition was seen among the eventual options.

(10) Also considered were plans for independence and apparently partition. It appears that the Averoff-Iksel talks of 6 October 1956 were instrumental in the discussion of the last mentioned solution. Such allegations were of course, strenuously denied by both Averoff and by the Greek government. Evidence suggests however, that Averoff was the *"secret weapon"* of the British at the Greek foreign office.

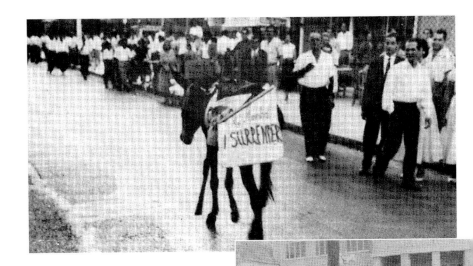

*Above:* EOKA's reply to the new plans "I Surrender".

*Right and below:* Regular demonstrations and arrests, including that of children.

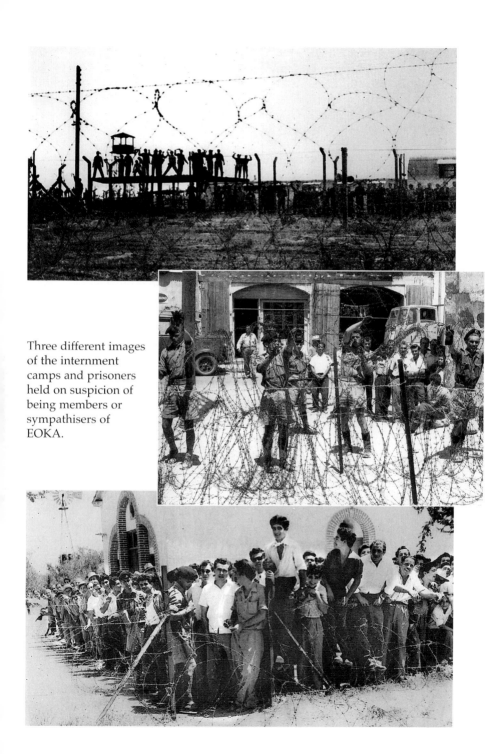

Three different images of the internment camps and prisoners held on suspicion of being members or sympathisers of EOKA.

In March 1957, Britain, following pressure from the United States, announced that Makarios and the other deportees could leave the Seychelles but should not return to Cyprus at such an inauspicious hour. The archbishop and his co-exiles left Sans Souci on 6 April and boarded the Greek ship *Olympic Thunder* bound for Madagascar. They arrived in Athens at 10.00 a.m. on 17 April where they were given a hero's welcome. The Greek capital became the archbishop's new base. He gathered men of real calibre around him and commenced once more his difficult task for keeping world opinion informed of the continuing tragedy of Cyprus. What were Britain's motives for releasing the deportees?

1)  Following the recent Radcliffe proposals, Whitehall was pledged to changes in the island's status.

2)  Britain's middle eastern policy had failed, especially after the Suez misadventure of late 1956 early 1957. Sir Evelyn Shuckburgh was able to record on 28 February 1956 that *"we have no diplomacy at all, no flexibility "*. Of the PM (Eden) and Foreign Secretary (Selwyn Lloyd), he recorded in his diaries that the former had *"deteriorated"* and the latter was a rather *"nervous official"* who had neither the *"inclination"* nor the *"courage to take decisions of any kind"*. With so much uncertainty and failure in other theatres, military strategists were saying that *"Cyprus should not be abandoned"*. Undoubtedly, Britain was torn between its commitment for democracy and the rule of law and the contradiction of empire, trading routes and its geo-strategic interests.

It is important to note that between September and November, Cyprus was prepared for and used as a launch pad for the allied anti-Nasser operation. It was a massive failure. Stung by such an unprecedented collapse, snubbed by the Americans, who were originally in the dark about the timing of the invasion, faced by an escalating economy and with EOKA once more on the offensive, HMG was in total disarray. Its present thinking, though in private much earlier, showed another shift: it was stated that not the whole of Cyprus but parts of it would be sufficient for future military needs. It may be added that before the previous decade closed, Britain offloaded a substantial part of its overseas responsibilities. Washington generally viewed this so-called *"end of an era"* with scepticism. Needless to say Britain's commitment to sharing electronic intelligence remained intact. Eden highlighted another issue. In a widely publicised speech at Norwich, East Anglia, on 1 June 1956, he said *"No Cyprus, no certain facilities to protect our supply of oil. No oil, unemployment and hunger in Britain. It is as simple as that"*. It must not be forgotten that British companies (Shell and BP) handled 1/3 of all the oil in international trade and that 1/2 of that oil came from the Middle East.

*Above:* The detention camp of Kokkinotremithia, one of several such camps established by the authorities where around 4000 Cypriots were detained without trial.
*Below:* Lena C. Jegger addressing a pro-Cyprus rally at Trafalgar Square in 1956.

3) The British at last admitted publicly that only Makarios could stem the escalation of violence. Grivas in fact announced a truce on 14 March 1957 to facilitate negotiations as soon as the ethnarch was released.

4) British troops and personnel in the island were becoming highly exasperated due to Whitehall's paralysis in formulating a fair and democratic positive plan for Cyprus.

5) Britain was bitterly criticised at home and abroad. What was needed was the resumption of meaningful negotiations based on a constructive policy. Since early 1956 Whitehall was saying, in private at least, that in the face of new realities Britain did not need the island as a base but needed only a couple of airstrips so that atomic bombers might fly off in pursuance of the West's defence obligations.

6) Pressure, both official and unofficial, was exerted by the US. At the Bermuda Conference which opened on 21 March 1957, Britain and the US, in all probability, agreed on the future course of the Cyprus question. Macmillan considered giving up sovereignty and retaining only military bases. Being economically dependent on America, the latter's policy prevailed. In fact the inglorious end to the Suez crisis (beginning of 1957) had left Britain impotent and bereft of any real authority in the Middle East. A just and peaceful solution to this so-called 'thorny problem' was demanded.

7) For Britain, which desired to improve its international image on the Cyprus question, Makarios was proving an embarrassment because there was no recognised leader but himself to conduct any meaningful negotiations.

8) Just as Greece had earlier turned to the UN for support against the British policy of perpetual sovereignty, so in June 1956 it turned to the Commission (under section 24) established by the European Convention on Human Rights for support against the British policy of repressing opposition within the island. This procedure became a powerful instrument of Greek policy.

With Makarios' release a new wave of diplomatic activity began. He wrote to Macmillan on 28 May 1957 recalling the wording of UN resolution 1013 (XI). Yet Macmillan recorded in his diary that 'we still have no clear or positive plan'. He went on to say that very reluctantly he began to feel that partition 'will be the only way out'. By July a new scheme was worked out. On the 16th the Cabinet discussed Cyprus and there was wide agreement on the 'tri-dominium' concept. The governments of Greece and Turkey were sounded out on the possibility of a conference. Meanwhile from late July, the archbishop was orientating himself towards a solution that envisaged independence. The foreign office, of course, was strongly opposed to independence which would have meant rule by Makarios or worse the communists *'who were popular'*. Grivas, on the other hand, was greatly disturbed and urged continued insistence on self-determination. The dice however was cast! During the summer of 1957 NATO mooted the idea of Cyprus becoming independent. Consequently, *'guaranteed independence'* (a solution especially favoured by President Eisenhower) and preferably by NATO powers was at the top of the agenda in secret discussions held at the US embassy in London on 12 September between the foreign office and American officials.

In November 1957 Harding retired on completion of the two-year tour of service previously agreed. He was replaced by **Sir Hugh Foot**, a liberal colonial civil servant, who arrived on 3 December. He was not new to Cyprus having served as colonial secretary from 1943 to 1945. The new governor appeared to have two major objectives: to relax tensions in the island and to work out some plan for settling this multiform problem. He visited detention camps, walked through the streets of Nicosia, spoke to leading local personalities, rode through villages and argued in coffee shops. The famous *'honeymoon period'* was in full swing.

Within a month he was back in London with his recommendations. He was very pleased because he had a *'positive policy'* to take to his superiors. Within ten days a new initiative was agreed upon. This was immediately rejected by Turkey. However, the failure to find common ground for a settlement induced HMG to revert to its own policy. By May 1958, a draft agreement embodying Foot's plans for internal self-government and the earlier proposals for the external solution of *'tri-dominium'* was agreed upon. The **Foot-Macmillan Partnership Plan** was presented to the Commons on 19 June 1958. Macmillan made it clear that Cyprus was now not a *'colonial problem'* but an *'international one'* - a drastic switch from his attitude three years before when he said at the tripartite conference that *'the internal affairs of Her Majesty's possessions cannot be discussed with foreign powers'*. He now suggested an *'adventure in partnership'* between the island's two communities and between the British and their two allies:

1) For seven years the international status of Cyprus would be unchanged.

2) The administration of the island as a whole would be directed by a council composed of the British governor, representatives of the Greek and Turkish governments and six Cypriot ministers, four elected from the Greek assembly and two from the Turkish.

3) External affairs, defence and internal security would be matters specifically reserved to the governor acting after consultation with the Greek and Turkish government representatives.

4) The government said that it would welcome any arrangement which would give Cypriots, Greek or Turkish nationality while enabling them to retain British nationality.

The Greek and Turkish response was disappointing. It was stressed by the Greeks that if applied the proposals would lead to an intense antagonism between both the majority and the minority of the population and between the governments of the countries involved in the island's administration. Thus the plan prejudged the future by preparing the ground for the islands' partition. The Turks were also critical. They went so far as to say that the plan was a *'stepping-stone to enosis'*.

In Cyprus the reaction was an increase in violence. EOKA intensified its activities and the British armed forces hit back hard. The problem of racial strife in 1956 and 1957 was not serious. The Turkish underground organisation *Volkan* (The Volcano) was simply anti-Greek and was determined to achieve partition. Its *'leader'* was **Rauf Denktash** - an admirer of Menderes the Turkish Premier. Officially proscribed in November 1957 it was succeeded by the *Turk Mudafaa (or Mukavamet) Teskilati* - Turkish Defence or Resistance Organisation, known as the **TMT** for short. The scheme it drew up was code-named *'Reconquering Cyprus Plan'*. Its first leader appears to have been Colonel Riza Vuruskan.

The TMT, though cruder, smaller and less well organised, modelled itself on EOKA. Hence the boycott of British goods which EOKA had ordered on 6 March 1958 was now applied by the Turks to Greek produce. Turks caught smoking Greek cigarettes or using Greek shops were beaten up by groups of youths. Any Turk who deviated from the national line that co-existence with the Greeks was impossible was liable to be denounced as a traitor. By mid-1958 pro-partitionist Turks were absolutely sure that soon the tide would turn their way. This confidence stemmed from several related factors:

i) As in 1955, Ankara was determined to show the world the strength of its feelings on the Cyprus issue. The press and Ankara radio were responsible for whipping up agitation and building up anti-Greek and anti-British resentment.

ii) Loss of confidence in Britain's ability to settle the problem without detriment to Turkish interests encouraged the pro-partionist Turkish Cypriots to step up their agitation for *taksim* (partition). The partitionist report which appeared initially in November 1956 under the name of Professor Nihat Erim was faithfully followed right through to 1974.

iii) Tension was exacerbated by the government's prolonged delay in publishing its new plan for Cyprus. Fearing that the policy,

The most revered hero of the Cyprus liberation struggle – Gregoris Afxentiou who died on 3 March 1957, following a last-ditch battle at his hideout.

WANTED PERSON

AFXENTIOU, Gregoris Pieri

*Above top:* Two images of the hero.
*Left:* As an officer in the Greek army and *Right* 'Father Chrysanthos' was Gregoris' disguise. *Above:* The remains of Afxentiou's gun. *Left:* Wanted poster.
*Below:* Makheras Monastery, close to his hideout where he died fighting.

announced on 19 June, would not provide for partition, the Turks, as we shall see below, intensified their activities and serious communal strife broke out on the night of 7 June 1958.

iv) Such over-confidence was fostered by the firm belief that Turkey would, if necessary, send troops to their assistance. Behind the scenes especially, Ankara certainly made such threats. The fact that in the island the Greeks outnumbered them by four to one was no deterrent. In a fair number of Turkish houses, posters were displayed showing Cyprus partitioned across the figure of a helmeted Turkish soldier.

v) The conviction that Turkey's allies, the manipulators of the Cyprus scenario, would not *'dare'* disregard their alleged interests.

The year 1958 was even more eventful. In January seven Turkish Cypriots were killed by security forces during anti-British demonstrations. Other incidents increased Turkish hostility towards the British. Then in June and July violent clashes broke out between the two communities. A bomb explosion outside Turkey's press office in Nicosia on the night of 7 June marked the beginning of the most acute phase of racial tension the island had seen.[11] Passions reached a climax on 12 June when eight Greeks were massacred by the Turks during a clash near the Turkish village of Guenyeli. A report by the commission of inquiry (it sat from 20 to 28 June with Sir Paget Bourne, Chief Justice of Cyprus, as the sole commissioner) published in Nicosia on 9 December 1958 found that the Greeks were rounded up by the British security forces and surprisingly released on the same day near Guenyeli, seven miles from where they were arrested and some distance from the nearest Greek villages. The incident has gone down in Cypriot history as the **Guenyeli Massacre** - organised by the British and executed by the Turks.

Arson, murder and destruction continued for two months. In the end 56 Greeks and 53 Turks had died. Sir Hugh Foot ordered an island-wide standstill for 48 hours on 22 July. The TMT was proscribed and around 60 Turks and 2,000 Greeks were arrested. Apart from the actual casualties there was a further disturbing factor: the Turks, with a view to partition, began to withdraw their minorities from predominantly Greek areas and evicted Greeks from areas where Turks formed the majority. In one week alone over 600 families left their homes of which 2/3 were Greek. Suffice it to say that many of the Turks who left the Greek areas at this stage did so largely under intense pressure from Turkish agitators.

---

(11) The Yassiada Trials (Turkey) of 1960-61 established that the bomb was planted by Turkish terrorists. *"They faked a bomb incident"* wrote Major General D.A. Kendrew. See WO 216/915

Another highly disturbing factor became more prominent in 1958. When EOKA's campaign opened in April 1955, AKEL was quick to condemn violence, pointing out that armed conflict would lead to only greater complications. The party also expressed its misgivings when it learnt that Grivas, a fanatical anti-communist, would lead the Cypriot struggle. This uneasy alliance endured many strains. However, during these early years armed masked men began to appear in villages seeking out *undesirables*. The victims tended to be members of left-wing families which often meant that the workers in them belonged to the *old* trade unions dominated by AKEL.

The shooting of left-wingers in Lyssi and Koma tou Yialou by masked men on 21 January 1958 heightened tension. On the following day PEO called a 48-hour strike to be observed throughout the island and there were demonstrations in most of the big towns. A cable to the archbishop in Athens begged him to use his influence to stop such incidents. Makarios' answer, given 48 hours after the murders, was surprisingly a call for unity and not a condemnation of the killings. A few weeks later news leaked out that EOKA had formed a special unit to deal with communists. AKEL had by now come out openly in favour of independence and Grivas' pamphlet *The Communist Leadership Against the Cyprus Struggle* helped to widen the breach between them.

Perhaps the worst flare-up between the two factions was in August 1958 after clashes between Greeks and Turks had already brought the island to the verge of civil war. At Milia (near Famagusta) a so-called *left-wing home guard* formed to protect the village against possible Turkish Cypriot attacks was instead ambushed by EOKA. Two people were killed and around twenty injured - nearly all left-wingers. An urgent appeal to Makarios to intervene resulted in another belated call for unity. Similarly, TMT was responsible for the killing of Turkish progressives who spoke out for full co-operation between the two communities.

Not surprisingly, the British took advantage of these *domestic squabbles* and put forward final proposals for the solution of the problem. Macmillan made arrangements to visit both Athens and Ankara. Accompanied by Foot, the British Premier held discussions in the Greek capital on 8 and 9 August. He pleaded for peace and for a seven year period with provisional solutions but without prejudice to any final settlement. He repeated that *partnership was a fine and noble ideal*. The Greeks disliked partnership as a principle since that would have been equivalent to admitting de jure a Turkish presence on the island. Ankara and Nicosia were also visited. As a result of Macmillan's shuttle diplomacy Whitehall concluded that certain modifications to its general policy, announced in June, were needed; in particular, Greek and Turkish government representatives were to have no seats in the general council although they were to be consulted by the governor as originally envisaged.

Political rallies – *Above:* Greek political gathering outside the archbishopric
*Below:* Turkish demonstrators carrying their own flags

Even though agreement was not forthcoming the British planned to put their policy into operation. September 1958 was the month of *'shifts and turns'*. On the 7th Makarios told the Greek government privately that he was now willing to accept independence for Cyprus under UN auspices. On the 22nd he made his views known to **Barbara Castle MP** vice-chairperson of the British Labour Party.[12] She, in common with many others, believed that parts of the Macmillan Plan if applied would have regrettable consequences. On that date, Makarios authorised Mrs Castle to give the news to the press. The date coincided with the decision of the UN General Assembly to include the Cyprus question in its agenda.

Under constant pressure from Britain and the US, Greece decided to seek NATO mediation. On 23 September **Spaak**, the Secretary General, arrived in Athens. It was agreed that he should submit the following *'personal proposals'* at the NATO council meeting which was to take place within the next few days:

1) The Macmillan plan to be neutralised.

2) A seven-point plan to be adopted which included provisions for a single legislative chamber with the future of the island remaining open.

3) A conference should be held under the aegis of NATO with all interested parties present.

This NATO initiative, once more, failed to secure wide support. The impasse continued and the date for the application of the Macmillan Plan - 1 October - was approaching. Back stage diplomacy reached fever pitch. The work done by the British and American secret services, especially in Athens, was of primary importance. The stage reverts once more to the UN. Draft Cyprus resolutions were put forward by various countries; eventually an Iranian one which urged something more than the tripartite conference which the British had suggested in 1957 was accepted with several amendments. On 4 December the Political Committee accepted it by 31 votes to 22 with 28 abstentions. The US, Britain, Turkey and most of the other countries voted in favour while Greece was amongst the opponents.

Yet on that same evening an event took place which ultimately led to the **Zürich-London Agreements of 1959** which finally set up the Cyprus Republic.

At the entrance of the Political Committee hall where the vote was taken, Zorlu approached Averoff and congratulated him on the splendid fight he put up in the debate. They agreed to *'meet'*. A compromise motion

---

(12)  FO 371/136441/RGC 1782/109

was upheld by the General Assembly on 5 December. Resolution 1287(XIII) was adopted by 57 votes to none with one abstention. It recalled resolution 1013 (XI) of 26 February 1957 and expressed confidence that continued efforts will be made by the parties to reach a peaceful, democratic and just solution in accordance with the Charter of the UN.

In the delegates' lounge of the UN building on the morning of 6 December, Zorlu and Averoff talked for two hours. The rapprochement between Greece and Turkey led to the Paris talks of 18 December when the two ministers, together with Selwyn Lloyd, their British counterpart, had informal discussions on Cyprus during a NATO meeting. Zorlu had with him a draft agreement which had been approved by the Americans. A 16-part Plan known as the *"Paris Sketch"* was taking shape. The two sides met again on the following day and yet again in Paris between 18 and 20 January 1959 during an OEEC (Organisation for European Economic Co-operation) meeting convened to discuss problems connected with the European Common Market.

Why such a sudden change in the attitude of both Greece and Turkey? Among the reasons are the following:

1) The international community, tired of the prolonged problem, loss of life etc., had *'ruled'* towards the end of 1958 that both enosis and partition should be discarded and suggested talks between the three governments and Cypriot representatives.

2) Turkey became more accommodating because, for the moment at least, obtaining a *'share'* of the island was the best scenario possible. Moreover, Russian officers arrived in Iraq and with Syria *'uncertain'* its southern border was under threat. Hence it did not want hostilities with Greece, its NATO ally, to the west. Moreover, after the Iraqi coup of July 1958, Turkey and Israel, with the blessing of the US, entered into a wide-ranging secret military pact.

3) For Greece, such a face-saving compromise and an independent Cyprus was better than the other suggested solutions of confederation, tridominium or worst of all partition.

4) Both Greece and Turkey were duly rewarded with massive economic and military aid. In addition, both the British and the US secret services bought influence by adding key members of the two administrations to their payroll.

5) As Sir Hugh Foot explained in March 1959 it was the Macmillan Plan which laid the foundation for the settlement and that it was HMG's determination to press on with it which *"broke the deadlock and forced the issue"*.

The Turks insisted that at the following top level meeting the Premiers of both countries should be present. Zürich was chosen as the next venue. On 11 February a declaration was initialled by the two countries confirming that Cyprus would become an independent state with a Greek Cypriot president and a Turkish Cypriot vice-president and detailing the *'basic structure of the Republic of Cyprus'*. With the Zürich concordat under their belts the two Foreign Ministers flew to the British capital and conferred on the same evening with Selwyn Lloyd. The London Conference of 17 February held at Lancaster House was widened to include two separate delegations headed by Makarios and Kutchuk. The purpose of the three governments, which had agreed previously on the plan to be implemented, was to present the Cypriots with a *fait accompli* which they would be forced to accept. On 19 February the London Agreements were finally signed.

The settlement that evolved had two main parts: a draft constitution for Cyprus and three treaties. British rule in the island was to end not later than one year after 19 February 1959. The Republic finally came into being on 16 August 1960. Before it could be established the constitution and the final texts of the three treaties had to be drafted and administrative arrangements made for the transfer of power and for the holding of presidential, parliamentary and communal elections.

Three ad hoc committees were immediately set up. The Transitional Committee in Nicosia, composed of the governor and Cypriot members, was responsible for the adaptation of the government machinery in preparation for independence. The London Joint Committee, composed of representatives from Britain, Greece and Turkey and from the two Cypriot communities, was charged with drafting the final treaties. The Joint Constitutional Commission, composed of representatives of the two communities and of the Greek and Turkish governments with legal advisers, had the task of drafting the constitution. It was however bound by the 27 articles laid down at Zürich.

The sovereignty of the island was safeguarded by Britain, Greece and Turkey under the Treaty of Guarantee which precluded under Article I either the union of Cyprus with any other state or its partition. The Treaty of Alliance provided for co-operation between Greece and Turkey and the Republic in common defence, for the stationing of Greek and Turkish military contingents (950 and 650 respectively) on the island and for the training of a local army. The Treaty of Establishment was concerned with the retention of British bases (BSBs) and ancillary facilities on Cypriot territory (at the end of 2004 such facilities were drastically reduced in number) and problems of finance and nationality arising out of the end of colonial rule.

Hence the turbulent years of 1955-58 were at an end. Peace was preserved on the south eastern flank of NATO. In real terms the total

British military and internal security expenditure between December 1954 and December 1959 was estimated at £90 million. In human terms lives lost since July 1954, owing to armed action and civil disturbances, were 142 British and 492 Cypriot. However the 18 months prior to independence day were nearly as troubled as the months before the Agreements were signed. The early preparations for independence took place against a background of lawlessness. The archbishop, after an absence of almost three years, returned to Cyprus on 1 March 1959 and was given an overwhelming welcome by a crowd estimated at 200,000. He had the unenviable task of persuading the diverse segments of the Greek Cypriot majority to accept the spirit of the Agreements and of convincing the Turkish Cypriot minority that its future on the island could best be served by emphasising the unifying rather than the divisive elements of the compromise settlement.

The Cypriot state was gradually taking shape. On 27 March 1959 agreement had been reached on the allocation of portfolios in the first provisional government which was to hold office until the island officially became self-governing. Domestic irritants continued to make problems;[13] However attempts were made by all sides to eradicate the major sources of tension. Hence, polling day on 13 December 1959 went off peacefully. Makarios received 66.82% share of the total vote. Preparations for independence went ahead as scheduled - though postponed several times. The constitution, consisted of 199 articles and 6 annexes, embodying the Zürich-London Agreements and forming the fundamental law of the new state, was taking shape. On 16 August 1960 Makarios was invested as President of Cyprus and Kutchuk as Vice-President. Through resolution 1489 (XV) Cyprus became in1960 (20 September) the 99th member-state of the United Nations; it became a member of the Commonwealth (13 March 1961) and the 16th member-state of the Council of Europe on 24 April 1961. It became a full member of the enlarged European Union in May 2004.

---

(13) Deep-set enmity between Makarios, Grivas, the bishops and their supporters; between the various political groupings and finally between the two communities. The interception of the Turkish gun-running motor-boat ('Deniz') on 18 October 1959 by a mine sweeper H.M.S. Burmaston exacerbated suspicions and tension even further. See FO371/144692-3.

The heroes finally return:
*Above:* Archbishop
Makarios amongst some
of the ex-EOKA fighters

*Left:* EOKA fighters
return *"home"* led by
Polycarpos Georgadjis
*(left)* and Yiannis Matsis

Autonomy however did not entail an independent economy nor did it entail a sovereign state free from all foreign troops. This in turn implied the impossibility of an independent political line being pursued by the infant state. Ever since 1960 Cyprus has been subjected to the influences and pressures of the respective governments of Greece and Turkey and the political instability in both these nations has been allowed to spill over and create tension within the republic and between its people. Added to the above was the imposition of an unworkable constitution which required only a few flash points to destroy the island's unity completely. The powder keg was therefore ready and the fuse already ignited.

The settlement in fact was further complicated by three other 'agreements' which remained secret for many years:

1) The Gentlemen's Agreement signed by Karamanlis and Menderes on 11 February 1959.[14] It concerned agreement regarding NATO bases in Cyprus, the prohibition of communist activities there etc.

2) A bi-lateral Greek-Turkish document presumably also agreed at Zürich.

3) An Agreed Minute signed by the three Foreign Ministers on 19 February. It included the commitment to safeguard the US's facilities and installations in Cyprus.

In reality, it was a settlement with a little of every solution that anyone ever thought of throwing into the pot - *'faute de mieux'* as the foreign office explained. It was a compromise that fulfilled none of the disputants' aspirations. Henry Kissinger even recorded in his memoirs, that *"in 1959, Britain brokered an agreement which was doomed from the start"*. The treaties were certainly irrational; democratic principles were violated beyond comprehension. Thus in the first years of independence Cyprus was to pay dearly for the precarious settlement granted her by the allied western powers.

---

(14) See CAB 109/96. Folio 137-38

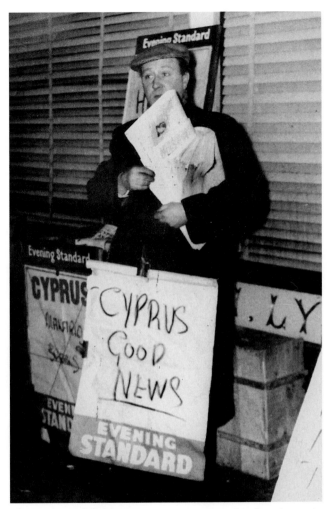

The signing of the Agreements was greeted in London
with great relief and became front page news ...

The hoisting of the Cyprus Republic's flag in the newly built House of Representatives on 16 August 1960

# Chapter FOUR

## THE INFANT REPUBLIC

The setting up of the Cyprus Republic meant, in theory at least, that a number of Greeks who had earlier led the struggle for enosis and a number of Turks who had successfully led the resistance to it would come together to collaborate in running the new state. Such co-operation was not easy in view of:

1) the recent enmity between EOKA and TMT;

2) the complexities created by the settlement;

3) the imposed rifts within the two communities which were not conducive to creating harmony or promoting the Cypriot consciousness and

4) more generally, the relationship between the two opposing nationalisms; Cypriots were conscious of their Greekness or Turkishness (their national leaders never stopped reminding them of that) and their first loyalties were to their own communities and leaderships.

It soon transpired that the immediate objective of the Turkish Cypriot leadership was to accept the new constitutional order but its long term policy was to find ways of proving it unworkable and thus to argue that partition was the best solution. In Ankara such an arrangement was seen as the best setting for its declared partitionist policy and even of its 'future' annexation of the island. To the Greeks the many weaknesses of the constitution produced an imbalance and an injustice. Governmental dualism and ethnic separatism between the two communities were institutionalized. The constitution had brought into being a state but not a nation.

Conflict, inevitable given the peculiarities of the constitution, intensified as the majority tried to show that only a unitary system of government would work while the minority took every opportunity to block government business whenever they felt that their rights were infringed or their needs unmet. Soon they were deadlocked on a host of issues including civil service staffing, the army, separation of municipalities[1] and the use of the Turkish Cypriot veto on central government taxation.

Hence, the complex and rigid settlement imposed on the Cypriots by British, Greek and Turkish diplomats, who rejoiced over the triumph of goodwill and international understanding, soon broke down. On paper the constitution was incomprehensible. In application it was a legal monster. Cyprus in fact was given two governments - a majority one and a minority one - functioning together and overlapping. As pointed out by

---

(1) The divisive article 173 was probably the greatest source of trouble in the 1960 constitution. For a skeleton summary of key articles see FCO 9/1919. Folio 84.

The ceremonial formalities are over – Cyprus is no longer a colony but a new nation constitutional and legal experts **Cyprus was the first country in the world to be denied majority rule by its own constitution**. Undoubtedly, the accords gave the Turkish Cypriot community quite a disproportionate, if negative power.

Inevitably, the new state was arrested in infancy. The last attempt to reach a mutually acceptable solution to the so-called *'battle of the five towns'* was made in December 1962. On Christmas Eve, after negotiations lasting late into the night, it looked as if a compromise had miraculously been achieved. A joint communique drafted by Clerides and Denktash was issued announcing an agreement *'in principle'* but within 24 hours Kutchuk had repudiated it.

Separation, which became an end in itself bred tension and afforded the opportunity for diehards to plunge the country into strife. Such extremism was shown earlier in the year (1962) when two London educated barristers were murdered by TMT gunmen on 23 April. **Ahmed Gurkan** aged 38 and **Ayhan Hikmet** aged 33 were leaders of the Turkish Cypriot People's Party which was in opposition to the majority NFP[2] led by Kutchuk and Denktash. Hikmet was the editor of the weekly

The Turkish Cypriot trade unionist and journalist Ahmed Gurkan. Assassinated by Turkish extremists.

newspaper *Cumhuriyet*, founded by Gurkan, which advocated closer association between the two communities. The murders were unreservedly denounced by influential persons of both communities. Especially vociferous in their condemnation were Ali Dana, the Turkish Cypriot mufti and Emin Dirvana, the Turkish ambassador in Nicosia. Following Denktash's protests the moderate Dirvana was shortly afterwards recalled to Ankara and replaced by Mazkar Ozgol, a hardliner, in September 1962. Thus all the obstacles were now removed to the Turkish Cypriot *'insurgence'* and gradual separation long prepared for by extreme chauvinists both in Cyprus and in Turkey.

---

(2) National Front Party; successor to the Cyprus is Turkish Party - Kibris Turktur Parti.

*Above:* The historic signing ceremony. Cyprus became an independent country. *Sitting from left to right:* Archbishop Makarios; Sir Hugh Foot and Dr F. Kütchük.

*Below:* A triumphant Makarios accompanied by George Grivas. Just behind them is Glafkos Clerides.

The precedents for such terrorism were certainly there. In 1958 progressive Turkish Cypriots were the targets of TMT. The ethnocentric elements who were determined to divide and rule attacked their leading compatriots who were members of AKEL and the united trade unions in order to force around 3,500 of their brethren, organised in the joint Greek and Turkish trade unions known as PEO, to leave such all-Cypriot unions and form exclusively Turkish ones. Furthermore, prominent Turkish Cypriot members of AKEL and other democratic individuals were attacked and a number of them murdered in cold blood because they fought for friendship and co-operation between the two communities against colonialism and imperialism and for independence.

Even though acts of violence, arson and destruction of property were a regular occurrence, the colonial administration reacted by arresting Turkish democrats, political and labour chiefs instead of their reactionary leaders and their diehard supporters who were responsible for such civil and criminal disobedience. Thus when, on 17 June 1958, Francis Noel-Baker MP asked Lennox-Boyd, Secretary of State for the Colonies, what action the authorities of Cyprus intended to take against Kutchuk and Denktash in view of their repeated violations of the emergency regulations, the curt reply was *'no proceedings have been taken'*!

During the first months of 1958 relations between the two communities were strained even further. Ankara radio spoke daily in very strong terms of the impossibility of the two communities living together in peace. It emphasized that since they had completely different political, religious and cultural backgrounds they could not co-exist under a single political system. The Turkish ruling elite therefore demanded that the island should be partitioned, with Turkey fully controlling financially, politically and militarily *'its'* sector. In such an atmosphere it was easy for their supporters to brand as traitors all those who disagreed with its crazy pro-imperialist policy.

Even so hundreds of Turks joined with their Greek compatriots in the 1958 May Day celebrations, as they had done in previous years. The marchers, shouting anti-imperialist slogans and protesting against the divisions being enforced by the western powers, paraded through the streets of Nicosia with their national flags and vowed to fight for the common ideals of the working class.

The reaction of the fanatical right-wing Turkish leadership was vicious. On that very night TMT activists looted the Turkish sports and cultural club of Nicosia, set fire to it and then accused its members of having been sold to the Greeks. The crime took place under the noses of the security forces, yet no one was arrested. The burning of the club gave the signal for a general attack to exterminate the progressive and peace-loving Turks. The assassins continued their work unpunished. Sir Hugh

Foot wrote in September 1959 that he was *"greatly concerned at the continued violence by Turks against Turks"*.

Back in December 1962 the Greek majority in the House of Representatives rejected a Turkish proposal to extend the existing municipal laws for one year from1 January 1963. On 2 January the council of ministers brought the town councils under the direct control of the central government by setting up development boards to run the main towns. The Greek municipalities surrendered their powers to the board but the Turkish ones refused to do so; the Turkish communal chamber declaring that the separate municipalities were still legal.

The Turkish Cypriot leaders consulted Ankara and referred the dispute to the Cyprus Constitutional Court, whose neutral president, Dr. Ernest Forsthoff (a West German Professor from the University of Heidelberg who later resigned), ruled on 25 April that both moves were illegal. Since the same court had already decided on 8 February that the Turkish veto on the tax laws in 1961 was illegal it meant that the government had no authority to collect customs duties and income tax; both central and local government were henceforth threatened with paralysis. On 4 April 1964, Sir Arthur Clark (British High Commissioner in Cyprus) informed his superiors that *"during the period 1960-63, the Greek government behaved well, constantly counselling restraint on the Greek*

*Left:* A local publication with a Greek description: "The Independent Cyprus Republic is born" on 16 August 1960.

*Above:* The first postage stamp of the Republic

*Cypriots. But the Turkish government unfortunately bolstered up the Cypriot Turks to insist on every pound, nay ounce of flesh that they could extract from the Zurich constitution".*

On 9 April 1963 Makarios explained that the blocking of the taxation laws had caused *'great difficulties'*; that the insistence on separate municipalities in the five main towns was *'unreasonable and wastefully expensive'*; and that *'real damage'* had been caused by the Turkish obstruction of proposed legislation for setting up a development bank. Nevertheless, the first five-year plan (1962-66) concentrated on developing the economic potential of the island by mobilizing all unemployed resources, thus providing the necessary infrastructure for the diversification of the economy with a view to removing the causes of the pre-1960 economic instability. Despite the internal problems of the island the plan succeeded in getting the productive resources moving and restored internal and foreign confidence in the economy. See next chapter for details.

Yet in 1963 Cyprus was without an income tax law, a customs law and a municipalities law and the two communities seemed headed for a major confrontation. Convinced by now that the Turks would not consider any change in the constitution by agreement and that their ultimate aim was to partition the island, the Greek Cypriots began to talk of removing the divisive and negative elements of the constitution. At the same time the Turkish Cypriots threatened that any Greek effort to amend it without their approval would meet with Turkish might and would result in *'partition or death'*. A strong Greek Cypriot lobby had even suggested that the government should use the good offices of the UN to carry through the proposed amendments. Makarios' apparent endorsement of the 1963 **Akritas Plan** - a secret programme to use UN pressure to remove the restrictions on enosis imposed by the Treaty of Guarantee and the Treaty of Alliance - was very unfortunate. The plan was leaked and with it the suggestion that the Greek Cypriots would use this freedom to conduct an *'enosis referendum'*, which by sheer weight of numbers they were bound to win.

On 4 August 1963 Makarios said that he had finally made up his mind that the constitution was in dire need of a change. He would seek this revision since certain provisions of an inapplicable character threatened to *'paralyse the state machinery'*. In reply Kutchuk declared on the 22nd that the Turks might resort to civil disobedience if the Greeks attempted a unilateral revision of the constitution which would *'not be binding on the Turkish community'*.

The president however, in his desire to facilitate the smooth functioning of the infant state and remove the causes of intercommunal friction, submitted, on 30 November, concrete proposals (glossed over by

Sir Arthur Clark) for amending the constitution. These were transmitted to Kutchuk (Makarios even requested that his vice-president should propose some himself) and copies were sent to the governments of Britain, Greece and Turkey for *'information purposes only'*. These proposals, as set out below, were intended to establish a more unified state and were, in logic, undeniable":[3]

1) The right of veto of the president and the vice-president was to be abandoned.

2) The vice-president was to deputise for the president in case of temporary absence or incapacity to perform his duties.

3) The Greek president of the house of representatives and the Turkish vice-president were to be elected by the house as a whole and not, as before, by separate Greek and Turkish majorities within the house.

4) The vice-president of the house of representatives was to deputise for the president of the house in case of his temporary absence or incapacity to perform his duties.

5) The constitutional provisions regarding separate majorities for the enactment of certain laws by the house of representatives were to be abolished.

6) Unified municipalities were to be established.

7) The administration of justice was to be unified.

8) The division of the security forces into police and gendarmerie was to be abolished.

9) The numerical strength of the security forces and of the defence forces was to be determined by law.

10) The proportion of the participation of Greek Cypriots and Turkish Cypriots in the composition of the public services (70:30) and the forces of the republic (60:40) was to be modified in proportion to the ratio of the population of Greek to Turkish Cypriots.

11) The number of members of the public service commission was to be reduced from ten to five.

---

(3) His 13-point plan appeared to have been designed to remove the constitutionally entrenched minority rights and replace them with expressions of goodwill. They were bound to be rejected by Turkey and the Turkish Cypriots. Makarios had no intention of ever provoking the Turks. The role of HMG, during the drafting stage of these proposals, is clouded in doubt. There are even accusations that HMG 'forced' Makarios to take such action!

12) All decisions of the public service commission were to be taken by simple majority

13) The communal chambers would be abolished and a new system devised. Should the Turkish community however desire to retain its chamber in the new system, such a course would be open to it.

Meanwhile the two *'mother countries'* were going through a political crisis. Just before Christmas both were left simultaneously with unrepresentative governments. In Greece, the eight-year reign of Karamanlis came to an abrupt end on 11 June 1963. In Turkey, the situation was even worse and after several attempted coups, Inonu's government fell on 2 December 1963.

It was in the middle of this crisis and when Greece, after inconclusive elections on 3 November, was also struggling to form a government, that Makarios *'chose'* to make his first formal bid to change the *'Cyprus constitutional oddity'*. Kutchuk, to whom the proposals were addressed, failed to reply, although at press interviews he reiterated that the constitution could not be changed. However, on 7 December F.K. Erkin, the Foreign Minister, announced that Ankara had rejected them and on 16 December Ozgol, the Turkish ambassador, handed to Makarios Turkey's written rejection. Makarios however refused to accept the rejection, pointing out that the recommendations had been sent to his vice-president for reply and not to any foreign government. Did Makarios overestimate London's role and underestimate Ankara's part and determination?

On 20 December 1963 the Foreign Ministers of Cyprus, Greece and Turkey met in Paris to discuss the situation. Within a few hours of their first encounter shooting broke out in Nicosia. An initial attempt to bring intercommunal tension to boiling point had been averted on 3 December. The government managed to cool tempers after a bomb exploded at the base of the newly erected statue of Markos Dracos, a revered hero of the EOKA campaign. Who was responsible? Who gave the order? Who took the final decision? Evidence so far is inconclusive.

However in the early hours of 21 December a police patrol car with Greek Cypriot officers driving down Hermes Street in the old city of Nicosia (the same area which had been the scene of arson and looting by Turkish extremists in 1958) stopped a car for a routine check. Shots were fired and one of the policemen was wounded. The officers returned fire. A young Turk was killed and a Turkish woman wounded, dying on her way to hospital. Within minutes shooting broke out in various quarters of the city. By 5.00 a.m. an angry Turkish crowd started moving into the Greek quarter and by 6.00 p.m. one Greek and one Turk had been brought to hospital with gunshot wounds. There were further incidents on 22

December and by midday all Turkish Cypriot government employees and policemen had left their posts. The Turks fortified themselves in their own areas; their defence proving to have been well prepared in advance. In order to further their partitionist aims they forced several thousand innocent and contented Turkish peasants to abandon their farms and animals and move into their overcrowded quarter of Nicosia. Thus the aim of partition, camouflaged by propaganda as *'federation'*, was relentlessly pursued regardless of loss of human life and the human misery created. However, this so-called *'first phase'* of the invasion of Cyprus by Turkey only partly succeeded, since well over half of its brethren refused to obey instructions to abandon their homes for the predetermined enclaves.

The clashes had caught the leadership of the two communities completely unprepared. To date, there is no hard evidence to suggest that the outbreak of violence had official sanction. In fact Makarios and Kutchuk met Greek and Turkish Cypriot ministers at the Paphos Gate police station and there was another call to the public for calm and for the shooting to stop. Undoubtedly, both had difficulty in reconciling and disciplining their own trigger-happy dissidents.

Did they therefore, get the the tacit approval of their leaders for such violence? On 23 December the acting British high commissioner and the US ambassador called on the president and expressed the grave concern of their governments at the turn of events in Cyprus. They appealed for moderation from both communities. Athens and Ankara also appealed for an end to intercommunal violence. Such pleas were too late.

At 2.25 p.m. on 23 December, Turkish Cypriot extremists moved into the Armenian quarter of Nicosia and forced the inhabitants to leave their houses, shops, church, school and clubs. On the same day some Turkish patients at the Nicosia General Hospital disappeared from their beds - possibly killed. Shortly afterwards British servicemen and civilians were shot at in Larnaca and Lefka by TMT gunmen. A ceasefire was hastily arranged on 24 December. It failed because of clashes on the outskirts of Nicosia but a new accord was concluded on Christmas Day.

At these and subsequent discussions between Major-General Peter Young (GOC Cyprus) and the Greek and Turkish army commanders on the island, agreement was reached on the establishment of a headquarters for the joint peace-keeping force. British troops began patrolling Nicosia and Larnaca on the same day and a **'green line'** (reminiscent of EOKA days and regularly likened to the more famous Berlin Wall) was subsequently established on 29/30 December in Nicosia to separate the Greek from the Turkish Cypriot quarters. This demarcation line, guarded by British troops, cut straight across the mixed suburbs of Omorphita and Neapolis and put the entire Armenian quarter as well as the Greek areas of Kermia, Ayios Kasianos and Ayios Iakovos behind Turkish lines.

It was so named from the colour of the talc with which Major-General Young traced and retraced it over his map. It must not be forgotten that the Joint Intervention Force (JIF) or tripartite truce force consisting apparently of 1,500 British, 1,000 Greek and 800 Turkish soldiers, was established under the command of the British. In addition, a Tripartite Patrol Organisation (TPO) was set up to provide the mediating element of joint forces activities and to be the facilitator of communal re-engagement. Its UNFICYP successor was known as the Joint Patrol Organisation (JPO). HMG warned (at a meeting at No.10 on 26 December 1963), that Archbishop Makarios should be made to understand that if the dispute was not solved by peaceful means *"we might be compelled to endorse a partition of the island as the only alternative"*. A US contingency plan to allow a *'controlled'* Turkish occupation in northern Cyprus was also discussed with Britain in February 1964.

The renewal of the Cyprus conflict brought Greece and Turkey once again to the brink of war. The joint plea for peace issued by the protecting powers on 23 December was followed the next day by rumours of a Turkish invasion. Late on 24 December the Turkish army contingent in Cyprus marched out of its appointed camp and took positions on the northern outskirts of Nicosia and along the Nicosia-Kyrenia road which leads to he northern coast. On the following day, Turkish jets screamed low over the rooftops of Nicosia and naval units were spotted manoeuvring off the island's coast. Following suit the Greek army contingent also left its barracks and took up positions to counter a possible invasion. Cyprus had become *'the new apple of discord'* between the two countries. In the circumstances the peace-keeping force was composed essentially of British troops.

For the reasons mentioned below NATO became an interested party and tried to forestall, albeit unsuccessfully, international initiatives:

1)   The island's three guarantor powers were integral members of this organisation. The western alliance could not simply disregard this dispute as it had already done other colonial conflicts.

2)   There was a real fear at the beginning of the crisis that the Soviet Union might exploit the position of the Cypriot left to acquire a foothold on the island.

3)   It was widely believed that if the conflict continued the island might eventually become a *'Mediterranean Cuba'*. Makarios' non-aligned policy was viewed with great concern by the western alliance. President Kennedy however, even as late as 1962 appeared to have been encouraging Makarios to pursue such a policy. The US Pentagon, sensing the coming tensions in the Middle East, considered him too vague and uncertain a quantity and saw that ultimate

A historic photograph between Archbishop Makarios and President Kennedy, June 1962. Kennedy referred to Makarios as a *"fighter for freedom"*.

stability for the bases could be achieved only if the island was brought under NATO control. Alternatively, Makarios and all other opposition should be removed.

Up to the beginning of 1947 the US State Department was favourably disposed to the idea of Britain ceding Cyprus to Greece. Yet by 12 March, President Truman revolutionised the pattern of eastern Mediterranean strategy by announcing the first of America's moves to defend its interests by strengthening the states bordering on Russia - the famous programme of aid to Greece and Turkey. US planners were very busy studying Turkey even before 1947. It was destined to feature in several ways in this US grand strategy. Almost immediately, both the State Department and the US Chiefs of Staff informed London that they attached great importance to Britain retaining its position in Cyprus. The same view was expressed at a conference of US representatives in the Middle East held at the end of 1949. In the 1950s the Americans installed and operated CIA-run signal monitoring stations and during the next decade the island became an integral part of the US global electronic intelligence network.

While the Cyprus government relied on non-alignment for the removal of its constitutional shackles, the Turkish Cypriot leadership relied on anti-communist orientation to preserve its rights. There was little internal opposition to this since the Turkish left, as we have already seen, had been suppressed. Thus between 1960 and 1963 Kutchuk was particularly opposed to the expansion of trade with the socialist countries and the government's association with the Afro-Asians. After the outbreak of fighting in 1963 he appealed to President Johnson of the US to prevent Cyprus from being turned into another Cuba by *'communist armed infiltration"*.

4)   Cyprus was of direct strategic interest to NATO and the organisation was concerned with the security of the British bases there. In the long term of course, the development of long-range nuclear bombers and ballistic missiles might change the requirements for the Cyprus bases. Maybe!

The NATO philosophy therefore was that serious inter-member conflicts should be avoided and that if such disputes occurred they should be settled quickly and peacefully. In fact the threat of war between NATO partners was avoided by the swift action of the British who arranged, as already noted, a cease-fire. Such a desire to safeguard the status quo was instrumental in saving Cyprus from further catastrophe.

Meanwhile on 26 December the Cyprus government requested the intervention of the Security Council. It called for an urgent meeting to consider charges that Turkey had committed aggression and intervened in the internal affairs of Cyprus by violating the island's air space and territorial waters. Turkey denied the charges and the Security Council adjourned the debate without taking any action. At all times of course the Cyprus government insisted that the UN was the only international forum at which the crisis could be resolved. The Americans, however, were saying that winning resolutions at the UN would only *"buy you a cappucino"*!

Kemal Gursel, the Turkish president, also cabled a plea to various foreign capitals to *'prevent further acts of genocide'* on the island and for the second time jet fighters were sent to buzz Nicosia. Although the government had withdrawn its earlier request for UN intervention, the threat of a such an invasion prompted Foreign Minister Spyros Kyprianou to telephone envoys in Nicosia to apprise them of the situation. In the last

*Above:* The early years of the peaceful republic. President Makarios, Vice-President Kütchük and other leading personalities attending the Platres festival.

*Below:* Makarios inspects a guard of honour of the National Guard.

days of December the Soviet Union denounced any attempt at foreign intervention in Cyprus and President Johnson sent cablegrams to Makarios and Kutchuk calling for a peaceful settlement of the dispute.

On 28 December Duncan Sandys, Secretary of State for the Colonies and Commonwealth Relations, arrived in Cyprus and suggested a conference to discuss the island's future government. The conference, with Sandys in the chair, opened at Marlborough House, London on 15 January 1964. The Greek and Turkish delegations were led by their respective foreign ministers, Palamas and Erkin and the two Cypriot delegations by Clerides, Kyprianou and Denktash. The conference could not suggest a settlement since those who attended it had completely different views on the Cyprus problem. On 10 February it ended in complete failure. Demetris Bitsios, a young Greek diplomat recalled:

"The British and with them the Americans, wanted above all to prevent the internationalization of the problem. They were disturbed also by the support given to the Archbishop by the Soviet Union. Besides, they wished to buy out the Turkish desire to use military force against Cyprus with the promise that no solution would be granted which did not satisfy their views."[4]

Makarios now sought the assistance of the UN. Simultaneously however the US, pulling strings to make the UN take its time, proposed a NATO solution. At a Department of State meeting on 25 January, Ball, whose initial response was negative, mentioned the possibility of using the NATO Mobile Force (ACE) totalling roughly 3,000 men. He believed however that a bigger force, in excess of 20,000 was needed. Moreover, he was worried about the 1,500 Americans on the island. An Anglo-American scheme (later termed the 'Sandys-Ball Plan') for a NATO force was formally submitted to the parties concerned on 31 January. The scheme involved the landing of 1,200 US combat troops and a NATO mixed force of 10,000 to be used for peace-keeping duties and a neutral mediator to search for a political solution. Security considerations would then make its permanent presence necessary with the island becoming a NATO base; Makarios' neutralist tendencies would be discouraged and a de facto condominium of Greece, Turkey and NATO would perpetuate allied military influence.

The British Labour Party, then in opposition, voiced its disagreement to such a scheme. During question time in the Commons on 30 January,Harold Wilson declared that 'the sooner it is possible to give that force a UN status, the better it will be for peacekeeping and the reputation of the UN'. However, Turkey and Greece were persuaded to back the Anglo-American initiative. Paraskevopoulos, the caretaker Prime Minister,

---

(4) Krisimes Ores. (Critical Hours). 1973. Pages 143-144

Despite disagreements on the political front, the vast majority desired to live peacefully side by side.

*Above:* Young athletes from both communities parade before the start of a major competition.

*Left:* Greek and Turkish Cypriot strikers on a picket line.

made some objections which were immediately overruled after a lightning visit to Athens by the NATO Commander in Europe, General Lyman Lemnitzer. Makarios proved adamant. Yet he stated that he would accept an international force under the Security Council. The plan America had in mind was in fact double *enosis* through partition - the whole island thus becoming a NATO base with Britain relegated to a secondary role. Natofication of Cyprus was of course, one of the favourite solutions which was suggested in 1964.

George Ball (acting as US Secretary of State, in Dean Rusk's absence) was dispatched to Cyprus but even he could not *'bully'* Makarios (they met on 12 and 13 February) into accepting the plan. Ball visited London, Athens, Ankara and Nicosia between 9 and 14 February. The governments of Britain and of the US drew up a revised version of their plan which was accepted by Greece on 8 February and by Turkey on the following day. Makarios did not yield an inch. He thus succeeded in sidetracking a trap laid for him to recognise the American position, which was to make Cyprus a NATO responsibility. In this he had the support of the USSR. On 7 February, Krushchev strongly protested in a letter to the heads of government of Britain, Greece, Turkey, France and the US against the proposals for a NATO force which he described as *'a case of crude encroachment on the sovereignty, independence and freedom of the Republic of Cyprus'*.

It appeared at this stage that the American contingency plan was aimed at allowing Turkey to invade Cyprus and occupy a large area to the north of the island and if necessary to occupy an enclave in the west. It also appears that Britain had a similar plan. Makarios was to be confronted with a *fait accompli*. Accept or go! It is interesting to recall the teletype conversation between George Ball in Nicosia, the British Foreign Secretary (R. Butler) and Dean Rusk in Washington DC at 12.30 p.m. Thursday 13 February 1964. In a *"highly emotional"* private meeting with the archbishop, Ball pleaded for the acceptance of the American plan. He reveals that Makarios was a *"prisoner"* of his three young ministers (Clerides, Papadopoulos and Kyprianou) who *"unhappily"* were all lawyers. He concluded by stating that *"I have very little hope of succeeding since I am convinced that the gangsters have given Makarios his instructions and he is too scared to depart from them"*.[5] In the end however, Makarios' determination prevailed. He was also backed by the strong administration of George Papandreou, who was sworn into office on 19 February after a decisive victory at the polls; as far as he could Papandreou resisted American pressure. Hence he sent a message to the archbishop on 25 February assuring him of the solidarity of the Greek nation and government. On 13 April, after a meeting with Makarios in

---

(5) FO 371/174747/C.1015/693

Athens, it was announced that complete agreement had been reached on the handling of the Cyprus problem. At that meeting a critical decision had been made. Papandreou proposed, and Makarios accepted, that troops and arms should be sent to Cyprus to prevent a future Turkish invasion. By mid-summer an estimated 10,000 officers and men, fully equipped, were in the island. Some however, were students, volunteers and even deserters. The bargaining strength of the Greeks and of the Greek Cypriots was greatly reinforced.

Makarios was henceforth assured of the support not only of the USSR and the neutralist world but also of a leading member of the western alliance. Behind Greece, ready to profit from the dissensions of western polycentrism, stood France (the Gaullist notion being that Europe's destiny was not America's concern), unwilling to see the Cyprus crisis taken up by NATO and willing to back Greece in its dispute with the other member of the western alliance, Turkey.

The archbishop had several motives in seeking refuge at the UN:

1)  to secure a guarantee against a possible Turkish invasion;

2)  to gather enough support to nullify in due course the treaties of Alliance and Guarantee;

3)  to make the UN directly responsible for the solution of the Cyprus problem and thus escape from the straight jacket of new negotiations with the three guarantor powers alone or with NATO: since 1955 Makarios feared all American-backed Anglo-Turkish combinations against Greece and himself;

4)  to isolate, as far as possible, the Turks who had evidently fewer friends at the UN than at NATO headquarters;

5)  to rule out partition; and

6)  to pave the way for a unitary state with majority rule: Makarios, though paying lip-service to *enosis*, desired Cyprus (and there were many reasons), to remain a neutral state.

On 15 February, one hour before Zenon Rossides, the Cypriot ambassador, was to make his appeal to the UN, Britain asked for an early meeting of the Security Council to deal with the on-going *'dangerous situation'*. Two days later **U Thant**, the UN Secretary-General, submitted certain proposals to the Greek Cypriot delegation led by Kyprianou and Clerides. The Cypriots, though pleased with this initiative, gave no encouragement to proceed further. On 25 February, during the Security Council meeting, Kyprianou asked whether the Treaty of Guarantee gave the three guarantor powers the right to invade Cyprus. Denktash on the other hand, three days later expounded the theory that symbiosis between the two communities was impossible.

However, on 4 March 1964, the Security Council through resolution no. 186 unanimously recommended the establishment of a UN peace-keeping force and the appointment of a mediator *'for the purpose of promoting a peaceful solution and an agreed settlement of the problem confronting Cyprus, in accordance with the Charter of the UN, bearing in mind the well-being of the people of Cyprus as a whole, and the preservation of international peace and security'.* The force was to be stationed in the island for three months and all costs were to be met by the states providing contingents, by the government of the island and by voluntary contributions. In effect, the Cypriot authorities accepted an international force funded and manned largely by NATO members but controlled by the Security Council. A tentative evaluation of resolutions passed from March 1964 to 13 June 2002 suggests that some 10% related to Cyprus. A phenomenal statistic!

On 12 March Turkey rejected Rolz-Bennet of Guatamala as the mediator on Cyprus and on 25 March Sakari Tuomioja of Finland was appointed instead. Following the death of Tuomioja, Senor Galo Lasso Plaza, ex-President of Ecuador, succeeded him on 16 September. On 27 March the UN force became operational and was placed under the command of **Lt. General P.S. Gyani** of India. By 8 June its strength was 6,411, composed as follows:

| Military (UNFICYP) | | Police (UNCIVPOL) | |
|---|---|---|---|
| Austria | 55 | Australia | 40 |
| Canada | 1,122 | Austria | 33 |
| Denmark | 676 | Denmark | 40 |
| Finland | 1,000 | New Zealand | 20 |
| Sweden | 954 | Sweden | 40 |
| Ireland | 639 | | |
| UK | 1,792 | | |
| **6,238** | | **173** | |

The resolution of 4 March however, failed to reduce tension in the island. On the following day Turkish armed bands fired the first shots around the Saint Hilarion fortress and on 6 March a bomb exploded in the building of the Turkish Cypriot communal chamber. The aim, as in 1958, was to put the blame on the Greeks and thus provide an excuse for further strife. Outbursts of shooting and killing continued unabated. Neither side was blameless.

*Above:* A cartoon from a Greek newspaper showing Britain's involvement in Cyprus being satisfied with obtaining its bases, while Makarios as head of the Republic is left with numerous problems. eg economic, Greek–Turkish police, dismantling of EOKA etc.

*Below:* UN officers enjoying a chat with local villagers.

Two views of British soldiers as part of the UN peace-keeping force on the island

On 13 March Turkey made further threats and demanded that Makarios should put an end to he fighting, release Turkish hostages and restore freedom of movement. Stavros Costopoulos, the Greek Foreign Minister, replied that if Turkey used military force against Cyprus his country would also fight. At 6 p.m. on 13 March the Security Council met and adopted resolution no. 187, calling upon all members to comply with its resolution of 4 March and to refrain from any action which might worsen the situation.

Events now moved very fast in Cyprus. On 4 April 1964, Makarios denounced the Treaty of Alliance with Greece and Turkey. On 11 and 26 April heavy fighting was centred around the Saint Hilarion fortress. On the following day U Thant explained that in spite of the presence of UN forces there had been 126 outbursts of shooting in the past month. On 29 April he reported that the UN mission had no hope of succeeding until all the irregulars on the island were disarmed. Nevertheless, in a memorandum to Tuomioja on 14 May, Makarios set out his proposals for a Cypriot unitary state containing wide guarantees for the Turkish minority. Turkish plans on the other hand had previously recommended partition into two cantonal states with a federal government responsible for foreign affairs, finance and defence. It must be noted that, throughout April and May, Lieutenant Commander Martin Packard - a Greek speaking intelligence officer - and others, worked tirelessly for reintegration and had talks with all the island's leaders. He was mysteriously removed on 11 June and sent back to London! The clash between *'peacekeeping'* and *'peacemaking'* is surely an issue that needs very careful analysis when the year of 1964 is discussed. It's a very important issue. Packard's forthcoming publication will surely shed light on this dark episode in the island's history.

The month of June was particularly critical. On the first day conscription was introduced and three days later the first recruits were called up. Almost immediately Turkey threatened another invasion. The US again intervened and George Ball undertook his second mission to Athens and Ankara, inviting both premiers to visit Washington. On 5 June Johnson sent a secret letter to Ismet Inonu that, in the latter's words, *'included all the juridical thunderbolts that could be assembled'*. According to Ball it was the *"diplomatic equivalent of an atom bomb"*. The President argued that:

1) The Turkish decision to intervene by military force to occupy a portion of Cyprus was unwise and fraught with far-reaching consequences.

2) The purpose of such intervention would be to effect a form of partition and thus produce a solution which was specifically excluded by the Treaty of Guarantee.

3) Such an invasion would violate a number of international commitments: first, a commitment to complete consultation with the US before any such action was taken; second, a commitment to consult with the other two Guarantor Powers, which had by no means been exhausted; third, a commitment to NATO not to undermine the strength of that organisation or to run the risk of involving the Soviet Union; and fourth, a commitment to the UN to act in a manner consistent with its efforts to bring peace to the island.

4) Under the US-Turkey Agreement of 12 July 1947, American consent was required for the use of military assistance for purposes other than those for which assistance was furnished. *'I must tell you in all candour that the US cannot agree to the use of any US supplied military equipment for a Turkish intervention in Cyprus under present*

*circumstances'*, the president continued. It must also be pointed out that economic aid from the US to Turkey from the inception of the Marshall Plan in 1948 to 1958 amounted to $1,065,234,000. In addition, Turkey is among the largest recipients of US military assistance.

Replying on 13 June, the Turkish Premier stated that *'the necessity of a military intervention in Cyprus has been felt four times since the closing days of 1963'*. Inonu also expressed great concern that the pending report of the Secretary-General to be submitted to the UN on 15 June would result in another defeat for Turkey *'similar to the one we all suffered on 4 March 1964'*.

The Cyprus crisis of 1963-64 marked a watershed in US-Turkish relations. The specific event which triggered the reaction, after long-simmering discontent, was Johnson's letter. Numerous anti-American demonstrations were staged in Ankara throughout the summer of 1964 and there was strong opposition in the Turkish press to US efforts to restrain Turkey from military intervention. In fact, as in the 1950s, there were guaranteed demonstrations in Greece or Turkey whenever it was seen that American policy was tilting against either country. Thus the US-Turkey honeymoon which had lasted since 1947 was at least temporarily interrupted. This incident in particular and there were a few others, disabused the Turks of the belief that their interests were in every respect identical and that they could count on American support in every eventuality. It must be remembered that the Pentagon's global strategy is based on long-term planning, politically stable and predictable allies, and the search for alternative and/or fallback positions in case traditional allies fail to measure up to future expectations.

On 20 June UNFICYP was extended by resolution no.192 for a further three months. General **Kodendera S. Thimayya**, also of India, succeeded Gyani as commander of the force. Towards the end of the month the US made mediation moves via its seasoned diplomat **Dean Acheson**, Secretary of State from 1949 to 1953 and then adviser to both Kennedy and Johnson. He went to Geneva where Tuomioja was to be stationed. Before the month was out Tuomioja informed Bitsios, the Greek permanent representative at the UN, that the differences between the two sides were virtually unbridgeable, that war between Greece and Turkey was a distinct possibility and that he needed Acheson's help in Geneva to enable him to carry out his task. The Americans had of course stated on several occasions that they viewed with pessimism the role and functions of the UN mediator. **June also witnessed the return of Grivas to Cyprus**. (By whose orders[6] and was there a secret agenda to get rid of Makarios?) By

---

(6) According to Athens, the Americans were the ones who issued the order *"Grivas must go to Cyprus"*. The view of the Foreign Office was that such ordering was done by the Hellenic government. See PREM 11/4710 and FO 371/174757/C.1051/65

15 August he had succeeded General Karayiannis as supreme commander of the island's national guard.

In that climacteric month both Inonu and Papandreou visited he US. The latter met Johnson at the White House on 24 June (Inonu met him on 22nd and 23rd) and his son Andreas, present at that fateful meeting, recorded that it had not been a discussion but a monologue, which soon became a brainwashing operation with Johnson, using at times undiplomatic language, insisting that what was needed to resolve the crisis were summit-level negotiations between Papandreou and Inonu. Senior officials moreover pointed out that in the event of Turkey attacking Cyprus and or Greece, the Americans would be *"unwilling to lift a finger"*.

US pressure on the Greek government was intensified in July. As early as May, Senator Fulbright, Chairman of the Senate Foreign Affairs Committee, was dispatched to Greece and Turkey to convey the sense of urgency felt in the US regarding the restoration of order in the island. On 2 July Johnson sent a letter to Papandreou urging him to come to terms with Turkey. Specifically, he appeared to have suggested an exchange of territories under which Cyprus could be united with Greece. It appears that *'enosis'* with appropriate concessions to Turkey (whether it be a base in the Karpas peninsula, Cape Greco, one of the Sovereign Base areas or elsewhere) was the solution which was very much favoured in 1964. *'Compensated'* enosis was at the top of the agenda. But Johnson warned that in the event of war, which Turkey was bound to win, the US would be obliged to stand aside.

Meanwhile further fighting in Cyprus was used as an excuse for the expulsion of Greeks from Istanbul. On 17 July U Thant warned the Greek, Turkish and Cypriot governments that military preparations in Cyprus were leading to greater risks of a showdown. On the previous day Turkey had gone through the motions of preparing for a landing on the island. Top level Graeco-British talks in London on 20 July proved abortive since Whitehall was presenting only a more polished version of the Washington formula. While these talks were under way President Gursel was threatening to bomb the island. On 27 July, in Athens, Makarios agreed with the Greek government on 27 July to take the Cyprus issue to the General Assembly of the UN instead of merely to the Security Council.

In the meantime Acheson was in Geneva where he was in almost daily contact with Tuomioja and the Greek and Turkish representatives. These discussions in which Ball insisted that no Cypriot should participate, were aimed at the final settlement of the Cyprus problem and were held in the greatest secrecy. The now famous '**Acheson Plan**' was taking shape. Cyprus as an independent state was to be eliminated. The key provisions appeared to have been the following:

*Above:* A demonstration rally by Greek Cypriot organisations.
*Below:* The early years of the popular Wine Festival in Limassol.

The early years of independence resulted in a major revival of Greek art, culture and history from the majority of the Greek Cypriots.
*Above:* A performance of an ancient Greek tragedy at Courion Theatre.
*Right:* Traditional Cypriot dancers at a festival.
*Below:* Boy scouts planting trees.

1) Cyprus was to be united with Greece, in return for a 30-40 year lease of a military base to Turkey. The Turks would have sovereignty over the base, whose size was to be approximately equal to one-fifth of the island i.e. *'to engulf most of the Turkish Cypriot population'*. Castellorizo, a small island in the Aegean, was also to be ceded to Turkey.

2) Cyprus would be cantonized, creating two parallel governmental structures, one for each of the ethnic groups.

3) A joint military command for Greece and Turkey would be set up.

4) Compensation would be paid to all Turkish Cypriots who wished to leave the island.

The US's direct and active interest in the dispute was intended o safeguard the south-eastern flank of NATO and to curb Soviet infiltration of the area. In fact Greece was to eliminate AKEL's influence and neutralize Makarios' capability for political action. The return of Grivas in June 1964 was intended to serve as a countervailing force to the president.

The Turkish government accepted the above proposals as a basis for negotiations. It saw the plan as another variant of partition or double *enosis*, the bargaining being centred on the size of their area. For exactly the same reason it was rejected by both Athens and Nicosia. Moreover the Greek Cypriot leadership was increasingly identifying itself with a policy favouring independence with neutrality but without *enosis*. It was also believed that greater reliance should be placed on the UN, both for peace-keeping functions and as a guarantor of the independence and territorial integrity of Cyprus. Thus the Acheson proposals of 28 July were found to be inconsistent with existing realities and therefore unacceptable.

In August 1964 however, the supply of arms by sea from Turkey into the Mansoura-Kokkina Turkish stronghold had reached large proportions and it was felt that an attempt to link up with either Lefka or Polis would be made thus effectively cutting off the western road from Xeros to Paphos. A strong national guard contingent directed by Grivas was moved in to cut off any intended armed attack. As the Greeks pushed forward, four Turkish air force jets appeared and fired warning shots out to sea off Polis. By the early hours of 8 August the Turks had been pushed out of Mansoura and Ayios Theodoros and retreated into Kokkina. Moreover, in the afternoon some 30 Turkish jets (F100s) appeared and on the following day 64 similar jets machine-gunned everything in sight. Peaceful villages and other targets were indiscriminately bombed with napalm bombs. Hospitals were hit and scores of women and children, as well as doctors and nurses, were either killed or wounded. Makarios even sent a telegram(8 August) to Queen Elizabeth II expressing his disgust over such *"unprovoked and indiscriminate attacks"*.

The irony of this ghastly episode was that the planes and napalm bombs were supplied by the Americans for NATO defensive purposes but were used instead to attack a smaller state, a member of the UN, the Council of Europe and British Commonwealth. Furthermore, the US Sixth Fleet (*'the grey ghost of the Mediterranean'*), which had been in the vicinity for some time, did nothing to prevent the outrage.

At the Security Council the Turkish representative explained on 8 August that Cyprus was being bombed on a *'limited and restricted basis only'*. He told everyone to sleep well since there would be no further action. Yet shortly afterwards napalm bombs were used.

Athens retaliated by warning that if the bombing did not stop *'intervention'* would be the only answer. The Greek telegram, resembling an ultimatum, was delivered at the Security Council; Platon D.Morozov of the Soviet Union supported the Greek demands. Both Johnson and Khruschev, the Soviet leader, once again made it clear to Turkey that they would not approve an invasion. In fact, the Soviet Union was pushing the US to say *'no'* to a possible Turkish invasion. The Turks complied and the Security Council, after denouncing its action, passed yet another resolution (no. 193) on 9 August calling for a cease-fire. Two days later it noted with satisfaction that *'the cease-fire is being observed throughout Cyprus'*.

On 9 August it was also announced in Nicosia that the Cyprus government had appealed to the USSR and Egypt for military aid to protect the sovereignty and independence of the island. In reply to this appeal the Kremlin emphasized on 15 August that *'if a foreign armed invasion of the island takes place, the Soviet Union will help Cyprus to defend her freedom and independence.... and is prepared to begin negotiations on this matter'*. Consequently a joint communique was issued in Moscow on 1 October stating that agreement had been reached between the two countries on *'practical measures of assistance'* to be given by the Soviet Union to Cyprus for *'safeguarding the freedom and territorial integrity '* of the latter. It appeared that such aid was being provided with *'no strings attached and no conditions whatsoever'*.

The Acheson proposals as already shown, were abortive, but the talks were resumed in August and on the 20th the American *'trouble-shooter'* suggested a revised (final) version of his plan. He proposed *enosis* in return for a NATO base in Cyprus under Turkish command. The base would be leased to Turkey for a *'reasonable'* number of years. Acheson, at one stage even suggested a north-south dividing line just west of Komi

Kebir. Both the Turks and Makarios answered *'no'* but a sizeable proportion of the higher Greek establishment believed that the plan should be accepted. Professor Andreas Papandreou, a leading proponent of Cypriot independence, explained: *'The King, in his eagerness to maintain positive relations with the US, took the initiative in promoting this plan and pressure was put on our government by the Americans to denounce Makarios' policies as a prelude to the execution of the plan'.*[7]

At the UN, resolution no. 198 was adopted on 18 December. The Security Council recalled its earlier resolutions and asked members to abide by them; informed all of a marked improvement in the internal condition of the island and, extended UNFICYP for another three months.

The search for a solution was now centred on the UN mediator. On 26 March 1965, the Secretary-General transmitted a report by **Galo Plaza** to members of the Security Council. The report, composed of 173 paragraphs, was a full background investigation into all the issues. After a careful examination of the internal aspects of the Cyprus puzzle and the positions of the parties concerned (Britain, Greece and Turkey), Plaza made specific observations on the prospects of dealing with the situation. In fact the report was intended to serve as a basis for a new solution. Its main points were:

1) Cyprus should remain an independent state, renouncing its right to unite with Greece. The report stressed that *'if Cyprus should become fully independent by being freed from the 1960 treaty obligations, it would automatically acquire at the same time the right of self-determination'.*

2) The island should be *'demilitarized'*. The question of the British bases was set aside for later consideration.

3) There should be *'no partition or physical separation of the two communities'.* Turkish Cypriots *'wished'* to be physically separated from the Greek community but this separation was utterly unacceptable to the majority community and could not be imposed except by force. Nevertheless, Turkish Cypriot rights should be guaranteed by the UN and supervised by its commissioner on the island.

4) A settlement should depend in the first place on agreement between the people of Cyprus themselves and talks should take place between the two communities.

---

(7) Democracy at Gunpoint. 1977. Page 140

Plaza concluded by reiterating his conviction that *'every endeavour must continue to be made to bring about a peaceful solution and an agreed settlement of the Cyprus problem consistent with the provisions of the UN Charter'.*

The Plaza Report was in general sympathetically received by Greece and the Greek Cypriots. Turkey and the Turkish Cypriots rejected it as *'unacceptable'*. In fact the government of Suat Hayri Urguplu, which had taken over from Inonu, was a caretaker administration formed to fill the gap until the national elections of October 1965. A weak government, conscious of the army in the background, it felt obliged to take a strong line in public over Cyprus. It not only rejected the plan outright but also rejected Plaza himself as a future mediator, proposing instead direct talks between Greece and Turkey. As Plaza himself stated (paragraph 107), the Turks continued to insist that any settlement must contain two elements: *the prohibition of enosis and the geographical separation of the two communities under a federal system of government.*

The Plaza Report was noted by the Political Committee of the General Assembly and so it can be said to have been approved to that extent by the UN. Moreover, on 18 December 1965 the Cyprus government succeeded in securing the adoption of resolution 2077 (XX) by the General Assembly which supported its claim for the *'unfettered'* independence of Cyprus and discounted the Turkish claim to the right of intervention based on the Zurich and London treaties. The resolution, carried by 47 votes to 5 with 54 abstentions and 11 nations absent, called on all sides to respect the sovereignty, unity, independence and territorial integrity of the island. Surprisingly, the Cyprus government did not demand a Security Council meeting to discuss the actual rejection of the Plaza Report. The 5 negative votes were cast by the US, Turkey, Iran, Pakistan and Albania.

The Foreign Office has since admitted that Tuomioja, the first UN mediator, devoted much of his time in exploring the positions of the Greek and Turkish governments and subsequently to providing *'cover'* for the unsuccessful partitionist efforts of Dean Acheson at Geneva. (summer 1964). Plaza (his successor) on the other hand, insisted that any viable and lasting solution *'must be built around Archbishop Makarios'.*

In Cyprus meanwhile the two communities followed their antithetical directions . The Turkish Cypriot leadership, not content with keeping the two groups apart by persuasion, force, threats and killings, now set up regulations to keep them at a distance. A makeshift administration was set up in the main Nicosia-Kyrenia road enclave with representatives in other areas, a separate civil service, police force (the crescent star replacing the republic's insignia) and radio station.

Despite intercommunal divisions the majority of Cypriots embarked on an economic miracle which included the emergence of tourism as a major source of income. *Above:* The golden beaches of Famagusta and *below* the picturesque Kyrenia harbour *Left:* Road construction was a priority.

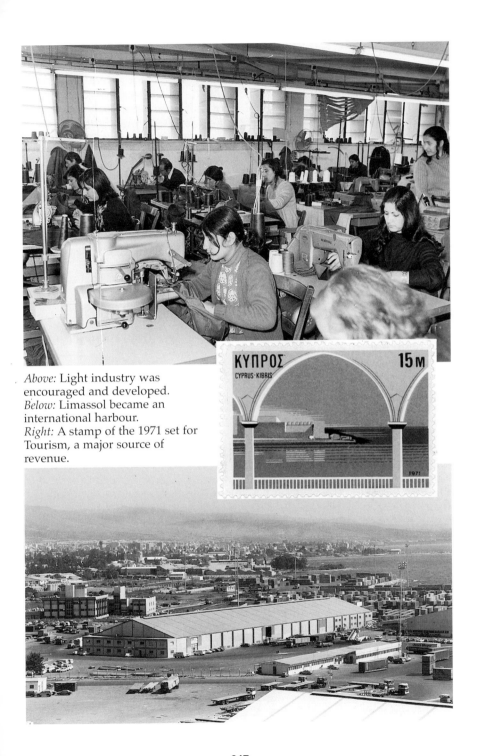

*Above:* Light industry was encouraged and developed.
*Below:* Limassol became an international harbour.
*Right:* A stamp of the 1971 set for Tourism, a major source of revenue.

Consequently, Turkish Cypriots abandoned many of their villages and gathered for *'self-protection'* and the facilitation of partition in the more densely populated areas. According to UN figures around 25,000 so-called *'refugees'* were forced to relocate in this manner. Greek Cypriots were not permitted to enter these areas nor were the Turks allowed to leave without permission from their leaders. Confined in such places without sufficient resources, they survived as a *'separate'* entity only with direct economic aid from Turkey (between £10 and £12 million annually). However, despite harassment from their leaders and pressure from armed gangs which had arrived from Turkey after 1963, a far greater number of Turkish Cypriots, for many reasons, remained in government controlled areas.

The demand for partition or, as a second best, the geographical separation of the two communities, never wavered. Glafcos Clerides, writing in 1966, explained:

"Turkey proposes to break up the unitary state by reshuffling the population on the basis of communal criteria to create predominantly Turkish areas, with the apparent intention of creating two federal states; but with the real intention of preparing the ground for partition, which today is physically impossible owing to the fact that the Greeks and Turks live side by side in the same villages and towns of the Island"[8]

Galo Plaza also pointed out in his report that he was reluctant to believe, as the Turkish Cypriot leadership claimed, in the *'impossibility'* of the two communities learning to live together again in peace. He showed that in those parts of the island where movement controls had been relaxed and tensions reduced they were already proving otherwise. A survey conducted on the damage caused to Turkish Cypriot properties induced the government to launch a rebuilding programme to encourage them to return to houses they had left during the fighting. Moreover, contacts had already been established where they had been severed: commercial dealings for example had been restarted within days of the fighting. In fact, there was in the economic sector an almost total unity and mutual dependence.

However, in order to counter the Turkish separatist moves the Greeks, having secured absolute control over the government, enacted legislation in 1964-65 which incorporated most of Makarios' 13 proposed amendments to the 1960 constitution. They also offered their compatriots a Bill of Minority Rights. In fact the structural and functional changes to the 1960 constitution had been directed towards establishing a unified

---

(8) Middle East Forum. Volume 42. No. 1 Page11

state with unfettered independence. There was no intention of reverting to the conditions before December 1963. Plaza also emphasized that the problem of Cyprus could not be resolved by attempting to restore the situation before the outbreak of intercommunal strife, but that a new solution must be found consistent with the provisions of the UN Charter.

The Acheson failure was soon followed by other *'initiatives'*. In 1965 Henry Labouisse, the new American ambassador to Greece, *'prepared'* a five-point programme for the pacification of Cyprus over a six-month period. The terms were intended to satisfy the pride of the Turks and to improve their relative military position. Petros Garoufalias, Greek Minister of Defence, who went to Cyprus in mid-March to meet the Cypriot cabinet and present the Labouisse plan, returned empty handed. Makarios, supported by Papandreou, maintained his unyielding stand and declared that he would never deviate from the line that the Cyprus question was exclusively a matter within the competence of the UN and *'cannot be the object of Graeco-Turkish negotiations'*.

It was around this time that the first news of an attempt to remove Papandreou appeared in the press. In early April 1965 the Cypriot media carried the story that the king was searching for a way to overthrow the elected government, to form a cabinet of national unity and to close the Cyprus question on the basis of the Acheson plan. According to Andreas Papandreou, *'Cyprus lay at the heart of the tragic political developments that led to the death of democracy in Greece'*. Instability in government led to less than desirable results.

About this time the Americans, presumably after sounding out other interested parties, were *'kicking around'* some ideas aimed at solving the Cyprus problem. One such idea was the surrender of a SBA on lease to the Turks. Such a move however should be in *"residual sovereignty'* (recognised under international law as very long leases) since Britain was committed to return to the island's government any part of either base over which it gave up sovereignty. And the plot thickens! A handwritten note (on the margin) by an FCO official in June 1967, stated that *"the Greek-American solution will have to come about without the agreement of the Cyprus government"*.

The Greek elections scheduled for 28 May 1967 were never held. On 21 April a small gang of junior officers, under the leadership of **George Papadopoulos** and closely associated with the intelligence services of Greece and the US, put into effect a NATO-elaborated contingency plan called *'Prometheus'* and thus plunged the country into a ruthless military dictatorship. As the coupists had boasted, they *"kept the country in plaster for seven years"*. President Bill Clinton, a highly skilled and instinctive politician, admitted in Athens (November 1999) that the US was *"misguided in backing the ultra-rightist military coup in 1967"*.

Following the coup many Cypriots feared that the large number of Greek troops in the island might attempt to overthrow Makarios and forcibly achieve *enosis*. In early August, Papadopoulos, then Minister to the Prime Minister, visited Cyprus and tried to concert a plan for *enosis* with the island's government. At the same time the Greek leadership declared that *'Greece and Turkey are bound by the need to confront jointly the common enemy - communism - and to consider all outstanding differences of view as secondary to this primary interest'*. Cyprus was soon to be auctioned and leading the bidding were the two *'mother'* countries.

On 9 September the Greek and Turkish delegations headed by their two Premiers, Constantine Kollias and Suleyman Demirel, met at Kesan, a small Turkish village about 18 miles from the Greek border and on the following day (lasting eight hours) at Alexandroupolis in Thrace, Greece. Both countries agreed that Cyprus must be integrated into the western defensive system, thus preserving the security of the Turkish mainland and of the island's Turkish Cypriots and nullifying the communist danger from the north. From the joint Evros communique the following issues were not given any publicity:

1) what percentage of the island's territory and how many military bases did Turkey demand in return for *enosis*;

2) whether the Greeks offered Turkey the British sovereign base of Akrotiri;

3) whether the Greeks offered territorial concessions in Thrace in return for *enosis*; and

4) whether the above proposals were also suggested to the Turks by Stephanopoulos in 1966. He had been premier from September 1965 to December 1966 and had always been at loggerheads with the Cypriot leadership.

It was agreed however that the restoration of good relations and cordiality between the two countries primarily depended on a just solution of the Cyprus problem. The fact that both countries belonged to the same alliance was also reiterated.

In Cyprus meanwhile, both sides were extending their fortifications and consequently, according to UNFICYP, over 600 shooting incidents took place in 1967 . The Ayios Theodoros-Kophinou incidents of 15 November, in which 24 Turkish and 2 Greek Cypriots were killed, have been fully documented by an eye-witness, Brigadier Michael Harbottle, then chief of staff of UNFICYP, in his book *The Impartial Soldier*.

An acute crisis was caused by the incidents in these two villages. In Ankara the Grand Assembly met and decided to fight if necessary. Planes flew over Nicosia and 30 warships stood by in the channel separating the island from Turkey. In Ankara and Istanbul violent anti-Greek riots erupted and the best units in the Turkish army were rushed to Alexandretta (Iskenderun) on the northeast coast facing Cyprus. In Salonica, the principal port for garrisoning and supplying the Greek army on the island, there were unusual troop movements. Across the Evros river, with guns at the port, Turkish and Greek armoured units faced each other.

The build-up by both countries continued. Papadopoulos, who for various reasons wanted peace, (evidence suggests that he had been on the CIA payroll since 1952), worked tirelessly to avoid such a confrontation. On 21 November he offered bilateral talks, an act contrary to the spirit of the Plaza proposals, but his offer was turned down while an estimated 80,000 people in Istanbul and 30,000 in Izmir demonstrated for war and blood donors volunteered at various hospitals. In Athens, air-raid shelters were being cleaned and according to several reports key contingents received sealed battle orders.

Meanwhile peace initiatives to avert war were forthcoming. The UN sent a special envoy, Signor J. Rolz-Bennet, NATO sent Manlio Brosio, its former Secretary General (1961-64) and President Johnson sent **Cyrus Vance**. Whilst the last was in Turkey, President Sunay warned world leaders on 24 November that his country intended to solve the Cyprus problem *"once and for all"*. Yet Demirel had earlier informed Kosygin at a Kremlin dinner on 20 September that, *"we are wholly and entirely guided by our desire for a peaceful solution of this problem"*.

At midnight on 17 November 1967, Turkey delivered an ultimatum to Greece demanding that certain conditions should be agreed to instantly or its troops would land in Cyprus to defend the island's Turks. The five major demands were:

1) General Grivas should be recalled. To lower the temperature the Greeks decided on his immediate recall. He was flown to Athens on 19 November and on the next day resigned his supreme command of the Cyprus forces.

2) All Greek troops stationed in Cyprus since 1964 should be removed. The withdrawal of this estimated 10,000 strong contingent began on 8 December, yet, the admittedly smaller number of Turkish troops that had infiltrated Cyprus since 1963 remained on the island.

3) An indemnity should be paid for the Turks killed plus damages for the property destroyed.

4)  Greek Cypriot organisations should be disarmed, including the national guard.

5)  Pressure on the Turkish Cypriot community should cease.

It appeared that there was agreement on these and on certain other issues (26 November). Cyprus was not invaded. Turkey had triumphed and the agreed withdrawal of the Greek troops meant that Greece and the Greek Cypriots had lost an important bargaining card. In a message to Makarios on 29 November, President Johnson pleaded for the *"highest degree of wisdom, courage and statesmanship"* in order to *"resolve the current crisis"*. In this political climate, the Turkish Cypriots on 28 December instituted a separate authority which they named the *'Provisional Turkish Cypriot Administration'*. The UN was not informed until the day after and U Thant expressed his misgivings.

Even though intercommunal tensions eased after the clashes of 1967 the situation in Cyprus remained at an impasse. On the initiative of the island's government the question was again brought before the UN, where U Thant offered his good offices by proposing the commencement of direct negotiations between the island's two communities. The *intercommunal talks* began under his auspices in Beirut on 11 June 1968.

Hence the pro-government faction changed its immediate geopolitical goal to independence; other groups continued to seek enosis. Those who sought independence decided to negotiate with their Turkish compatriots and therefore undertook political and economic actions to facilitate such discussions. Those who continued to seek enosis as an immediate goal were determined to continue their *'fight'* not only against their cohabitants but also to take up arms against their co-religionists who wanted independence.

For six years the two negotiating teams met regularly. Even though agreement was reached on most matters, considerable differences divided the two sides over the authority to be vested in local government and the international guarantees to be given to the new constitutional order. Excuses? Or did the die-hards of both communities prevail?

The chief stumbling block seems to have been the Turkish insistence on a separatist policy based on a federal state composed of two communities; i.e. a state within a state. It was termed by some as *'loose'* or *'relaxed'* federation. A breakthrough, a 'near' agreement, was very nearly achieved in both 1972 and 1973 and finally in July 1974 but it appears that Ankara suddenly objected. Partition under the euphemism of federation had been its persistent objective. Some analysts even claim that it was Makarios who torpedoed the talks. Hence they failed to achieve a formula for more *"jaw not war"*. Much more research is needed to expose the flaws of such a massive failure.

Ioannis Christophides, the Cypriot Foreign Minister, informed the UN General Assembly in November 1976 that the Turkish Cypriots had plans to partition the island in 1963. He quoted extracts from a secret document dated 14 September 1963 bearing the signatures of Kutchuk and Denktash which revealed planned self-segregation as the first step to partition. In the following year Kemal Satir, a former deputy Prime Minister of Turkey, publicly declared that *"Cyprus will be divided into two sections, one of which will join Turkey"*. A secret document issued on 18 April 1964 by Ismet Inonu clearly laid out the partitionist plan of his country which was named by him the '**Attila Plan**'. This scheme was proposed in 1965 by Kutchuk to the UN mediator and appears in Plaza's report of 26 March 1965 to the UN Secretary-General. The plan covered essentially the area which Turkey occupied following its invasion of Cyprus in July 1974 - the area coveted by Turkey for so many years. Inonu also explained quite emphatically on 17 May 1964 that: *"one day Greece will agree to a peaceful partition of Cyprus with the help of NATO. As long as the Greeks refuse, the battle will go on - Turkey will not recede in any hopeless position - Turkey will use her right of intervention in the island."*

On 8 September 1964 Inonu informed the National Assembly that *"officially we promoted the federation concept rather than the partition thesis"*. In fact geographical federation is simply a disguised form of partition. In June of that year F.C. Erkin, the Turkish Foreign Minister, stated in Athens that the *"radical solution would be to cede one part of Cyprus to Greece and the other, closest to the Turkish Asiatic coast, to Turkey"*. British documents for 1964 reveal that in view of the UK's interests in the Eastern Mediterranean and Middle East the problem of Cyprus *"is primarily the problem of Turkey"*. Moreover, Turkish politicians continued right through to December 1964 to re-state the *"classic Turkish position"* of *"partition or double enosis"* and *"the maximum physical separation of the two communities"*. The UK also stressed that the *"best"* solution was enosis with Greece or partition and union of the Greek and Turkish parts with *"their mother countries"*.

Turkey's intentions emerged once again on 1 February 1974 when, following a long parliamentary crisis after the elections of the previous autumn, the coalition government under **Bulent Ecevit** signed a protocol in which it declared that only *'federation'* would be accepted in Cyprus. The call for such a system was repeated with great regularity.

Such statements (Greek Cypriot enosists were equally disruptive) thwarted all efforts to reach a settlement in accordance with the previously accepted principles that the solution of the constitutional problem of Cyprus should be on the basis of an independent, sovereign and unitary state. Turkey, seeking a pretext to enforce its plans, set its invasion machine in motion. The opportunity soon appeared in the form of a *coup d'etat* by the Greek junta and its proxies against Makarios on 15 July 1974. Five days later, Turkey invaded.

The years since 1968 were notable for several other important events. Firstly, Makarios announced on 12 January 1968 that elections would be held during the following month. On 25 February he was re-elected president. He received 220,911 votes (94.45 per cent) and his opponent, a Nicosia psychiatrist Dr. Takis Evdokas, within weeks leader of DEK (Democratikon Ethnikon Komma - Democratic National Party), received 8,577 (3.71 per cent). DEK (the *'predecessor'* of EOKA-B and ESEA) was formally set up in March/ April 1968 and Evdokas began publishing *Gnomi (Opinion)*, a weekly newspaper that sharply criticised the government's policies and advocated *enosis* as the only guarantee against communism. On 15 February, Kütchük was returned unopposed as vice-president. In fact, Judge Zekia had been persuaded to withdraw his candidature.

A second major event was the attempted assassination of the Greek *'military'* leader. On 13 August 1968 Alecos Panaghoullis unsuccessfully tried to blow up the car of Papadopoulos. During the enquiries that followed curious links were revealed between Panaghoullis and the Cyprus government which led to the resignation of the enigmatic **Polycarpos Georghadjis**, a former EOKA district leader and at the time Minister of the Interior and Defence. Georghadjis himself was mysteriously assassinated on 16 March 1970.

Thirdly, the Greek Cypriots found themselves plunged into a domestic political crisis. The government's policy of abandoning *'genuine enosis'* for the *'attainable solution'* of a peaceful, independent, sovereign Cyprus was opposed both by the extreme right of the island and by the junta in Greece. Enosis was finally *'buried'* and Makarios was accused of being its *'undertaker par excellence'*. By 1972 a new underground organisation called EOKA-B was created and quickly infiltrated into the government, civil service, clubs and associations. Its political front ESEA (*Epitropi Sindonismou Enotikou Agonos - Co-ordinating Committee for the Enosis Struggle*), with **Photis Papaphotis**, ex-EOKA district leader, as its general secretary, had regular contacts with the island's senior churchmen and with the Greek embassy. The conspirators were both numerous and well armed.

Plots to assassinate Makarios became frequent. The first assault, coded *'Hermes'*, was made on 8 March 1970; power was to be seized by means of a coup. Grivas, reportedly disguised as a priest, returned to Cyprus in September 1971 to direct the anti-Makarios forces. Ankara, which in 1967 was instrumental in removing him from the island, did not raise a murmur in 1971! In the same year, the UN described the situation as one of *"negative stability"*, quiet on the surface but strained, abnormal and fraught with serious danger of an armed clash.

In 1973 there were several armed clashes between the *'rebels'* and security forces. After the creation of EOKA-B the government in 1972 formed the Auxiliary Police (or tactical reserve) Force. Christos Vakis, the Minister of Justice, was kidnapped on 27 July. Another attempt was made on Makarios' life at Ayios Serghios on 7 October. Earlier in August, police discovered machine-gun positions on the Nicosia-Troodos road and at Kokkinotrimithia, from which assassination attempts were to be made against Makarios. The president was not the only target. Since 1969 pro-*enosis* groups had embarked on a campaign of terrorism, raiding police stations to steal arms, bombing British military buildings and vehicles, shooting and wounding the chief of police and making several bomb attacks on government ministers and other political leaders. One such attack was outside Papaioannou's house on 14 October 1969. Next day the AKEL leader accused the CIA of preparing a plan which entailed the assassination of progressive MPs, the arming of Greek and Turkish bands to provoke incidents, the overthrow of Makarios and the imposition of partition.

At the same time the Greek military government, subservient to foreign interests and for the sake of maintaining its power, followed a double policy on Cyprus. Though it officially supported the intercommunal talks it undertook a campaign to corrode the Cyprus state by financing and encouraging elements working to overthrow the island's

Archbishop Makarios addresses a mass rally in the archbishopric square in Nicosia on 8 February 1973.

legitimate government. The Athenian cabal (known popularly as the *'changing of the guard'*, Papadopoulos being replaced following the *'popular'* rising of 16 November 1973 by the hidden strongman **Brigadier Ioannides** on 25 November) worked conscientiously for the virtual partition of Cyprus. Thus Papadopoulos told a Turkish reporter on 31 May 1971 that if Greece and Turkey came to a mutual agreement *'our children in Cyprus would also consent to bury their differences'*.

As early as November 1967 the Pipinelis-Cyrus Vance talks seem to have proposed to partition the island.[9] At the June 1971 NATO Foreign Ministers' Conference at Lisbon, the two countries by all accounts, promised to split their differences and divide Cyprus. Relations between Papadopoulos and Makarios deteriorated and their meeting on 3-4 September 1971 proved futile. The Greek dictator was furious because the president, amongst other things, had visited the Soviet Union between 2 and 9 June of that year.

Makarios therefore had been under constant pressure from the mainland clique. Athens now insisted that he should dismiss ministers considered hostile to Greece. A provocative note dated 11 February 1972 demanded that a government of national unity must be formed and should exclude communists but include moderate representatives of Grivas. The *demarche* delivered by the Greek ambassador (Panayotacos) urged the Archbishop to hand over the Czech[10] arms to UNFICYP and explained that Athens was the metropolis of hellenism. On 3 March the British high commission informed London that the present climate was more favourable than before for *"Grivas to seize power"* since he could represent the Archbishop as being in conflict with both the national centre (Athens) and his own Church. Yet, after the failure of the anti-Makarios coup (February 1972), the Americans were starting to come to terms with the Makarios whom they felt was henceforth a *'stabilising'* influence in the region. But for how long? The president did not resist the pressure for long. A coup *'scheduled'* for the evening of 14/15 February was averted but on 5 May Spyros Kyprianou, the Foreign Minister,who had been the main target of the junta's hostility resigned (his dismissal having been demanded since 1971), together with two other ministers. In June the cabinet was reorganised.

---

(9) In December 1966, the talks in Paris between the Foreign Ministers of Greece and Turkey - Admiral J. Toumbas and I.S. Caglayangil - appeared to have had the same double enosis content. Did they exchange a secret memorandum along the lines of the Acheson proposals?

(10) Intended to be used by the government against the rising state of lawlessness. The arms arrived on the island in late January 1972. They were sufficient to arm 8 battalions. See FCO 9/1509. See also FCO 9/1968. Folio 2. They were placed under the custody of UNFICYP.

After 1973 *enosis* adherents prepared such plans as *'Apollo'*, *'Gronthos'* and *'Aphrodite 3'*. The conspiracy was in full swing. In the spring and summer of 1974 EOKA-B intensified it activities. Police stations were raided and there were hundreds of bomb explosions. Makarios was to be removed and the Karpas and Troodos areas were to be seized. When Grivas died on 27 January George Karousos assumed command of the organisation. However, by the end of February control of the movement appeared to have passed to Kikis Constantinou and Lefteris Papadopoullos. In reality it was directed from Athens and financed at the rate of C£1 million a year. On 25 April it was declared unlawful. Makarios reacted by sending a letter, dated 2 July but delivered the next day, to President Phaidon Ghizikis of Greece demanding, amongst other things, the withdrawal of mainland officers in the Greek contingent and national guard on the grounds that they were plotting against the island's legal government. No reply was received.

By this time the plot coded *'Hermes'* was an open secret. On 3 July the Greek Foreign Minister S. Tetenes, his aides and several officers resigned in disgust. On 5 July *Apoyevmatini*, a Nicosia newspaper, printed an account of the plot against Makarios, adding that the Greek officers and their EOKA-B henchmen planned to kill the president and put a puppet in his place. On 7 July Cypriot newspapers published the archbishop's letter under banner headlines. Surprisingly however nothing was done militarily to prevent it.

On 2 July, at the office of General Gregorios Mbonanos, chief of the Greek armed forces, the coup preparations took their final shape. Those present were Mbonanos, Ioannides, Georgitsis and Papadakis. The last two[11] were to carry out these plans in Cyprus. In order to confuse the island's government, the political representative of Greece in Cyprus departed for the Athens on Friday 12 July.[12] The dangerously volatile and unpredictable Ioannides (anti-Turk to an extreme degree) needed a diversion in order to stave off Turkish action in the Aegean (over oil rights) and restore the prestige of his regime. His target was Cyprus.

The fateful day was Monday 15 July 1974. The first announcement of the *coup d'etat* came from the Cyprus Broadcasting Corporation (PIK) at around 8 a.m. and it contained the following points:

1) The National Guard intervened on 15 July to stop internecine war between Greeks.

---

(11) Chiefs of the Greek armed contingent and supreme command in Cyprus.

(12) On 13 July, the Hellenic government gave the impression that it was going to answer Makarios' letter on Monday 15th. Such tactics were deceptive and misleading.

2) The main purpose of the National Guard is to maintain order.

3) The matter is an internal one among Greeks alone.

4) The National Guard is in control of the situation and Makarios is dead.

5) Anyone who puts up resistance will be executed at once.

It is ironic however, that the coup provoked no immediate action by the Security Council nor from the Cypriot delegate to the UN.  **Nicos Sampson**, believed to be the fourth choice, was installed as president. Makarios however escaped and on 15 July confirmed reports that he was alive by broadcasting to his people from Paphos.  The message, transmitted by the Free Cyprus Broadcasting Corporation, urged the entire Greek Cypriot population to continue its resistance against the dictatorship.  From Paphos he was flown by helicopter to Akrotiri and then by RAF plane to Malta, where he spent the night at Valetta as the guest of the Mintoff government.

On 17 July Makarios arrived at RAF Lyneham, Wiltshire, and proceeded to have talks with Harold Wilson at 10 Downing Street and then at the Foreign and Commonwealth Office with James Callaghan. He was not only promised unqualified support at the UN but also that HMG would not recognise the island's '*existing*' administration since he and none other was the acknowledged leader and elected president. The archbishop called for the restoration of his country's independence and sovereignty. The Americans however were not so accommodating. On 18 July and, according to some reports, Makarios was received in New York as archbishop and not as president. By the same title, it appears, he was received on 22 July by **Kissinger** in Washington . Furthermore, on 19 July the US fought hard at the Security Council to achieve two objectives:

1) to allow the representative of the Sampson '*government*' to speak on an equal basis with Makarios; and

2) to prevent this body from reaching a decision which could have impeded a Turkish invasion.

Kissinger failed on the first but succeeded on the second and far more important issue.  It must be emphasised that throughout his presidency (1969-1974) Richard Nixon backed the Athenian cabal which repeatedly tried to eliminate Makarios.  Though difficult to substantiate, covert operations (the work of the CIA and other intelligence operatives) and official governmental action (State Department/Pentagon and American embassies worldwide) sometimes functioned within different wavelengths.

The condition of the archbishopric after being attacked by the insurgents

In Turkey meanwhile there was a news black-out in its eastern regions and on17 July two journalists were arrested in Mersin for trying to send out news of military movements. Troop activity in the Mersin-Alexandretta districts had been evident since early June. Whitehall received a request from Turkey on 16 July for consultation with the government under the terms of Article 4 of the Treaty of Guarantee. Bulent Ecevit arrived on the following day and appears to have proposed joint action by Anglo-Turkish forces to restore the status *ante-bellum*. The British Premier refused to use force, hoping that the crisis would be resolved diplomatically. Wilson reveals that the object of Ecevit's visit was to seek British approval for a Turkish invasion, to protect the Turkish minority there. *"To this end, he asked us to allow him to use the sovereign base at Akrotiri for the purpose. He received a courteous but declaratory 'no'...."*[13] However, research conducted by B.O'Malley and I. Craig[14] suggests that the UK came close to war with Turkey in 1974. Wilson, who was leading

---

(13) The Final Term. The Labour Government, 1974-76. 1979 Page 62

(14) The Cyprus Conspiracy: America, Espionage and the Turkish Invasion. 2001. Page 198.

a minority government (calling elections in October 1974, he was restricted to an overall majority of three i.e. 319 to 316), went on to say that apart from the lunacy at Suez, this was probably the nearest Britain came to war with another nation, and especially an ally, since 1945. The Americans, it may be added, vetoed such a course. Amongst other considerations, it did not want to jeopardise its top secret electronic spying facilities in northern Cyprus. The story of Cyprus as a Western intelligence asset *has* to be written. Surely there is so much to be learned!

**Makarios' escape route**

- ➔ By Car.... Nicosia to Paphos
- By Helicopter....Paphos to Akrotiri ⎤ Operation
- By Plane...Akrotiri to Malta ⎦ *'Skylark'*

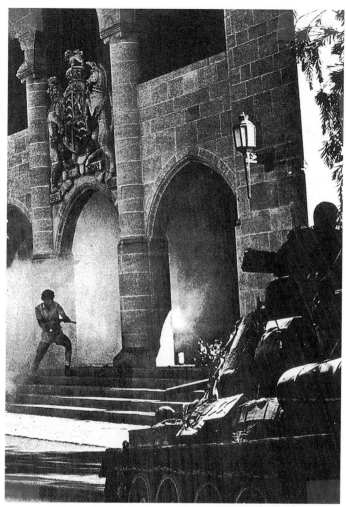

The tragic storming of the Presidential Palace by anti-government troops during the coup of Monday 15 July 1974

The invasion started. The air bombardment was indiscriminate, destroying many residential areas in towns and villages

Chapter FIVE

# THE COUP & INVASION OF 1974:

Effects on
Cypriot Society

Fairly early on the morning of 20 July, Turkey invaded Cyprus; the decision to launch the attack had already been taken on 15 July. Ecevit recalled that "**the coup was the green light for our invasion**". For this operation the full might of the Turkish military machine, supplied by America and NATO, ostensibly to defend the country's and Allied interests, was used against Cyprus. A country with an estimated population of 50 million plus and an army of well over $1/2$ a million invaded an unprepared island, member of the United Nations, Commonwealth and Council of Europe, with 630,000 inhabitants and an army comprising around 10,000 national guardsmen, the 1,000 Greek contingent and approximately 5,000 others - all it may be added, armed with outdated weapons. This is well documented in British official papers released in 2004/05.

Turkey landed its troops in Kyrenia and its paratroopers inside the Nicosia-Kyrenia road enclave and then bombed the capital and Famagusta. Following strong protests and a warning from Britain the Turks desisted from attacking Nicosia airport because, as Harold Wilson explained, there would have been casualties among the UN forces of which the biggest component was the British, including the 16th/5th Lancers; moreover had Ecevit *"proceeded with his design we should not hesitate to order our fighters to shoot down his aircraft"*.[1] Even more revealing is the fact that in the aftermath of C.I.D. (Coup, Invasion, Disaster), Britain was willing to withdraw from Cyprus and abandon its military bases. The idea was supported by the chiefs of the defence staff and outlined by the defence review but vetoed by Henry Kissinger, Secretary of State in the Nixon administration.[2] It was later explained by Whitehall officials that such a willingness to quit was *"a temporary aberration, and that the Cyprus bases were as much a part of Britain as Devon and Cornwall"*. In fact, under the 1959-60 Agreements, Britain maintained, and does to this day, two Sovereign Base Areas (SBAs) of around 99 sq miles, or 2.5% of Cypriot territory and a Government Communications Headquarters listening post on the Troodos Mountains (in addition to other training sites etc.) which eavesdrops on the former Soviet Union, Eastern Europe and the Middle East and feeds information into America's National Security Agency. Whatever their significance now, contemporary military literature describe the bases and other *'retained sites'* on the island as *"the UK's most important interests"*. They remain key strategic assets in a troubled region; their logistic benefit as a forward mounting base was demonstrated during the Gulf Wars (1991 and 2003) and they provide valuable training facilities.

---

(1) Final Term. The Labour Government 1974-76 1979. Pages 63-64. See also PREM 16/19

(2) The Guardian. 2 April 1988. Page 1. See amongst others: FCO 46/1178, T 225/3905 and PREM 16/21

# What were the new Cypriot realities and new developments?

Undoubtedly, the year 1974 was something of an *"annus horribilis"* in the recent history of Cyprus.

1) Around 37.5% of the island's territory is still (mid-April, 2005) under Turkish occupation and approximately 142,000 Greek Cypriots were ousted from their ancestral homes - less than a few hundred now remain in the occupied north. These refugees constituted 69% of the area's population and about 24% of the island's total inhabitants. Added to the figure of 142,000 displaced persons must be that of about 19,500 enclaved who were subsequently driven out of the occupied area. By any international standards, the volume of refugees proportional to the ethnic population was enormous - some 40%. This has made the problems of absorption, rehousing and perhaps eventual resettlement correspondingly complex. By contrast, the 40,000-odd Turkish Cypriot refugees (some *'ousted'* for the second or even third time since the mid-1950s) did not face such problems of shelter provision. The Turkish occupied sector has succeeded through various means - renaming settlements, comprehensive dehellenisation, erection of monuments to the 1974 *'liberation'* etc., - to convey the message of permanent separation and independence. For the Greek Cypriots a contrasting ideology exists: such a permanency is not accepted.

2) Following the invasion, ¹/₃ of the Greek population became completely dependent on state aid. Around 15% of the island's employed force and 10% self-employed people were left without a job. The government was faced not only with a massive rehousing problem but with the added unprecedented difficulty of *'finding'* jobs for the *'unemployed, displaced and dispirited refugees'*. In a series of Emergency Action Plans (1975-1986) the government successfully rebuilt the shattered economy. Within a few years after the events of 1974, economic activity returned to the pre-invasion levels with unemployment virtually eliminated, productive resources replaced, refugees rehoused and confidence in the economic future restored. This upsurge has been described by independent observers as an **"economic miracle"**. Per capita income in1987 was well over US$ 6,000 (at a rate of C£1 - US$2), certainly one of the highest in the Middle East and Southern Europe. So rapid has been Cyprus' economic progress that it is now classified as a *'high-income country'*. According to the World Bank (World Economic Indicators), the per capita Gross Domestic Product (GDP)[3] for the island, calculated on a purchasing power parity basis reached EUR 14,250 in

---

(3) GDP is the annual total value of goods produced and services provided in a country. In 2003 tourism for example, constituted 20% of GDP

Cape Andreas
Rizokarpaso

FAMAGUSTA
Cape Greco

Lefkoniko
Marathovouno

Kythrea

LARNACA
Cape Kiti

**Positions of the Turkish
Invading Forces – 1974**

On 22 July
On 30 July
On 8 August
On 16 August
After 16 August
British Bases

KYRENIA
Karavas

NICOSIA

Dhali

Lapithos

Cape Kormakiti

Morphou

LIMASSOL
Cape Gata

Pyrgos

TROODOS MOUNTAINS

Cape Arnaouti

PAPHOS

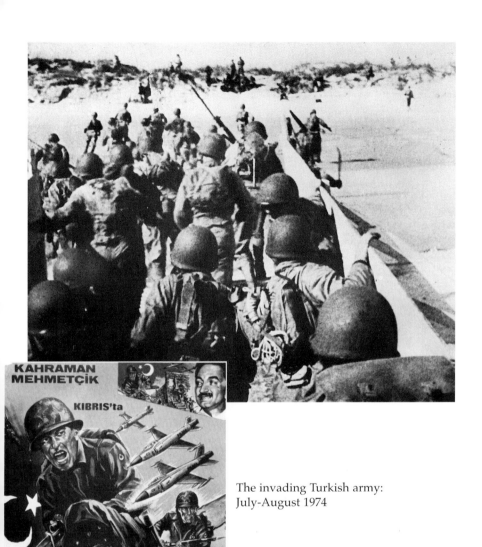

The invading Turkish army:
July-August 1974

2000, ranking it 16th worldwide. If other aspects of social welfare are considered (income distribution, educational levels, health and housing conditions), then the standard of living in Cyprus ranks even higher. The recent Strategic Development Plan 1999-2003, envisaged not only steady but higher growth estimated at 4.7 per cent in 2003. The one for 2004-06 aims, amongst other things, to utilise to the greatest possible extent the opportunities offered through the accession of Cyprus into the EU.

Three further remarks must be brought to the notice of readers:

*Firstly* , it must be remembered that tourism played a major role in the island's economy. The main tourist centres of northern Cyprus are now under Turkish control. Kyrenia, *'the tourist's dream'* was occupied and Famagusta *'the riviera of the Eastern Mediterranean'* became and still is, an empty *'ghost'* town. To make up for the loss of such accommodation, new hotels, apartments and various other *'attractions'* have been built in many coastal areas. An entirely new town is **Ayia Napa**. On land sloping down to first class beaches, it is built round a small fishing village and an old, high-walled monastery near the southeastern corner of the island. Protaras and Paralimni are other major post-1974 tourist destinations.

Together with the friendly hospitality of the people, the excellent and healthy climate, the beauty of the countryside, the beaches and the blue sea, the long and rich history, Cyprus attracts numerous visitors - many of them returning year after year. In 2002 around 2.6 million tourists went to Cyprus of which over 50 per cent were from the UK. The above number representing $3^1/_2$ times the local population, brought to the island an income of over C£1,150 million or US$ 2,253 million. Two new airports at Larnaca and Paphos were built or extended to cater for this upsurge and for the island's other needs.

*Secondly*, it must be stressed that in 1972 Cyprus signed an Association Agreement with the European Economic Community (E.E.C.) for the establishment, through two successive stages, of a Customs Union between the two parties. The first stage of the Association Agreement expired at the end of 1987. The second stage became effective in January 1988. This stage consisted of two phases, the first was for a duration of ten years and the second of four or five years. These provisions led progressively to a Customs Union and to a free movement of goods between the two parties; this undoubtedly opened new prospects for the use of Cyprus as a base for the production of goods by enterprises based on the island. In 1990 Cyprus applied for full membership and in 1998 started the negotiation process to become a full member of the European Union. In 1999 some 53% of Cyprus' trade was with the EU of which more than 12.5% was with the UK. Exports to EU countries, primarily the UK, Germany and Greece absorbed in 2002 some 55% of Cyprus' exports. Around 20% went to countries of the Arab world and some 25% to the rest of the world. Cyprus in fact, was in a position to implement fully the *acquis communautaire* of the EU. In December 2002 it was fully accepted to become a full member of the enlarged European Union in 2004. This was achieved on 1 May of that year.

The *third* related issue that needs brief comment is the one of state involvement. Cyprus continues to operate a mixed economic system with the government supplementing private initiative. It will continue to promote and maintain favourable investment conditions that will permit entrepreneurs to participate directly in the process of economic development. The broad goals of this policy may be summarised as follows:

a)   Maintenance of a high rate of economic growth.

One of the cartoons of the time depicting the severity of the invasion

*Above:* Mr Eagleton, an American Senator visited the Lefkaritis refugee camp.
*Below:* The result of Turkish air bombardment.

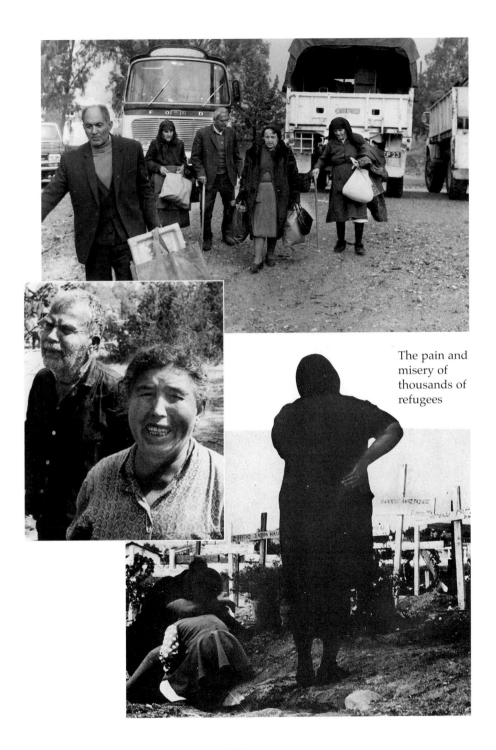

The pain and misery of thousands of refugees

b)    Diversification of the productive base of the economy. [4]

c)    Maintenance of full employment and price stability.  In 2002, unemployment peaked at 3.2 per cent (4.3 per cent less than the EU average)  Moreover, the number of foreign workers in mid-2002 was 33,153 representing some 10.7 per cent of the total workforce.

d)    Promotion of exports and improvement in the balance of payments.

The ultimate national economic goal remains the improvement of the quality of life and the welfare of the population.

3)   In simple economic terms therefore, the total assets under Turkish control following the events of 1974 were as follows:

>    70% of the gross output.
>    65% of the tourist accommodation
>    87% of the hotel beds under construction.
>    83% of the general cargo handling (Famagusta)
>    56% of the  mining and quarrying output
>    41% of the livestock production
>    48% of the agricultural exports
>    46% of the plant production, and so forth

4)   The invasion also cost the island 3,000 dead; 2,192 *'missing'* and 20,000 Greek Cypriots enclaved in various parts of the north.  Due to a wave of expulsions only a few hundred remain today.  Furthermore, and with the intention of changing the demographic character of the island large numbers of Turkish settlers - totalling approximately 140,000 (to date)  - have been uprooted from their homes and transferred to Cyprus. Correspondingly however, the indigenous Turkish Cypriot population has decreased by around 25% - from over 100,000 to some 80,000 - with Australia and Britain being the chief emigration destinations.  Displaced for the second or third time!  The  islanders surely, deserve something better.

5)   The impact on the lives of the refugees has been dramatic.  The pain and a long list of problems - adjusting to a new environment and very often with a depleted family, developing a new local status and new family guidelines (behavioural and workwise) etc. - have tested extensively the virtues and stamina of this large section of the island's inhabitants.  Thus, whilst the intention has been, through the housing and

---

(4)  Prior to 1974 agriculture engaged 36% of the working population but only 21% in 1984 and around 10% in 2003.  Tourism provided employment (2003) for around 15% of the country's population

economic programmes, to integrate and reactivate, at the same time the distinctiveness of the refugees who are still committed to repatriation, has been accentuated.

Also the massive propertylessness which such refugee status had generated, greatly unbalanced the structure of Cypriot society. In the island, property ownership played and, continues to do so, a crucial role in the family life-cycle, setting parameters for family patterns and helping in the solution of urban problems of adaptation.

6) Of particular importance - and often forgotten - is the impact of the invasion on women. Apart from the moral degradation faced by them when trapped by undisciplined soldiery, it has since been calculated that out of every 100 married women at least three lost a husband (male protector and breadwinner), brother or child, either dead or missing. This is a frightening statistic and one that has had dramatic effects on the renowned Cypriot close family unit. Whether it is a sign of the times or simply due to or accelerated by the effects of the new situation the age-long supportive family entity has shown signs of cracking - and, at times, directly from the centre.

Life in a refugee camp was harsh. It was back to basics!

7) In cultural, educational and social fields, Cyprus once more, has not stood still. In relation to population, it ranks among the first countries in the world in terms of university degree holders. The establishment of the Cyprus University in 1989 has given a further boost to the educational standards of the islanders. It must not be forgotten that a large percentage (31.20) of elementary schools and an equally impressive proportion (38.80) of higher education schools remained behind Turkish lines in 1974.

The state encourages all worthwhile intellectual creativity - an activity which is a fundamental element in any country's existence. Cypriots in fact have survived as a people through so many adversities in the course of time because they created a culture, an identity and kept it. Poets, literary writers and others are essential to the preservation of a culture as blood is to the continuing functioning of the human body. Creativity, courage, determination and initiative are all deep-set aspects of the proud inhabitants of Cyprus. Worldwide, the islanders have excelled themselves in many fields.

Two other related social phenomena must be added. Cyprus is a law-abiding society and a safe place to live and operate from. Yearly Interpol statistics reveal that the volume of crime stands at very impressive levels compared to other EU countries. Secondly, it must be emphasised that Cyprus is an epidemic-free country with first class medical and health care facilities. There are general hospitals in all the towns and also a good number of specialist clinics. Life expectancy currently stands at around 81 years for females and 76 years for males.

8) Also of great significance is the fact that a large part of Cyprus' centuries-old cultural heritage, represented by archaeological sites, monuments and museums, are now either damaged or destroyed and thus in great need of preservation and care. Undoubtedly, the cultural heritage of a people is its most important asset, its identity and sense of continuation through time. Listed below is a very brief description of some of the major monuments of this inestimable archaeological wealth, which has formed the basis of the cultural existence and heritage of the island and the chief factor of its tourist development:

**Salamis** the illustrious kingdom of Evagoras, Onesilos and Nicocreon and the glorious and cosmopolitan capital of the island during classical, Hellenistic and early Byzantine periods with its unique treasures - theatres, gymnasium and baths, forum and temples - is perhaps the greatest casualty of the 1974 invasion.

**Enkomi-Alasia** one of the most significant commercial centres of the period 1,600 to 1,050 BC, is another area rich in such monuments.

**Medieval Famagusta** the unrivalled commercial and cultural centre of the eastern Mediterranean in Frankish and Venetian times, is another casualty. The Venetian walls, which are preserved in their entirety,

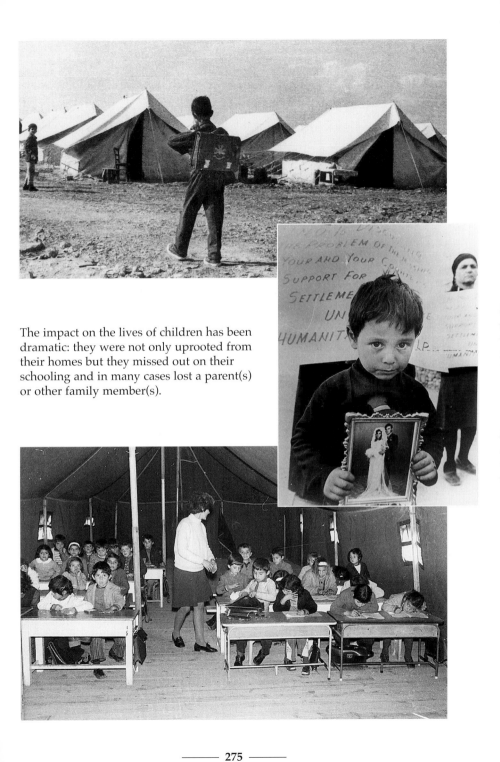

The impact on the lives of children has been dramatic: they were not only uprooted from their homes but they missed out on their schooling and in many cases lost a parent(s) or other family member(s).

Othello Tower and the stately Gothic Cathedral of St. Nicholas are amongst the most important medieval monuments of the island.

**Bellapais Abbey** is the only Frankish monastic establishment preserved in the island and together with the Cathedral of St. Sophia (Nicosia) and St. Nicholas (Famagusta),represent the island's Gothic monastic and church architecture.

**The Medieval castles** of Kyrenia, St. Hilarion, Buffavento and Kantara, so important in the defence of the island in years gone by, are also behind Turkish lines.

**Soloi** the kingdom of Philokypros and Pasikrates was one of the most famous cities of Classical, Hellenistic and Roman times.

**Vouni Palace,** the **Temple of Athena** and scores of other Byzantine monasteries and churches, with their superb exhibits and monuments are also in the occupied north.

9) Lastly, it must be stressed that in spite of the political and other hurdles, Cyprus has transformed itself from a relatively poor agricultural society into one with an enviable standard of living, a growing export-oriented industry, a modernising agricultural sector, an attractive base for big companies and an internationally recognised tourist centre. Moreover, the island has become an ideal place for business and inter-state conferences, international seminars and other specialist annual meetings. Cyprus' ideal geographical position, pleasant climate and excellent conference facilities are certainly factors which sway decisions in its favour.

So much for the effects on and present realities of the Cypriot scene. On the political field we must mention the following:

Turkey had at last realised its long-standing objective. Ecevit, hailed as the 'second Ataturk', at one time alleged that such intervention was made to protect the independence of the infant republic and restore its constitutional order. On another occasion, through Osman Olcay, its permanent representative at the UN, Ankara supported the view that the aim of the invasion was to protect and liberate the island's oppressed Turkish minority. Both arguments were propagated with relentless zeal since the mid-1950s

It is now universally accepted that the coup was not directed against the Turkish community, nor did Turkey bring to Cyprus peace other than 'the peace of the grave'. But as this naked act of aggression was bound to offend international public opinion, Turkey attempted to cover up her aims by invoking the 'legal fiction' that her armies came to Cyprus in exercise of her rights under **Article IV of the Treaty of Guarantee**. This reads as follows:

In the event of a breach of the provisions of the present Treaty, Greece, Turkey and the UK undertake to consult together with respect to the representations or measures necessary to ensure observance to those provisions.

In so far as common concerted action may not prove possible, each of the guaranteeing Powers reserves the right to take action with the sole aim of re-establishing the state of affairs created by the present Treaty.

It is, therefore, clear and unambiguous. Turkey could not intervene unilaterally unless common or concerted action proved impossible after consultation among the three countries. Even then intervention should have been limited to the sole aim of *'re-establishing the state of affairs created by the treaty'*, which is the constitutional order of 1960 and nothing else. Turkey's action was also contrary to the Agreed Minute signed by the Foreign Ministers of Britain, Turkey and Greece on 19 February 1959. It included the commitment, as guarantors, to consult among themselves regarding the common defence of Cyprus. Moreover, Article II of the Treaty of Alliance expressly states that *"the high Contracting Parties undertake to resist any attack of aggression, direct or indirect, directed against the independence or the territorial integrity of the Republic of Cyprus"*. Such action was also directly contrary to their obligations to NATO. Moreover, it was a smack in the face to all the universally acclaimed UN declarations and charters. Not only did Turkey, in furtherance of her ulterior motives, avoid meaningful consultations but she also spared no effort to dismember Cyprus and destroy what she herself had guaranteed.

The timely release of British documents in January 2005 - conforming of course to the 30 year rule stipulation - provide us with further evidence on which to base our conclusions. However, for the sake of clarification and historical accuracy, the following should be brought to the attention of readers. Even as late as 25 September 1970 the FCO was saying that, *"we take"* our obligation to *"guarantee the independence and territorial integrity of Cyprus...seriously"*. Was that the case in 1974?

In the face of this gross breach of such treaties and declarations, Britain and Greece avoided taking any action to protect the island. To quote the words of the House of Commons Select Committee on Cyprus which reported in 1976:

*"Britain had the legal right, a moral obligation, and the military capacity to intervene in Cyprus during July and August 1974. She did not intervene for reasons which the Government refuses to give..."*

Yet in other situations like the Falklands in April 1982, Britain

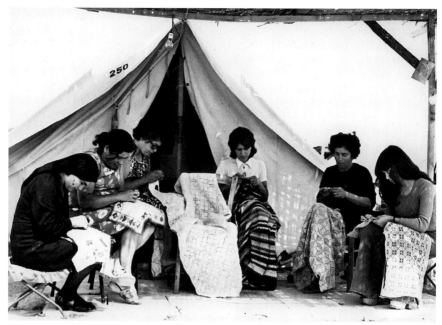

The reconstruction had to start without delay.
*Above:* Refugee women engrossed in making the traditional Cypriot lace –
popularly known as "Lefkaritica.
*Below:* A set of postage stamps showing an atmosphere of destruction and
reconstruction.

engaged in a war with Argentina for the sake of around 1,800 islanders situated in the South Atlantic and approximately 13,000 km from the UK. In the case of Cyprus, the British Foreign Secretary suggested that there was no moral obligation to intervene because the Treaty of Guarantee, though not formally abrogated, was in practice *'a dead letter'*. The fact remains however that Britain had not honoured its signature and its obligations as a guarantor of the independence and territorial integrity of Cyprus. Furthermore, all its actions point to collusion with and even capitulation to US foreign policy. Lord Caradon (formerly Sir Hugh Foot and last governor of the island) wrote in The Times on 17 April 1975 that:

> *"It is not possible to uncover or detect any British influence or initiative other than we should follow Dr. Kissinger. We have followed him with devastating and shameful results and failed to honour the British obligation as guarantor of the Cyprus people...."*

Britain had in fact sent a token task force to Cyprus. On its own however, it was not an adequate deterrent to prevent a Turkish invasion. Kissinger vetoed joint action and Greece's contribution was even less of an obstacle. Since there was no effective military opposition the Turks pushed ahead with their plans.

It must not be forgotten that as long ago as 1964 Acheson had attempted to partition the island. The double annexation of Cyprus would have meant the establishment of American and NATO bases there to serve the large western interests in the area. George Ball was even saying in 1964 that a Greek Cyprus would be hard for the Turks to accept but that it would be *"better than a Cuba off their shores"* and it *"would have the advantage of being in the NATO ambit"*. This solution would have filled the vacuum left by Britain in the Middle East. It was, as we have seen, rejected. Yet Acheson and others still persevered. Thus, in a speech at Salem College in North Carolina on 27 October 1966, he declared that a solution could be imposed on Cyprus by the use of superior arms. Furthermore, in November 1973, at a well-attended seminar in Rome, that seasoned US diplomat **Cyrus Vance** warned that if there was another crisis in Cyprus his country would not attempt to stop the Turks. Those present included Averoff, Bitsios, Clerides, Denktash and other leading politicians and scholars. In 1964 and 1967 however, the US managed to hold back the Turks after they planned to move in on Cyprus. Why not in 1974? Several possible reasons can be discerned;

1) The Cyprus question was dragging on for far too long and Turkey was growing impatient over the impasse. In 1974, Ecevit was able to tell Sisco, the American intermediary, described by Kissinger as a *"crisis manager par excellence"*, that *"this time sir, we will decide what to do"*. Of course the Sisco mission carried no proposals whatsoever. Did Kissinger re-activate the double-enosis partitionist plans of the mid-1960s?

An economic miracle followed the tragic events of 1974. Reforestation, new roads *(above)*, new industries, new airports and new harbours *(Limassol below)* contributed to the revival of the economy.

2) Cyprus' move towards the non-aligned camp and the fear of a possible leftist advance in the island. For many years the alarm over the advance of communism was at the centre of all western political thinking

3) The Greek military government's policy inconsistencies (tolerance, non-policy, misjudgements) were surfacing more and more. Popular resistance was certainly making a comeback. And, what can we make of the secret Graeco-Turkish negotiations over the fate of Cyprus especially in 1970-71?

4) The ill-prepared Cypriot forces were not capable of resisting any invasion of note. The internal chaos created by the activities of EOKA-B was highly significant if this factor is analysed carefully.

5) The unsettled and insecure Middle East situation was made more dangerous by the so-called Yom Kippur War, between the Israelis and Arabs, which broke out in October 1973. The Americans and Kissinger in particular, concluded as early as the 1950s that Cyprus was destined to serve as an allied staging post for the highly volatile eastern Mediterranean region. A similar role was earmarked for Britain itself in any European offensive.

6) The Soviet Union, unlike its declared strong pro-Cypriot independence position in 1963-64 and 1967, appeared to have taken a *'non-active stance'* over Cyprus during the crucial few months before the coup and invasion. Superpower collusion? Who knows? What did Kissinger and Gromyko discuss in June 1974?

7) It appears that the leadership of Ismet İnönü (1963-64) and Suleyman Demirel (1967) were very reluctant to take unnecessary military risks but in 1974, Ecevit was far more assertive and his generals were confident of carrying out a successful operation by land, sea and air.

Hence the US decided not to prevent this massive aggression. A war between Greece and Turkey would have put in danger NATOs vital *"southern anchor"* and would have opened the door to potential Soviet political and military exploitation in the eastern Mediterranean. Although the Americans thought that the Greek Cypriots had a fair case their regional and international strategic policy dictated that they should support Turkey. In this respect nothing has changed since the Truman Doctrine of 1947. America simply places greater importance to Turkey than to Greece. The US knew of the pending coup and invasion through the CIA and through its orbiting satellites but allowed it to happen and so can be accused of manipulating the whole Cyprus tragedy. In fact, an hour after the *'uprising'* had begun US intelligence had intercepted a message from the rebels to the Greek junta which read *"Operation President is underway and on schedule"*. Its indecision and obsession with not antagonizing Ankara only served to give Turkey a free hand in Cyprus. An American study mission report concluded in September 1974 that, '*US policy towards Cyprus seems to have been one of hasty improvisation which failed badly'*. Congressional debates and the American press also condemned the White House's ill-considered and short-sighted Cyprus policy. The administration proceeded to justify its actions by saying that, at worst, the Cyprus calamities were a result of a policy error and not of a conspiracy.

History is still too raw to judge Dr. Kissinger but his role, complicity or otherwise in this unfortunate tragedy is, to say the least, highly questionable. Those who contend that Kissinger was '*innocent'* explain:

1) He was simply reacting to developments and appeared therefore not to have had a Cyprus plan; his policy was '*undefined'* and '*uncertain'*. He was simply letting things take their course and had a '*softly, softly approach'*. He not only dismissed Cyprus as a study of "*ethnic conflict"* but he hardly ever cared about the island and often said that he did not understand the Graeco-Turkish conflict. Kissinger simply wanted Cyprus to go away and not bother him. He later explained that the tragic events in Cyprus were the result of a "*massive misjudgement"* by Ioannides. His apologists contend therefore that the coup and invasion caught the Americans by surprise.

2) His boundless energies were centred elsewhere. He stated that there were more pressing problems in other parts of the world. American diplomatic efforts in 1974 were largely reserved for the Middle East where Kissinger spent a great deal of time travelling from one country to another endeavouring to construct a lasting peace. With some justification the year 1974 was termed "*the year of revolutions"*. The overthrow of the Caetano regime in Portugal, of the junta in Greece and that of Emperor Haile Selassie in Ethiopia are massive examples justifying the above contention. In addition, the Arab oil embargo and the colossal increases in the price of oil, had far-reaching effects on the American decision making process. And, let us not forget the huge problems over Cambodia, Chile and East Timor. In addition the American-Chinese relations were in the "doldrums" and there was no prospect of a spectacular development on that front.

3) The Watergate scandal caused a temporary breakdown in Washington's action-taking procedures. On 5 August, Nixon admitted to the nation that he had been withholding information on Watergate. On the 9th he resigned. He was "morally convicted of political chicanery." Dr. Kissinger remarked that the conduct of American foreign policy under the "shoulder of Watergate was a nightmare."

4) It was suggested that Turkey would have opted out of NATO if at least some of its wishes were not adhered to.

5) Kissinger explained that he hated the colonels and hoped that their failure in Cyprus would lead to their downfall and to the return of

democracy in Greece. Yet, the CIA was very close to most of the junta leaders! Are we witnessing government on two levels? One official and the other 'unofficial'.

The anti - Kissinger lobby is equally vociferous. They argue that:

1) Kissinger was at the time of the crisis not only Secretary of State but also National Security Adviser. This dual role gave him unprecedented control over both foreign policy and covert intelligence operations.

2) Kissinger did not like Makarios or at least he could not tolerate him. According to him the Cypriot President was more of a *"nuisance than a menace"* and even described him as a *"high-wire artist"* but who was nevertheless *"a big man in a world not blessed with an excess of them"*. However, Kissinger's near pathological dislike of Makarios usually clouded his judgement.

3) Evidence suggests that Kissinger appeared to have neutralised all meaningful efforts undertaken by the State Department to avoid the escalation of the crisis. He simply ignored his own officials and even removed them from their posts. Witness the fate of Thomas Boyatt, head of the Cyprus desk at the State Department. His critics described his behaviour over Cyprus as *"fatal and highly undiplomatic'*. Undoubtedly, Kissinger was an extraordinarily intelligent man but manipulative and secretive who even wire-tapped his aides and officials. He has a temperamental, indeed mercurial personality and adapts tactics according to whether he is serious, irritable or frivolous. A man of very considerable intellectual and moral stature who did however have a tendency to "personify" his international relations.

One of the cartoons of the time depicting the suspicion over Kissinger's one-sided involvement

4) Historical research, to date, seems to imply that Kissinger's diplomacy was predominant both in 1973 and in 1974. Documents released lately in the US suggest that he carried on regardless of Nixon's wishes (a President who was absorbed, shamed and finally ousted from power by the events triggered by the Watergate scandal) and secretly confided (contrary to what appears in his memoirs and other writings) that both the Arab-Israeli War and the Cyprus invasion were *"best-run-crises"*. British records released in 1973 have unearthed a conundrum. Intelligence has concluded that the US, who came close to an armed conflict with the Soviet Union after the Yom Kippur War of 1973, appeared to have been ready to use force in order to seize the Middle East oil fields. Alternatively, the US was prepared to replace the existing rulers of Saudi Arabia, Kuwait and Abu Dhabi, with ones more amenable to Western policies and to provide them with military and other support. In other words US aims in the area, beyond those of deterring the Soviets and thwarting their influence and expansion are/were to bring Middle Eastern nations into the US-led orbit in order to ensure that they would cooperate strategically in wartime and allow therefore western corporations to develop and control their petroleum resources in peacetime. This was what the Truman Doctrine (1947) was all about, as well as the Eisenhower and Carter Doctrines of 1957 and 1980 respectively: *"Oil and Western/US control of it"*.

Whether it was action on his part or simply inaction, the events of 1974 in Cyprus could have been prevented if the necessary political will existed in the capitals of the interested parties. Blame, therefore must be shared, though not equally, between Washington, Ankara, Athens, Nicosia and Moscow.

Although the crisis of 1974 was only one of a series in the history of this tragic island, it was the greatest and most crucial because it threatened its destruction as a viable and independent state. From the beginning of the invasion Turkey followed its pre-arranged and well-organised '**Attila Plan**'[5] to remove the Greek population in the Turkish occupied areas; to alter the demographic status of Cyprus by the importation of Turks from the mainland; to ruin or usurp the sources of livelihood of the Greek Cypriots and to create such *faits accomplis* as would influence the solution of the Cyprus problem in favour of Turkey's objective. This objective is a *de facto* partition of the island under the guise of a loose federation, which would enable her, for the present, to exercise political and military control of the '*whole*' territory but would lay the foundations for the possible annexation of the entire island.

Four other events are worth noting at this juncture:

---

(5) Attila was the notorious King of the Huns c. 406-53 and is remembered for his savagery, murder and arson.

*Firstly*, the junta in Greece, under the pressure of public indignation, was forced to resign. After seven years, democracy had returned. Karamanlis was recalled from Paris and on the following morning (24 July) he was sworn in as Prime Minister. This transition however, on top of the other domestic and foreign difficulties, resulted in a brief period of complete inaction. Meanwhile Cyprus was burning.

*Secondly*, the illegal government in Cyprus established by the coup found itself unable to stay in office: Sampson resigned on 23 July and was replaced on the same day, by Glafcos Clerides, the President of the House of Representatives. He in turn gave way to Makarios when he returned in December 1974.

*Thirdly*, after the 20th, the UN limited itself to the passage of resolutions which Turkey completely ignored. It refused to comply either with Security Council resolution 353 of 20 July or with resolution 354 of 23 July which among other things called for an immediate cease-fire, urged an end to foreign intervention and the withdrawal of all foreign troops and finally requested the three guarantor powers to start negotiations for a settlement. The Greek Cypriots complied with the cease-fire demand of 20 July but the Turks did not. Meeting no resistance they repeatedly violated it, thus realising their objective of occupying about 37 per cent of the island's territory.

*Fourthly*, a preliminary cease-fire was reached on 22 July, leading to the first Geneva Conference. The Foreign Ministers of the UK, Turkey and Greece held lengthy negotiations from 25 to 30 July. Even though several ideas and suggestions were discussed, the cease-fire was continuously broken by the advancing Turkish troops. Nevertheless, the three delegations recognised the importance of setting in motion measures to regularise the situation in the island, having regard to the international agreement signed in Nicosia on 16 August 1960 and to resolution 353 of 20 July approved by the Security Council. The participants declared that in order to stabilise the situation the areas controlled by opposing armed forces on 30 July at 22.00 hours Geneva time should not be extended. They called on all forces, including irregular ones, to desist from all hostile activities. A new meeting in which representatives of the two Cypriot communities would participate was also outlined. However, the Geneva Declaration signed at 9. p.m. on 30 July proved to be worthless.

The second Geneva Conference attended by the three ministers for foreign affairs and on the following day by Clerides and Denktash, duly met on 8 August. Following heated arguments over the existence or non-existence of the 1960 constitution (Callaghan explained that he recognised only that of 1960) specific proposals for the settlement of the Cyprus problem were tabled by Clerides, Denktash and Gunes. It became clear that Turkey had not gone to Geneva to negotiate but to issue an ultimatum - the acceptance immediately of either of its two plans, both based on Turkish administration of 34% of the island's territory: in one case a single area in the north running from Limnitis on the west coast through Lefka, Morphou, the old city of Nicosia and ending at the old city of Famagusta, and in the other a smaller area in the north and five areas around the main towns. The second plan based on cantons put forward by Gunes had to be accepted by Greece and Cyprus on the spot. At 8 p.m. on 13 August, Mavros and Clerides asked for 36 hours to consult their governments. Gunes refused.

Callaghan explained that 36 hours' grace was justifiable and that all diplomatic avenues had not been fully explored. He accused his Turkish counterpart of being unreasonable. Gunes not only disagreed but remarked later that Callaghan was no more than a *"perfect telephone receptionist"*. The conference broke down at 3 a.m. on 14 August. Insistence on the bi-regional federation concept finally knocked the conference for six. At 4. 30 a.m. Turkish forces began operations which included the bombing of towns. Dhekelia was also threatened. Turkey's prearranged tactics had triumphed. Its forces had occupied that area defined at Geneva plus another 3% bringing it to 37%, thus instituting the 'Attila' or 'Sahin' (Falcon) line an artificial boundary separating the Greeks and Turks of Cyprus. The Attila II operation or second invasion was thus completed. Kissinger once more remarked that the Turks had cut *"the Gordian Knot"* and thus invaded Cyprus.

On 14, 15, 16 and 30 August, the Security Council issued new resolutions (making 8 since 20 July), calling for the immediate termination of military operations, the withdrawal of all foreign troops and the resumption of talks. These recommendations were once more wholly disregarded by Turkey. A General Assembly resolution 3212 (XXIX) adopted on 1 November 1974 by 117 votes, none against and no abstentions, which was of similar content, was also ignored by the Turks. The view expressed by the Americans was/is that winning resolutions or scoring points at the UN is *"useless"* since that *"will only buy you a cappucino!"* In fact the only agreement reached between the cease-fire of 16 August and the end of September was the one between Clerides and Denktash for the release of all prisoners of war. This was signed on 20 September.

However, the second phase of the Cyprus operation strained Turkey's relations with the UK, the USSR and finally the US. On 22 August Turkey, who were not alone, rejected Soviet proposals for a wider international conference. The US Congress voted repeatedly to cut off military aid to Turkey without however inducing it to make any concessions of substance.

On 7 December 1974, Makarios returned to Cyprus. Almost half the Greek population gathered in Nicosia on that day to welcome him.

Addressing his people from the archbishopric, he declared a general amnesty for those who were involved in the July coup by saying "*I forgive them all for their sins*" and also extended a hand of friendship to the Turkish community by repeating that talks were wanted "*for the bridging of our differences, for the finding of a lasting solution*".

Even though the intercommunal talks were resumed on 14 January 1975 the Turks used them as a pretext to gain time and bring about new

Some 200,000 Cypriots turned up to greet Makarios when he returned to Cyprus on 7 December 1974.

*faits accomplis.* The divergences in the views of the two sides on settling the problem have been described as being *'wider than the Aegean Sea'* - another and possibly greater, Graeco-Turkish irritant.

A comparison of the first two proposals by each side (taken from the abortive meetings of January-February 1975) will suffice to illustrate this contention.

Where the Greeks spoke of Cyprus as being an *'independent sovereign republic'*, the Turks desired to see an *'independent and secular republic'*. The Greeks wished that the *'constitution shall be that of a bicommunal, multi-regional federal state'*, but the Turks demanded that *'there shall be made a constitution for a bicommunal and biregional federal state'*. Thus from the Turkish point of view the only realistic solution was a federation composed of two ethnic groups. In their opinion any future political settlement should be based on three principles:

1) A bizonal federation;

2) The establishment of a central government with limited powers;

3) The participation of the two national communities in central government on an equal footing.

And in furtherance of their set policies, they proceeded on 13 February 1975 to proclaim a *'Turkish Federated State of Cyprus'* (TFSC) in the occupied area of the island . The Security Council met on 20 February to take up the complaint of the Republic's government about the illegal declaration. Resolution 367, adopted by consensus (without a vote) on 12 March expressed regret at this unilateral declaration. It also requested the UN Secretary-General to convene new discussions under his personal auspices.

Nicosia became a divided city and the once prosperous commercial area now became a ghost place

*(photo Doros Partasides)*

# Post 1974 Talks

Discussions took place in Vienna between 28 April and 3 May, (the *'first'* round) as well as between 5 and 7 June 1975. There was no progress. However, a *third* and *fourth* round soon took place in the Austrian capital between 31 July and 2 August and in New York on 8 and 9 September. At the third round it was agreed that 9,000 Turkish Cypriots from the Greek-controlled southern part of the island should be allowed to join their compatriots in the northern area and that the 10,000 Greek Cypriots already in the north should be allowed to stay and be joined by 800 of their relatives from the south. Other issues discussed included the jurisdiction of a possible federal government. Clerides told a press conference on 3 August that the Turkish Cypriot side had committed itself to produce a comprehensive plan for solving all aspects of the problem by the end of August. However, no such plan having been submitted, the fourth round of talks in New York was adjourned on 10 September after a brief formal session, no date being set for future negotiations.

Further talks were held in Vienna (*fifth round*) from 17 to 21 February 1976. The communiqué issued at their conclusion stated that:

1) Clerides and Denktash had held *'substantive discussions on the territorial and constitutional issues'*.

2) It had been agreed that an exchange of written proposals on both these issues would take place in Cyprus within the next six weeks.

3) The two negotiators would meet again in May *'with a view of establishing a common basis prior to referring the matter to mixed committees in Cyprus'*.

It seemed therefore that some progress towards a negotiated solution was achieved. The *fifth* round of talks were *'good, constructive and helpful'* according to Denktash. However, Clerides resigned on 7 April, after appearing to have made a secret *'procedural agreement'* with his co-negotiator without informing any member of the island's leadership.

The *'procedural agreement'* reached at the February discussions laid down that the Greek side would be the first to submit recommendations for a settlement and that the Turks would then have ten days in which to consider them before submitting their own proposals. But when Clerides tried to fulfil the agreement by handing Denktash a secret draft of the Greek proposals on 24 March, the latter reacted by disclosing publicly that he had received the draft and that he could not accept it. On the behaviour of the shrewd but highly unprincipled Turkish leader, a London-based newspaper recorded the following: *"There can be little doubt that his real aim in behaving as he did was to cause disarray on the Greek side and thus further delay any serious negotiation. He has already indicated that the replacement of Mr Clerides as negotiator by Mr Tasos Papadopoulos will entail a corresponding replacement of himself by a person with the same status."*[6]

The person chosen was Umit Suleyman Onan, then speaker of the TFSC constituent assembly. The first meeting between these two London trained lawyers took place on 27 May when they discussed humanitarian matters, principally the question of Greek Cypriots missing or living in the Turkish controlled north. At the time around 2,200 people were unaccounted for.

An event of much greater importance was to follow. More by design than by chance, Makarios received a letter from Denktash dated 6 January 1977 suggesting a meeting between them. They had not met since December 1963. The discussions took place on neutral UN ground on 27 January. Makarios stated later that the objective was *'to find common ground for a package deal'*. Denktash announced after this historic event that such fundamental aspects of the Cyprus question as the central administration, a federal system and the territorial issue were discussed.[7] In fact, the overall atmosphere had been friendly and a step had been taken towards the resumption of the intercommunal talks deadlocked for about a year. The meeting was described a *'breakthrough'*.

A second meeting between them, attended by Waldheim, took place (again in Nicosia) on 12 February 1977. It was agreed that the talks should be resumed. It appears that agreement, despite governmental murmurings, was reached on *four key guidelines*:

1) The aim was to establish an independent, non-aligned, bi-communal federal Republic.

2) The size of the territory under the administration of each community would be negotiated in the light of economic viability, productivity and property rights.

(3) Questions of principle such as freedom of movement, freedom of settlement and property rights would be open to discussion, taking into account the fundamental principle of a bi-communal federal system and certain practical difficulties which might arise for the Turkish Cypriot community.

4) The powers and functions of the central federal government would be such as to safeguard the unity of the country having regard to its bi-communal character.

---

(6) The Times. 15 April 1976. Page 15

7) For the first time the Turks voluntarily brought the territorial question under discussion which in the eyes of the Greeks was a matter of cardinal importance to any future settlement.

The UN Secretary-General (Kurt Waldheim) in direct negotiations with Cypriot leaders.
*Above:* With Makarios and Denktash, February 1977.
*Below:* With Kyprianou and Denktash, May 1979.

It was certainly a breakthrough and there was much optimism. In another effort to make further progress President Carter of the US dispatched Clark Clifford, a veteran White House confidant, on a nine day exploratory fact-finding trip to Europe beginning on 16 February 1977. On his return Clifford informed the international relations committee of the House of Representatives on 10 March that *with good faith on both sides a Cyprus settlement is definitely possible before the end of 1977*.

Vienna again hosted the *sixth* round of the intercommunal talks. They commenced on 31 March 1977. According to the map presented by Papadopoulos, 20% of the total area of Cyprus would remain under Turkish Cypriot administration. In the preparation of the map account was taken of the guidelines agreed between Makarios and Denktash in February on population, viability, productivity and land ownership. The Turks on the other hand, were talking of a weak central government to rule a strong bi-communal Cyprus and there were no territorial concessions. Although some progress had been made in clarifying positions, there was no hope of bridging the gap between the two sides in that round of negotiations. In accordance with the communiqué issued at the end of the talks (7 April) Papadopoulos and Onan met again in Nicosia on 26 May and 3 June but without making any further headway.

Meanwhile the embittered Cypriots went through another ordeal. At the age of 64, Archbishop Makarios died of a heart attack on 3 August 1977. After five days he was buried on a mountain peak overlooking the Kykko monastery following a funeral service in Nicosia attended by nearly 200 representatives from more than 50 countries. His premature death revived fears of renewed conflict in Cyprus. These fears however did not materialise. The mediocre, uninspiring but patriotic Spyros Kyprianou who succeeded him declared that he would *stay on the same course* in all fields. In fact, Cyprus was making advances everywhere. Culturally, economically and socially it achieved new heights - and the trend is still upwards.

The long-awaited Turkish *proposals* were handed to Waldheim on 13 April 1978 in Vienna. The procedural agreement reached when he met Kyprianou and Denktash in January was that detailed and comprehensive proposals should be given to him and that he should then hold consultations with both sides to establish whether or not they formed a basis on which he would be justified in recommending the resumption of the talks - suspended since April 1977. Instead, the UN Secretary-General was given a 34 page outline of the *main aspects* of the Turkish proposals and told that the full text would not be made available until the talks were reconvened. The Cyprus government rejected this proposition as *completely unacceptable* since it in no way formed a basis for the resumption of the intercommunal talks. Kyprianou said at a press conference on 19 April that they amounted to an attempt to *legalise and consolidate the faits accomplis and that their acceptance would mean a decision to commit suicide*.

*Above:* The highly popular President of Cyprus at a Commonwealth Conference, seen here in a *'privileged'* place, seated to the right of Queen Elizabeth II.
*Below:* The 'Great Father and Maker' of modern Cyprus died in August 1977. The roads leading to Kykko Monastery, his final resting place, were lined by thousands of grieving Cypriots.

Once again, the US attempted in 1978 to get some movement in the talks. Its so-called 'Framework for a Cyprus Settlement' was a 12 point plan, prepared jointly by the US, UK and Canada.[8] Although the document included several positive elements it was riddled with inconsistencies. It called however, for a reduction in the size of land held by the Turkish army and therefore for a return of a small part of the Varosha area (the modern suburb of Famagusta).

UN initiatives, however, resulted in a Kyprianou-Denktash meeting (18-19 May 1979) at which a *ten-point agreement* was reached.

1) The intercommunal talks should resume on 15 June.

2) The basis of the talks would be the Makarios-Denktash guidelines of 12 February 1977 and the UN resolutions relevant to the Cyprus question.

3) There should be respect for the human rights and fundamental freedoms of all the citizens of the Republic.

4) The talks would deal with the territorial and constitutional aspects.

5) Priority would be given to reaching agreement on the resettlement of Varosha under UN auspices.

6) All should abstain from any action which might jeopardise the outcome of the talks and special importance would be given to initial practical measures by both sides to promote goodwill, mutual confidence and the return to normal conditions.

7) The demilitarization of the island was envisaged and matters relating thereto would be discussed. It was submitted to the two communities in November 1978.

8) The independence, sovereignty, territorial integrity and non-alignment of the Republic should be adequately guaranteed against union in whole or in part with any other country and against any form of partition or secession.

9) The intercommunal talks would be carried out in a continuing and sustained manner, avoiding delay.

10) The intercommunal talks would take place in Nicosia.

The talks, the *seventh* round, which resumed on the agreed date (15 June) foundered on two major sticking points: the acceptance or rejection of a bizonal or bicommunal federal state and the Varosha issue. In an effort to break the deadlock, Waldheim proposed in 1980 various *alternative formulae* for the resumption of the talks. These were eventually

---

(8) It became known as the *Matthew Nimetz-Nelson Ledsky Plan*.

held on 9 August but again they proved abortive. So ended the *eighth* round of talks.

In 1981, expectations that during the summer there might at last be a step forward in the negotiations had been fuelled both by official statements and by press speculation. Firstly, a new cycle of discussions which began on 6 May gave the impression that they would be fruitful. Secondly, a report in the British Sunday Times on 24 May hinted that a solution envisaging two autonomous zones in loose confederation and the return of Famagusta, at first under temporary UN control, was on the cards.

Once more, nothing transpired. However on the same day that the above article was published, the people of the Republic went to the polls to elect a new house of representatives. The election was contested by seven parties and six independent candidates. In a turn-out of 95% there were no surprises.[9] It was dominated by AKEL, DESY, DEKO and EDEK parties. Between them they took over 93% of the total votes cast and all the 35 seats in the chamber of deputies. The electorate totalled 308,511 of which 1,505 were Maronites, 1,114 Armenians and 256 Latins.

Elections were also held on 28 June in the Turkish-occupied north. Comparing the results with those of the previous one we find:

|  | 1976 | 1981 |
|---|---|---|
| For Denktash as 'president' | 76% | 51.7% |
| For the 'assembly' of the TFSC and Denktash's National Unity Party | 53% | 42.6% |

The parties which increased their share at the expense of the NUP were the Communal Liberation Party (CLP) and the Republican Turkish Party (RTP), which stood against economic or political integration of the occupied areas with Turkey and Denktash's partitionist policy and called for a solution of real federation which would safeguard the unity of Cyprus. Omitting the votes of the mainland settlers, who constituted then around 25% of the population, it becomes evident that the overwhelming majority of the native electorate voted against Denktash and his policies.

There was yet another election in 1981. After 50 years of mainly conservative, and at times ultra-right rule, Greece elected on 18 October an unmistakably left-wing government. The long-awaited *'allaghi'* (change) had arrived. The Panhellenic Socialist Movement (PASOK) took 48.06% of the votes cast and 172 out of the 300 seats in the Vouli. The new government headed by **Andreas Papandreou** pledged its support for the territorial integrity and unity of the island.

---

(9) Voting is compulsory in Cyprus

In the same year an *'evaluation'* was prepared by Waldheim and was presented formally at the intercommunal talks of 18 November. As reported, this *'evaluation'* involved a negotiating basis allocating 70% of the area of the island (excluding the federal district) to the Greek Cypriots and 30% to the Turkish Cypriots but with the latter taking some 40% of the jobs in the public sector. It was also understood that the presidency would rotate between the two communities on an annual basis and there would be a six-member federal council in which four seats would be reserved for the Greek Cypriots and two for their compatriots. Moreover, each community would retain a large degree of veto power over major legislative and constitutional changes.

Nothing transpired from these *'proposals'*. On 13 May 1983, the UN General Assembly passed a resolution (37/253) calling, once more, for the withdrawal of all occupation forces from Cyprus and endorsed Kyprianou's call for a complete demilitarization of the island. The resolution was accepted by a vote of 103 to 5 with 20 abstentions.

Joining Turkey in opposing the measure were Pakistan, Somalia, Malaysia and Bangladesh. Denktash responded three days later by indicating that he would declare the northern part of the island an independent state. As we shall see below, he carried out his threat on 15 November.

A further *'initiative'* was undertaken by the new UN Secretary-General **Perez de Cuellar** on 8 August when he submitted a document to the two sides. He had undertaken to make a series of *'informal and confidential soundings'* in order to facilitate further discussion of the Cyprus problem. Again efforts were thwarted. On 15 November, the occupied part of the island was declared an independent state. This move was in contravention of all UN resolutions and was duly greeted with world-wide condemnation. Three days later, UN resolution 541/83 urged the international community not to recognise any Cypriot state other than the Republic of Cyprus. The resolution was adopted with 13 votes in favour, one against (Pakistan) and one abstention (Jordan).

The year 1984 opened very briskly. On 11 January a *'framework'* for a comprehensive settlement of the Cyprus problem had been submitted by Kyprianou to Perez de Cuellar. It was also explained to **Mrs. Thatcher**, the British Premier, on 18 January. Again all efforts proved abortive. Denktash proposed instead measures to legalise his *'illegal'* state. On 11 May 1984 the Security Council adopted resolution 550 by a vote of 13 in favour to one against (Pakistan) and one abstention (United States) and urged states to condemn all secessionist actions and requested that no one should recognise the purported state of the *'Turkish Republic of Northern Cyprus'*.

*Above:* Mrs Thatcher the British Prime Minister and Mr Kyprianou, President of the Republic during a meeting in January 1984.
*Below:* The Greek Prime Minister Andreas Papandreou during his visit to the island, in 1982. In Nicosia, he was warmly greeted by the Mayor, Lellos Demetriades and other prominent personalities.

Perez de Cuellar continued his initiative with a series of *'proximity'* talks. He met Kyprianou and Denktash in Vienna on 6-7 August. They agreed to enter into such talks in New York. The first round ended on 20 September 1984 and the second in October. The third round took place between 26 November and 12 December. It appeared that the Turkish Cypriots had agreed to reduce the area under their control to about 20% and to waive their claim to a rotating presidency. The Greek Cypriots also appeared to have adopted the principle of the equal representation of the two communities in the upper house of a bi-cameral legislature. *"Some optimism is justified"* remarked Mr. Kyprianou.

Summit talks opened in January 1985. The UN was very active with its draft plans. The Secretary-General had several meetings with Kyprianou and Denktash. These high-level direct talks which took place in New York between 17 and 20 January, intended to follow up the progress made at the proximity talks and conclude *"an agreement"*. Nothing happened. Shrewd commentators have pointed out that during the whole affair of the 1985 meetings in New York - where the Greek Cypriots were in the end perceived as the intransigent party - the UN Secretary-General became an appendix to the US State Department. The Greek Cypriots were outmanoeuvred and belittled by the US/UN combination. Support was evidently for the secessionist minority backed by Turkey. The Secretary-General however, in his efforts to find a breakthrough, submitted an *"integrated"* document in April, but Denktash proved uncooperative. Geneva and London then hosted a series of *low level* technical talks during the autumn and winter of 1985-86 under the auspices of the UN. At the end of three rounds the Secretary-General produced a *'Draft Financial Agreement'* which he submitted to the two sides on 29 March 1986.

Yet the Cyprus question remained at an impasse. The Soviet Union also put forward a plan on 21 January 1986. It called for a comprehensive, just and durable solution. Demilitarization was a must the proposals pointed out. Above all, international guarantees should rule out the possibility of any foreign interference. Hopes were raised however, by two events:

1) While attending the World Economic Forum at Davos, Switzerland on 30-31 January 1988, Papandreou and Ozal (the Greek and Turkish Premiers) held two day talks on bilateral relations. It was the first substantive meeting between the leaders of the two countries for ten years. Furthermore in June, Ozal paid the first visit to Greece by a Turkish Premier since 1952. It was said by officials that in the case of both Cyprus and the Aegean, a mechanism had been set up to begin resolving both issues.

This thaw in the relations between the two countries plus Turkey's desire to join the Common Market[10] has raised hopes for an early solution. *If* Turkey is serious in joining and *if* the other European countries stick to their founding Charter and insist on admitting only states with a clear-cut commitment to freedom, justice and democracy, then the world can rest assured that the islanders will celebrate a demilitarized and united Cyprus. Two big *ifs* but history has shown more difficult and delicate issues were resolved when justice, willingness, tact, courage and fairness prevailed over petty-mindedness, economic and military considerations.

2) On 21 February 1988, George Vassiliou was elected President of Cyprus for a 5 year term - securing 51.63% of the votes in one of the closest run-off elections in the island's history. At once Vassiliou proclaimed that he would revive the national council, as originally set up by Makarios, which would function as a permanent institution and aim to chart *"a collective policy and planning for the joint laying down of the strategy and tactics of the struggle for the salvation of Cyprus"*.

He also declared that he was willing to meet Denktash and or Ozal to study ways of approaching the island's problems thus leading to a final solution. Meeting in Geneva on 24 August, at a working lunch given by Perez de Cuellar, Vassiliou and Denktash agreed to resume intercommunal talks in Nicosia on 15 September. In a statement issued after the luncheon de Cuellar announced that both had agreed to mediate without preconditions and to attempt to achieve a negotiated settlement on all aspects of the Cyprus problem by *"1 June 1989"*.

Talks have continued since August under the new procedure that had been agreed in New York last November. According to this new formula a wide range of options were being considered on a non-committal basis in an effort to find common ground. Thus the propositions of the Greek Cypriots were submitted on 30 January 1989 to the Turkish leader. The proposals which took into account the concerns of the island's inhabitants, aimed at establishing an independent, sovereign, territorially-integral, non-aligned, federal republic. The document approved by the Republic's national council, was entitled *'Outline Proposals for the Establishment of a Federal Republic and for a Solution of the Cyprus Problem'*.

That round of intercommunal talks - designed to produce a lasting settlement of the Cyprus problem - began in August 1988. In a series of meetings since then, culminating at the session in New York (28-29 June 1989) Vassiliou and Denktash, in the presence of Oscar Camilion and or Perez de Cuellar, examined various *options* or *alternatives*, for all aspects of the problem. And in an effort to facilitate discussions the Secretary-General presented in July 1989 ideas which were described as *"food for thought"*.

---

(10) Now called the European Union. Greece a member since January 1981 can veto any Turkish (or other) application. Cyprus joined the EU on 1 May 2004

Two photos showing the intense talks that took place between the two leaders in 1988-89. *Above:* Seen on the table are Denktash *(left)*, George Vasiliou *(centre)* and Oscar Camilion *(right)* the special UN representative at the time.
*Below:* the two leaders shared a hopeful handshake which in the end did not produce results.

Cypriots and the world could only wait. It is important to note however that towards the end of May 1989 a decisive step was taken to reduce tension in Cyprus' divided capital. Twenty-four military posts along Nicosia's demarcation *(green line)* were *unmanned*. Was this a pointer towards a settlement? Once more, expectations were dashed. On 23 August, the *'assembly'* of the pseudostate in the Turkish-occupied part approved a resolution imposing conditions for the resumption of talks, to change the basis and procedure of such discussions by imposing new and unacceptable conditions. Nevertheless, the UN Secretary-General continued his efforts to find common ground for meaningful negotiations. The Non-Aligned Movement and other countries, such as the UK, were throwing their weight behind those activities.

The dramatic changes towards more open societies and freedom of movement in Eastern Europe and the destruction of the *Berlin Wall* on 8 November 1989 (Germany was re-united on 3 October 1990), brought new hopes to the Cypriots that 1990 will bring the desired solution. Nicosia, they said, must not remain the only divided city in Europe.

However, another high level meeting in New York between 26 February and 2 March 1990 again ended inconclusively. The Turkish side set unacceptable preconditions. This prompted the Security Council to adopt resolution 649/90 on 12 March reiterating the agreed basis of the Cyprus talks and rejecting Turkish Cypriot demands. However, the resolution, and probably for the first time, called upon the two leaders in Cyprus to cooperate with him on an *"equal footing"*. Even so, UN aides proceeded to bring the two sides within the *'agreement range'* for the convening of another meeting in New York and on 11 October 1991, (resolution 716) the Security Council unanimously reaffirmed its wish to see a settlement which excluded any form of union, partition or secession.

Following a series of meetings of his representative in Nicosia, Athens and Ankara, the new UN Secretary-General, Boutros Boutros-Ghali, issued a report to the Security Council on 3 April 1992. In it he included his suggestions that had evolved from such consultations. It endorsed his *'set of ideas'* with resolution 750 of 10 April 1992 which also reasserted its position that a settlement must be based on a state of Cyprus with a single sovereignty.

Further UN-sponsored meetings, described as a *'new critical round'*, took place between 15 July and 14 August 1992 in New York. Discussions during this period were based on an expanded version of the *'set of ideas'* on which a map was also annexed reflecting UN proposals on the territorial issue. Following the report of the Secretary-General on these meetings, the Security Council approved resolution 774 (26 August) which endorsed the expanded version of the *'set of ideas'* and the attached map as a basis for reaching an overall agreement.

The next round of meetings in New York lasted between 26 October and 11 November 1992 and at its completion the UN prepared a document codifying the positions put forward during the course of the previous months. The codification demonstrated how intransigent the positions of the Turkish Cypriot side were on most of the key issues under discussion. This was reaffirmed in the Security Council resolution 789 of 25 November 1992.

Following the presidential elections in Cyprus on 14 February 1993, Glafcos Clerides was sworn in as its fourth President on 28 February. The new government gave priority to the continuation of the talks and during the course of a high-level meeting in New York on 24 May 1993 the Secretary-General presented the two sides with a document for the implementation of a package of *confidence-building measures* (CBM's). The main measures provided for the return of some 16,000 Greek Cypriot refugees to the fenced part of the Turkish occupied town of Varosha and the re-opening, also under UN administration, of Nicosia's International Airport.

In July 1993, UN envoys started a new round of consultations in Nicosia, Ankara and Athens with a view to promoting the package of CBM's. Similar contacts were held by the representatives of the US State Department. During these meetings Rauf Denktash maintained his objections which led Boutros-Ghali to make the following statement in his report to the Security Council on 14 September: *"I am obliged to report that the Turkish Cypriot side has not yet shown the goodwill and cooperation required to achieve an agreement on the package. Its campaign of disinformation has been contrary to the undertaking by Mr. Denktash on June 1 to promote acceptance of the package"*.

Similarly on 30 May 1994, the Secretary-General issued his long-awaited report in which he stated that *"for the present the Security Council finds itself faced with a familiar scenario: the absence of agreement due essentially to lack of political will on the Turkish Cypriot side"*. Indirectly, he put blame on Turkey for the lack of progress. And, amid a number of negative Turkish statements, the Security Council approved resolution 939/94 of 29 July which reasserted its position that a Cyprus settlement must be based on a bi-communal, bizonal federal state with a single sovereignty and international personality and a single citizenship. It also called on the Secretary-General to begin consultations with all interested parties with a view to undertaking a fundamental and far-reaching reflection on the ways of approaching the problem in a manner that would yield results. The Greek Cypriot side welcomed the resolution whereas the Turkish Cypriot leadership, in unison with Ankara, rejected it. Moreover on 29 August the *'assembly'* in occupied Cyprus decided to abandon *'federation'* as the sole form of settlement. This decision was in gross violation of high-level agreements of 1977 and 1979, as well as with all UN resolutions.

In order to break the deadlock, the Secretary-General called Clerides and Denktash to hold informal meetings with his deputy special representative in Nicosia. Five such meetings took place between 18 and 31 October in which both the substance of the Cyprus problem and the package of CBM's were discussed. The effort ended in failure as a result of the Turkish Cypriot insistence on separate sovereignty. The year 1995

Glafkos Clerides, the veteran politician and the island's 4th president, 1993–2003.

was rather uneventful but in January 1996 the office of the US President announced a new American initiative for a solution within the context of the UN process. US, British and other diplomats visited Cyprus with a view to examining ways of restarting negotiations. The link with Cyprus' application to join the EU, became more and more apparent. Suffice it to say that as late as 1994 Washington and, therefore Ankara, were vehemently opposed to such an application. The critical turning point in Washington's policy appears to have come in 1995 under the stewardship of Richard Holbrooke, Assistant Secretary for European Affairs. Officials in Washington were apprehensive that a Turkey not integrated in the political institutions of Europe might drift towards radical ethnocentrism and fundamentalism. For Holbrooke, Turkey had to be *"anchored to the West"*. He believed that this was the critical component for stability in the highly volatile Eastern Mediterranean. A report by the US Pentagon in 1995 stressed that Turkey was at the crossroads of almost every issue of importance to the US on the Eurasian continent - including NATO, the Balkans, the Aegean, Iraqi sanctions, relations with the new independent states, peace in the Middle East, and transit routes for Central Asian oil and gas.   Washington also concluded that a Cyprus compromise, acceptable to Athens and Nicosia had to be implemented.[11]

Consequently, in Geneva in June 1996 Clerides discussed ways of starting negotiations with Boutros-Ghali.   Further talks were held with President Clinton in Washington, where emphasis was given to the issues of security and demilitarization and in London with Prime Minister John Major.   In 1997 the UN Secretary-General continued his efforts for the resumption of intercommunal talks for a comprehensive settlement.   In his efforts he was encouraged by the active support of the international community.   Yet Turkey continued to maintain its intransigent position which was coupled with its provocative attitude in the form of threats to use force and, if necessary, to invade in case the scheduled purchase by the Republic of the S-300 surface-to-air missile system was deployed in Cyprus.   In addition, Turkey also threatened that it would proceed with the 'integration' of the territory occupied by its forces if the EU proceeded with the accession negotiations with Cyprus.   The island's government protested to the UN against such threats which amounted to a blatant violation of international law, the UN Charter - which prevents the threat or use of force - and the numerous mandatory Security Council resolutions on Cyprus which inter allia called upon all states to respect its independence, sovereignty and territorial integrity.

Yet moves to find a solution continued.   The politics of make-believe carried on unabated.   It was always on top of the agenda but the problem was never tackled sincerely, fairly and conclusively.   A new phase of negotiations were again on the cards.   The year 1997 raised hopes for a settlement.   Clerides met the new UN Secretary-General, Mr. Kofi Annan, for the first time in January at Davos in Switzerland, where he was attending the World Economic Forum.   During the meeting they exchanged views on Cyprus' present status and on what should be done to break the impasses and move forward in an effort to solve the problem.   Clerides stressed that in his view the issue of the security  of both communities was of the greatest importance.   Therefore, he suggested that they should first deal with the issue which included demilitarization, the deployment of an international force under a UN Security Council mandate and the issue of guarantees.

Efforts to get the two sides together were intensified.   As a result Kofi Annan addressed a letter to Clerides and Denktash on 9 June inviting them for face to face talks for a comprehensive solution to this protracted problem.   There followed two rounds of talks.   The first in Troutbeck in up-state New York from 9-13 July 1997 and the second in Glion-sur-

---

(11)  Professor M.L. Evriviades - "Europe in Cyprus: The Broader Security Implications" in the Brown Journal of World Affairs. Vol. X Issue 1. Summer/Fall 2003. Pages 242-43.

Montreaux (Switzerland) from 11-15 August. The talks were chaired by Diego Cordovez. Also present in the wings (of the talks) were special envoys of several countries. During the talks the UN prepared and submitted to the two sides a document which was amended on the basis of suggestions made by the two sides and presented again to them. The paper was to be discussed by both sides separately and views would be expressed.

At Troutbeck, Clerides and Denktash agreed to meet in Nicosia to discuss humanitarian issues. They duly met on 28 and 31 July. On the agenda was the issue of the missing persons. There was some progress. During the second round of talks at Glion, the UN presented the two sides with two *'non-papers'* - a draft statement and an annex thereto. Clerides' reaction was positive but Denktash refused to hold any discussions on the substance of the Cyprus problem whilst the island's application to the EU was pending. Hence, what was described as the *"most elaborately prepared UN-sponsored peace talks since 1997"* collapsed. It must be noted, that Cyprus' accession process was finalised with the decision of the European Council in Luxembourg (12-13 December 1997) which set March 1998 as the day for the start of negotiations. Such discussions duly started on the 30th. In addition, an assertion by the EU summit in Helsinki (10-11 December 1999) emphasised that a settlement of the Cyprus problem was not a precondition for Cyprus' accession to the EU.[12]

Further diplomatic moves towards a agreement were made in 1999. On 20 June, the members of the G8 (leading industrialised nations including Russia) and the UN Security Council (on the 29th), through resolution 1250 urged Kofi Annan to invite both leaders to enter into comprehensive negotiations without preconditions, starting in the autumn of 1999 and to commit themselves in good faith to continue their discussions until an agreement was reached. US diplomatic pressure was also exerted although the Alfred Moses mission in October failed to unlock the path to a negotiated pact. Nevertheless, in the same month, President Clinton announced that he would take a personal hand in the Cyprus problem during his visit to the region in November. He kept his word. Some form of *'proximity talks'* were envisaged for December.

These indirect talks or talks for the sake of talks, aimed at preparing the ground for a comprehensive settlement, began at the UN headquarters on 3 December. Separate meetings, between Kofi Annan and Clerides and then with Denktash lasted until the 14th. The second round of UN sponsored *'proximity talks'* were held in Geneva from 31 January to 8 February 2000. The Geneva round, like the New York one, did not involve any face to face meetings between the two sides. Instead,

---

(12) The accession negotiations with Cyprus were successfully concluded on 13 December 2002 and the Treaty of Accession was signed on 16 April 2003. Following ratification of the above the island joined the EU on 1 May 2004.

the two delegations held a series of separate sessions with UN officials who sought to assess the positions of the two sides on the four core issues:

1) distribution of power under a settlement

2) property rights

3) territorial questions, and

4) security arrangements.

The third round was scheduled to begin in New York on 23 May and to continue into June and possibly beyond, However, these *'proximity talks'* were postponed when Clerides underwent an emergency operation in early May. It was hoped that the talks would commence in June either in New York or Geneva and in fact they began in Geneva on 5 July but went into recess on the 12th; resumed on the 24th and ended inconclusively on 4 August.

The fourth round took place in New York (12-26 September) and then in Geneva between 1-10 November which concluded the fifth round of these *'proximity talks'*. It is significant to note that on the 8th Kofi Annan met both Clerides and Denktash. He gave an oral assessment, or *'non-paper'*, citing the current status of the talks and the way ahead. On the 10th, Denktash called for the so-called *'non-paper'* to be invalidated. He later explained that the *'proximity talks'* had actually served their purpose!

The year 2001 was equally unproductive. In September, Denktash refused a UN invitation to resume talks. On the 26th the UN Security Council expressed its disappointment calling this decision as *"unjustified"*. In early November, however, Denktash made an unexpected *'volte face'*. He wrote to Clerides and called for face-to-face talks; the first since August 1997. Meeting under UN auspices in Cyprus on 4 December they agreed to resume negotiations, without preconditions, on 16 January 2002. In an apparent attempt to *'bridge the gaps'*, 56 sessions were held in New York, Paris and Nicosia. A further round was held in New York on 3-4 October. However, there was no breakthrough, there was no agreement.

# The Annan Plan

On 11 November 2002, the UN Secretary-General put forward propositions as a basis for agreement on a comprehensive settlement of the Cyprus problem. The 137 page document was delivered to Clerides and Denktash (through his adviser Ergun Olgun, since Denktash was convalescing in New York following a successful operation) and to governments of Greece, Turkey and the UK. Kofi Annan explained that his Plan was not a *"take it or leave it"* document and asked both sides to give him their first response by 18 November. Clerides met the deadline. Denktash did not.

The Plan also included several appendices, annexes and attachments. As it stood it represented what Kofi Annan believed to be a fair and honourable compromise which addressed the core interests, aims, concerns and even nightmares of each side. It foresaw a new partnership in Cyprus on the basis of equality, to ensure peace, security and prosperity for both communities in a united island.

Below is a summary of the key proposals:

1) It proposed a new state of affairs. The union of Cyprus, in whole or in part, with any other country or any form of partition or secession was prohibited. It should be noted that the status and relationship of the State of Cyprus, its *'common state'* government and its *'component states'* was modelled on the status and relationships of Switzerland and Belgium, their federal governments and cantons.

2) The *'component states'* will be of equal status. In addition, the *'common state'* and its *'component states'* shall be fully respected and not infringe upon the powers and functions of each other.

3) A single Cypriot citizenship was to be enjoyed.

4) Respect for human rights and fundamental freedoms shall be enshrined in the Constitution. There shall be no discrimination against any person on the basis of his/her gender, ethnic or religious identity or internal *'component state'* citizenship status. Freedom of movement and freedom of residence may be limited only where expressly provided for in this Agreement.

5) The *'common state'* Parliament, composed of two 48-member chambers, the Senate and the Chamber of Deputies, shall exercise the legislative power.

6) The Treaty of Alliance shall permit Greek and Turkish contingents to be stationed on the island. It appears that the scope of Article IV of the 1960 Constitution was to be enlarged. How could it be reconciled with the equality of states principle of international law and with Article 2 (4) of the UN Charter or for that matter Article 103. A UN peacekeeping force was destined to monitor the implementation of this Agreement.

7) The territorial boundaries of the *'component states'* shall be as depicted in the map which accompanied this Agreement. Territorial readjustments would leave 71.4 or 71.5% of the island (i.e. the area excluding the BSB areas) to the Greek Cypriot *'component state'* and 28.5 or 28.6% to the Turkish Cypriot *'component state'*, depending on the option chosen. This would allow the return of 85,000 Greek Cypriots out of some 161,500 displaced persons - that is 142,000 forced from their homes in 1974 and about 19,500 enclaved who were subsequently driven out of the occupied area through harassment and a denial of their fundamental human rights. About 60,000 of the 135,000 or so illegal Turkish settlers would also be repatriated. There would be limitations on the establishment of residency by members of each community in the other's *'component state'* and there would be compensation for property lost in 1974 rather than restitution.

8) Claims by property owners dispossessed by events prior to entry into force of this Agreement shall be resolved in a comprehensive manner in accordance with international law, respect for the individual rights of the dispossessed owners and current users and the principle of bi-zonality.

9) The Supreme Court would be composed of 9 judges, three from each *component state* and three non-Cypriots. Surely this is completely non-sensical!

After further intensive consultations, improvements were made and a revised format was suggested on 10 December 2002. The Plan, as it stood therefore, reflected nearly a year of intensive consultations and negotiations and stood on the shoulders of decades of talks before that. The differences between the new proposals and those of the British ones of 1956-59, were almost negligible! A second revision was presented to the parties on 26 February 2003. This took account of comments and objections made by the two sides. The Plan required a referendum before 16 April to approve it and therefore to re-unify Cyprus. The massive demonstrations in the occupied north (26 December 2002 and 14 January 2003) demanded the re-unification of the island within the EU.[13]

Supporters and opponents of the Plan abounded but no format can ever be perfect. Hence, there were both negative and positive elements. Kofi Annan explicitly stated to both sides that his Plan was not a *"take it or leave it"* document. However, he wrote that *"Cyprus has a rendezvous with history"* and that *"it should not be missed"*. In his report dated 1 April 2003, on his mission of good offices in Cyprus to the Security Council, Kofi Annan gave a full account of his efforts to achieve a viable settlement. The Plan was seen as an acceptable basis for a lasting agreement yet it was

---

(13) The latter demonstration was attended by more than 1/3 of the adult population of *'northern'* Cyprus. There have been others since.

not accepted and Kofi Annan said that Denktash *"bears prime responsibility"*. Earlier of course Denktash had declared the Plan as *"null and void"*. It was, however, also described by opponents as *"trap ridden"* and *"partitionist"*. Sceptics pointed out that:

1) UN resolutions to date called for territorial integration etc. of the Cyprus Republic, for the return of all refugees to their ancestral homes and the removal of all foreign troops. This Plan is simply not compatible with such resolutions.

2) Whereas in 1960 there was one state, in 2002/03 the Plan called for two states. To say the least, this is racist and, in a way gives legal sanctity to the events of 1974.

3) Certain provisions of the Plan were simply not well-suited with the European *acquis*, while others were strained to show compatibility. It is therefore, as anti-Annanists explain, contrary to international law and potentially catastrophic for the future of Cyprus.

4) Sceptics were also questioning the forcible exchange of properties, as implied in the proposals. Clearly, they say, this was not lawful. Moreover, was the property component of the Plan compatible with the 4th Geneva Convention of 1949? Accordingly, the UN is accused of violating its own Charter and resolutions by depriving Cypriots of their right to return to their own ancestral homes and property

5) The above proposals were in reality no more than a Hanney-Holbrooke inspired plan (apparently presented to the government of Cyprus in May 1998, but rejected) concerned above all with the security architecture of the Middle East. The *raison d'etre* appears to be an attempt to strengthen NATO and weaken European integration.

6) The voting provisions imposed on the two chambers, the monstrous exercise of executive jurisdiction, the equal parity of the legislative (law-making) power etc., in fact make the proposed settlement undoubtedly *"dysfunctional"*. It was described by one analyst as a plan of *"constructive ambiguity"*. A state of affairs, sceptics point out, which was acknowledged even by Alvaro de Soto.

The Greek Cypriots were prepared to accept the Plan as *"a basis for negotiations without terms or pre-conditions"*. Denktash however dismissed it as *"dead and buried"*.

Negotiations were temporarily interrupted in February 2003 due to presidential elections in which Tasos Papadopoulos was elected to succeed Glafcos Clerides.[14] Most of 2003 was a fallow period in terms of

---

(14) In a turnout of 90.63%. Papadopoulos received 51.51 percent of the valid votes cast and Clerides 38.80%. The remainder (9.69%) was taken by the other eight candidates.

constructive negotiations. Yet, Kofi Annan visited the island for the second time, on 26 February and presented to the two sides his third and final version of the Plan. It was agreed to meet again at The Hague. The meetings here (10-11 March), however, proved to be a diplomatic suspense story. Efforts, however, continued to find a comprehensive settlement of the Cyprus problem. The Security Council in resolution 1475 (2003) of 14 April gave its strong support for what was termed, a *"carefully balanced plan"* - namely, the *'Basis for Agreement on a Comprehensive Settlement of the Cyprus Problem'* dated 26 February.

Moving on to 2004, the parties in Cyprus were committed to negotiating in good faith on the basis of the settlement plan dated 26 February 2003, to achieve a comprehensive agreement through separate and simultaneous referenda before 1 May 2004. To this end they agreed to a three-phase negotiation and finalisation procedure:

In phase I of the effort, the parties negotiated in Cyprus between 19 February and 22 March 2004. There was no significant progress at the political level. Nevertheless, positive results were achieved at the technical level by experts from the two sides assisted by UN specialists.

In phase II of the effort, Kofi Annan convened a meeting of the two sides un Burgenstock, Switzerland, beginning on 24 March. Greece and Turkey were also invited to attend. Again there was no agreement on the final text.

In phase III, on 31 March, the Secretary-General finalised the text to be submitted later to referenda in Cyprus. Such referenda took place simultaneously on 24 April 2004. The 220-page document, accompanied by 9,000 pages and annexes, provided, amongst other clauses, for Turkey, Greece and Britain to maintain their role as guarantors of Cyprus' independence, for the island to become a federation run by a nine-member council, with one legal personality, a central bank, a unified economy and restrictions to freedom of movement between the *'constituent'* states for a number of years.

The people of Cyprus were asked to vote *'yes'* or *'no'* on Kofi Annan's Plan V. The results were as follows:

|  | Turnout % | Yes % | No % |
|---|---|---|---|
| Greek Cypriots | 89 | 24.17 | 75.83 |
| Turkish Cypriots | 87 | 64.91 | 35.09 |

Annan V was therefore dead and buried. The four provisions among many others, to which the Greek Cypriots were especially opposed were:

1) The reduced number of refugees who were allowed to return to their homes in the north. Property rights must surely rank as the most complex and most sensitive of the core issues facing Cyprus.

2) Security guarantees and the continued presence of Turkish troops in northern Cyprus. The Annan Plan expressly provided that the island should be demilitarised. This however, only refers to the existence of Cypriot military forces. On the contrary, non-Cypriot military forces shall remain in Cyprus according to the provisions of the 1960 Treaty of Alliance, which shall apply and operate *mutatis mutandis*, in accordance with the new state of affairs. Yet Kofi Annan argued that the presence of the Turkish army was simply '*symbolic*', since following 2018 or the European accession of Turkey, whichever is earliest, the Turkish contingent should not exceed 650 men. With today's sophisticated methods of warfare does this really make a difference? The House of Commons Foreign Affairs Committee on Cyprus concluded in its report published in February 2005 that, "Turkey has the power greatly to assist both a settlement in Cyprus and its EU aspirations, for example by withdrawing some of its thousands of troops from the island."

3) The issue of the Turkish settlers. The estimated number (including natural increase) has been estimated at over 135,000.

4) The financial and economic cost of implementation, was estimated to be too high, in fact prohibitive.

Greek Cypriots explained that even their basic and minimum aims were not met. In fact, their most substantial proposals were not accepted. The Annan Plan (mark 5) was therefore found wanting. It is hoped that Cyprus' entry into the EU might act as a catalyst for a lasting, viable and comprehensive settlement.

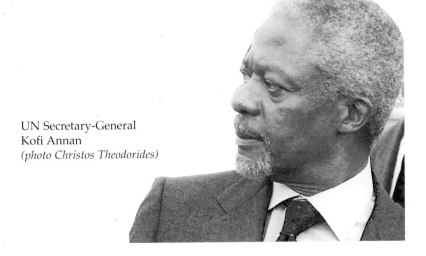

UN Secretary-General
Kofi Annan
(*photo Christos Theodorides*)

# After the Annan Plans . . . *The Future?*

Some months after the two referenda and Cyprus' entry into the EU, the European Council meeting held in Brussels on 17 and 18 December 2004, decided that accession negotiations with Turkey should begin on 3 October 2005. Turkey's commitment to sign the Protocol expanding the customs union to the ten new EU member states before 3 October, was included in the *'Conclusions'*. It seems that Turkey's progress was indissolubly linked to her improving relations with the Cyprus Republic.

Does this constitute formal legal recognition of Cyprus as a single entity? Legal experts are at pains to make a simple announcement. Tony Blair, on the other hand, explained to the House of Commons on 20 December that the Brussels statement *"does not"* constitute *"formal legal recognition"* of the Cyprus Republic. He proceeded to heap praise on Turkey by saying that it lies at the intersection of three areas of strategic importance to Europe - the Middle East, central Asia and the Balkans - and is a trusted NATO ally. In addition, he said, Turkey is a strongly growing economy which, has a market of 70 million or so people and imports over Euro 40 billion worth of goods from the EU each year.

According to the *'Conclusions'* however, the talks with Turkey are an open-ended process, the outcome of which cannot be guaranteed in advance. Such accession negotiations are likely to last at least a decade. Will the EU demonstrate its extraordinary capacity to heal the wounds of history?

It appears that fresh hopes for a lasting Cyprus settlement should henceforth be linked to:

1. Turkey's aspirations to join the EU, a group of nations of which Cyprus is a member state - a club of reconciliation and tolerance. It is certainly not in the European Union's interest to have countries within its ambit with issues of either *de facto* and or *de jure* recognition embedded in any element of doubt.

2 A fresh initiative by the UN to restart a *'new'* process, perhaps a more workable Annan Plan (number 6 or 7) and not a plan which was found wanting even by the most biased observers and international analysts. Cyprus requires a just, viable and functional system of government.

3. A fresh approach is needed, a new administrative formula and a movement away from the much maligned *zero sum* game, where one side's gain should be matched by the other side's loss. Gains and losses should never be equated in such a way. A solution must serve the interests of all the inhabitants of Cyprus irrespective of national origin or religious affiliation.

4. It would be politic for all interested parties to move away from their covert and often overt policy of wishing to see "*two separate state entities*" in Cyprus. Compassion and justice should be at the top of their agenda. Nationalistic small-mindedness should not be allowed to set in.

Finally, now that the Cyprus Republic is a full member of the European Union, it would be advisable that all efforts are focused on the reunification of the island. This would include the withdrawal of foreign troops, freedom of movement, freedom of residence, the safeguarding of property rights and respect for human rights and fundamental freedoms. Such provisions should be in accordance with the European *acquis* and with all universal declarations. In order that all adhere to the EU principles and values of human rights.

With such strong support, the island's inhabitants can prosper and live together side by side in peace.

A meeting of three veteran Cypriot leaders from left to right: Papadopoulos, Clerides and Denktash. *(Photo Christos Theodorides)*

# APPENDICES

# CYPRUS and the EUROPEAN UNION: A brief outline.

Since the early 1970s Cyprus had established and maintained excellent relations with the EU, an organisation which had its roots in 1957 when six countries signed the Treaty of Rome. The island was among the first countries which signed an Association Agreement with the European Economic Community (EEC). In 1971 it entered into negotiations with the Community which led to the signing on 19 December 1972 of the Agreement between the two parties, with the final goal of establishing, in two stages, and within a period of ten years, a Customs Union between Cyprus and the EEC. The Agreement came into force on 1 June 1973.

The Turkish invasion of 1974 and occupation of around 37.5% of Cyprus' territory and the subsequent catastrophic effects on its economy delayed the normal development of the various processes and in particular the implementation of its second stage. After successive extensions of the first stage, a protocol for the second stage of the Association Agreement was signed in Luxembourg on 19 October 1987, thus paving the way towards the progressive realisation of the Customs Union between the two parties. The Protocol came into force on 1 January 1988. In accordance with its provisions, the Customs Union between Cyprus and the EU was to be in two phases and to be completed by the year 2002 or 2003 at the latest. During the initial phase which ran until 1997, customs duties and quantitative restrictions on specified industrial and agricultural products were reduced. At the same time the Common Customs Tariff (CCT) was adopted.

On 4 July 1990, the island's government submitted its application for membership of the European Communities. The Council of European Communities examined the application and asked the Commission to give its Opinion (*Avis*). This it did on 30 June 1993. The Opinion recognised the European identity and character of Cyprus and its vocation to belong to the Communities. It confirmed that the island satisfied the criteria for membership and was suitable to become a member. The Commission also said that it was convinced *"the result of Cyprus' accession to the Community would be increased security and prosperity and that it would help to bring the two communities on the island closer together"*. It also said that its integration with the Community *"implies a peaceful, balanced and lasting settlement of the Cyprus question"*.

The Council discussed and endorsed the Opinion at its meeting on 4 October 1993. In its conclusion it invited the Commission to open substantive discussions immediately with the island's government to help it prepare for the accession negotiations to follow later on, under the best possible conditions, and *"to keep it regularly informed of the progress"*. Such discussions began in November 1993 and were completed in February 1995. For the purpose of such a dialogue the government established 23 working groups, each one of them dealing with a different chapter of the *acquis communautaire*. The deliberations were constructive and fruitful and helped Cypriot officials to familiarise themselves with the entire body of European legislation and to identify the areas in which local legislation needed to be harmonised with the *acquis*. After the completion of the substantive talks, the working groups produced reports on the level of the harmonisation of Cypriot legislation with the *acquis* and timetables for its progressive implementation. These were examined and approved by the Interministerial Committee on EU affairs.

A milestone in the development of relations between Cyprus and the EU was the decision included in the conclusions of the EU's General Affairs Council of 6 March 1995 which reaffirmed the suitability of the country for accession and stipulated that negotiations would start six months after the conclusion of the Intergovernmental Conference of 1996, taking account of its results. This decision gave new momentum to the relations of Cyprus with the EU and brought the prospect of Cyprus' accession closer to realisation.

On the basis of the 1995 decision, and the prospect of accession negotiations between Cyprus and the EU, a pre-accession strategy was formulated. This procedure included the establishment of a *"structured dialogue"* which consisted of meetings twice a year between the island's president and the heads of state or government of the *"15"* and meetings of ministers, as well as experts on specific issues such as social policy, justice and home affairs, financial and monetary matters, etc. Between 1995 and 1997, a large number of such meetings took place; these provided the opportunity for the island's officials to have a regular and in-depth exchange of views and ideas with their EU counterparts. This structured dialogue served as a useful instrument in helping Cyprus harmonise its legislation, policies and practices with the *acquis communautaire*, and prepare itself for a smooth and rapid transition to membership. The pre-accession strategy also provided, *inter alia*, for the participation of Cyprus in certain community programmes. '*Leonardo da Vinci*', '*Socrates*' and '*Youth for Europe*' were fine examples.

The way to EU enlargement was facilitated by the issuing, on 15 July 1997, of Agenda 2000, a Commission document which was a study of the possible effects of enlargement on the EU and the applicant countries and contained proposals on the future development of the policies of the EU. With regard to Cyprus, the Commission reaffirmed its 1993 Opinion noting the island's *"advanced level of development and economic dynamism"*. The Commission added that, *"the timetable agreed for accession negotiations to start with Cyprus means that they could start before a political settlement is reached"* and that if progress towards a settlement is not made before the negotiations are due to begin, *"they should be opened"* with the republic's government *"as the only authority recognised by international law"*.

Based on the results of the Intergovernmental Conference and the Commission proposals included in Agenda 2000, the European Council at Luxembourg (12-13 December 1997) took the necessary decisions so that the Union could launch the overall enlargement process, an action characterised as *"inclusive and ongoing"*. It was also decided to convene bilateral intergovernmental conferences in the spring of 1998 to begin accession negotiations with Cyprus, Hungary, Poland, Estonia, the Czech Republic and Slovenia. These were launched on 31 March 1998. The first stage of the enlargement negotiations which was initiated on 3 April involved the analytical examination of the *acquis communautaire* which was separated into 31 chapters for easy reference. During the stage (*"acquis screening"*), the European Commission presented and explained the *acquis* in a certain area, the applicant country presented its own policy in that sector, and the two were compared so that the necessary legislative or other changes needed to achieve harmonisation were identified. In the meantime, substantive negotiations on 7 chapters of the *acquis* began on 10 November 1998 and Cyprus submitted to the EU its position papers on 8 other chapters in December 1998 with substantive negotiations on these chapters beginning in the spring of 1999.

On 4 November 1998, the European Commission issued its first *"Regular Report on Cyprus' Progress towards Accession"*. It was noted that, *"in the economic field, developments since 1993 confirm that the Cyprus economy possesses the ability to adapt to the challenges posed by the adoption of the "acquis'"*. By December 2002 all the remaining chapters were closed and the harmonisation process was completed. In its resolution of 20 November 2002, the European Parliament reiterated that once a settlement was reached, there should be full respect for human rights and fundamental freedoms on the whole territory of the island. It also stated that the political settlement to be agreed should enable Cyprus to participate in the decision-making process and the policies of the EU and to ensure the proper application of EU law. During the European Council meeting in Copenhagen held on 12-13 December 2002, the Republic of Cyprus received a formal invitation to join the EU without any prerequisites and within the spirit of the 1999 Helsinki decision. That decision clearly stated that a solution of the Cyprus problem was not a prerequisite for the accession of Cyprus into the EU. In other words it accepted only *de facto* the Greek part and *de jure* the whole island.

On 16 April 2003, Cyprus signed in Athens, the Treaty of Accession to the EU. The Treaty Protocol said that the *acquis* will be suspended in areas not controlled by the republic's government. On 1 May 2004, the island became a full member of the EU.

The disadvantages emanating from Cyprus' entry into the EU cannot, as yet, be outlined with much conviction. The benefits, however, are much easier to tabulate:

1) Relations between the two communities of Cyprus will be improved simply by following the example of, and participating in the mechanisms developed by the EU. The EEC, from which the EU was derived, was born out of the bitter experiences of World War II and the realisation that the recurrence of such devastating wars could be stopped only by the nationalities and the states of Europe (and the whole world of course) coming together and developing common interests.

2) Improved security for all citizens of Cyprus, will emanate from membership of a community of nations and sovereign states that stresses its attachment to the principles of democracy, respect for human rights and fundamental freedoms and the rule of law.

3) The commitment to refer to the European treaties and the EU law in dealing with problems, thereby having a reference point for the resolution of disputes and problems that goes beyond the narrow interests of political groups, communities and pressure groups. This does not mean that EU law will determine everything, but rather that basic principles which form the foundation of the EU philosophy, such as the principle on non-discrimination, should be upheld.

4) The laws and standards will in most cases be upgraded and modernised. Social programmes will be brought into line with the high standards of the Social Charter, while a greater emphasis will be given to environmental issues and improvements in standards of safety and quality. Overall, a significant improvement in the quality of life is anticipated, especially in the less developed parts of the island which will be eligible for increased EU assistance.

5) More specifically, for the Turkish Cypriots the benefits will be massive from full membership of the EU and the solution of the Cyprus problem, both of which will bring about a sudden and permanent advancement in income and living standards and will give them all the benefits that citizens of Europe enjoy today.

President Papadopoulos addressing EU members and prospective entrants on the occasion of the signing of the Treaty of Accession, Athens 16 April 2003.

# APPENDIX – B

# Personalities involved with the Cyprus Question: 1950s to date.

## GREEK CYPRIOTS
### Archbishop MAKARIOS III 1913-1977

For his early career etc, please refer to section vi **(pages 171-174)**. In the early 1950s Makarios travelled extensively abroad and successfully gathered support for Cyprus' independence claim. Following the commencement of the armed struggle for national self-determination on 1 April 1955, and the break up of talks between Makarios and the British colonial administration, the Cypriot Ethnarch was exiled to the Seychelles in March 1956 - only to be released a year or so later.

After protracted negotiations, Britain agreed to grant Cyprus its independence. On 13 December 1959, Makarios was elected as the first president of the infant Republic and he assumed his duties on 16 August 1960. Cyprus became the 99th member-state of the United Nations.

From 1960 to 1977 he went through many trials and tribulations culminating in four attempts on his life and in July 1974 came the fateful coup and Turkish invasion.

Without any shadow of doubt the Archbishop had great natural dignity: he was very accessible, courteous and considerate even to the least important visitor who went to see him. He had a teasing but not unkind sense of humour and few could resist the charm and twinkling smile that was never far away.

The Cypriot Ethnarch was a dynamic and great leader. From the time he became Archbishop (1950) to the time of his death (5.15 a.m, 3 August 1977), he held the trust and worship of the Cypriot people. Makarios had a unique multi-layered authority: spiritually as Archbishop, communally as Ethnarch, nationally as unchallenged President, internationally as an acknowledged leader of the Commonwealth and the Third World and an apostle of non-alignment and world peace.

From 1950 Makarios had symbolised everything that was Cyprus. His life was simply the history of the island - *The Great Father and Maker of Modern Cyprus*: certainly a wise and apt description of the island's first democratically elected leader.

# George GRIVAS 1897/8-1974

For his early career etc, please refer to section vi (**pages 168-171**) In the 1950s Grivas focused his attention on Cyprus - he planned guerrilla tactics to oust the colonial regime and achieve enosis - Union with Greece.

During the early hours of 1 April 1955 a series of bomb explosions inaugurated the commencement of the national liberation struggle. On the same day, EOKA proclaimed its existence in leaflets signed '*Dighénes*'. This was Grivas' *nom de guerre* in his capacity as leader of EOKA. In the course of the struggle he was also called '*arkhigos*' (leader) and '*apiastos*' (the one that could not be captured).

After the Cyprus settlement (February 1959), Grivas left Cyprus and was acclaimed as a national hero by the Greek state. On 18 March 1959 the Vouli named Grivas, Lieutenant-General.

From 1964 to 1967, he returned to the island and commanded the Cyprus National Guard.

In 1967 Turkey demanded his recall but in 1971 he returned secretly to Cyprus and was in opposition to Makarios. He died on 27 January 1974.

As a military strategist he was much admired and respected.

# Spyros KYPRIANOU 1932-2002

Born in Limassol, he graduated from the Greek Gymnasium and proceeded to study economics and commerce and then law in London.

During his student days in the British capital, he founded the Cypriot Students Union (EFEKA) of which he was its first president during the period 1952-54.

In February 1952 he was appointed '*London Secretary*' to Archbishop Makarios and in 1954 he took the office of '*Secretary of the Cyprus Ethnarchy in London*' and was responsible for enlightening British public opinion on the rights of Cyprus.

From London he went to Athens in 1956 and from August 1956 to March 1957 he represented the Cyprus Ethnarchy once more in New York. From there he went back to Athens and then back to London.

On declaration of Cyprus' independence (16 August 1960), he was first appointed Minister of Justice but within a few days he was given the Ministry of Foreign Affairs. In this capacity he represented Cyprus in many international conferences, meetings etc and accompanied President Makarios on his state and other visits.

On 5 May 1972 he resigned (perhaps relieved of his duties) following a serious dispute with the military leaders in Athens.

In May 1976 he announced the establishment of the Democratic Party (DEKO) and was its first president. From 1976 to 1977 he was President of the House of Representatives.

On the death of Makarios on 3 August 1977 he became, under the Constitution, acting president of the republic and on 3 September he was unanimously elected President. He was subsequently re-elected unopposed in 1978 and again in 1983.

In the face of many difficulties, he served his country with dignity and courage. He died on 12 March 2002.

# Glafcos CLERIDES  1919 -

Born in Nicosia, he proceeded to study law at Grays Inn and Kings College, London.

He served in the Royal Air force during World War II and in 1942 his plane was shot down; he remained in a German prisoner of war camp until the end of hostilities.

He returned to Cyprus in 1951 and became a practising lawyer. In that capacity and as a member of EOKA (known by the pseudonym of '*Eperides*'), he successfully represented many Cypriots during the EOKA years of 1955-59.

From 1960 he was the first President of the House of Representatives - a post he held for 16 years. In that position he performed the duties of 'acting president' during Makarios' absence.

From 1968 to 1974 he was the chief Greek Cypriot negotiator in the intercommunal talks.

He was the founder of the Unified Party 1969-76 and the Democratic Rally Party (DESY or Democraticos Synagermos 1976-93)

An astute politician with an in-depth knowledge of Cyprus' history and current affairs. He was president of Cyprus from 1993 to 2003.

# George VASSILIOU 1931-

Born in Famagusta he completed his secondary education in Cyprus and later studied at the universities of Geneva , Vienna, Budapest and London.

Returning to Cyprus in 1962, he established the Middle East Marketing Research Bureau which at present is probably the largest research and consultancy organisation in the region. From 1980 to 1988 he was economic adviser to the council of the Church of Cyprus.

After victory at the polls  he assumed, on 28 February 1988, Cyprus' highest office as its 3rd elected President.   His election, coupled with the thaw in Graeco-Turkish relations, gave rise to new hopes for a solution to the Cyprus question.

A highly-principled, open-minded, hardworking and sincere individual. Has remained in politics after 1993 and now leads a peripheral (in terms of votes received at parliamentary elections) centrist party, (United Democrats) 'tied' to the EU ideology.

# Tassos PAPADOPOULOS 1934-

Born in Nicosia he attended the Pancyprian Gymnasium and then proceeded to study law at Gray's Inn, London.

He became a successful lawyer in Cyprus and went on to take an active part in the EOKA liberation struggle. He participated in the London Conference of 1959 which set up the republic of Cyprus. He was at odds with the Agreements and he signalled his opposition by casting, at such an auspicious moment, a negative vote on the critical issue of whether to accept the Agreements or not.

Following the island's independence he was appointed Minister of Labour and Social Insurance, a post from where he had an opportunity to prove his commitment to the principles of the welfare state. He served in other ministerial posts as well. Similarly, he represented the Greek Cypriot community at the intercommunal talks, at the UN and at the Council of Europe.

In 1970 he was elected to the House of Representatives (on the Unified Party ticket) and 30 years later he was elected unopposed president of DEKO, during the historic electoral congress at which Spyros Kyprianou, the founder of the party, stood down.

In February 2003, he was elected President of the Republic of Cyprus, defeating the veteran politician Glafcos Clerides.

## TURKISH CYPRIOTS

### Fazil KÜTCHÜK 1906-1984

Born in Nicosia he proceeded to study at the universities of Istanbul and Lausanne. He started his career as a specialist physician in 1938 in Cyprus.

In 1941 he founded the newspaper 'Halkin Sesi' and two years later joined the Cyprus Turkish Association (KATAK). In 1945 he established the 'Cyprus Turkish National Party'; ten years on it became the 'Cyprus is Turkish Party'.

Kütchük served as the first vice-president of the infant republic from 1960 to 18 February 1973. Ten years later, when the Turkish republic of northern Cyprus was declared, he said, "I feel reborn". Though a moderate, he espoused under pressure the divisive dictum/policy of communal separation.

On 15 January 1984 he died in London's Westminster Hospital where he was receiving treatment. Described by the British as, "friendly, well-disposed but unimpressive; inclined to be touchy; drinks heavily". Certainly one of the most charismatic figures of modern Cypriot political life.

### Rauf DENKTASH 1924 -

Born on 27 January in Ktima, Paphos. He was the youngest child of Judge M. Raif Bey. He studied law at Lincolns Inn in London, went on to practice law and from 1949 to 1958 he served in the Cyprus Legal Department, Attorney General's Office.

A key pro-partitionist, capable and a shrewd political figure of the post-mid-1950s period. An admirer of Adnan Menderes the Turkish PM of those years.

He was president of the Turkish Communal Chamber 1960-1973 and is still 'president' of the illegal Turkish federal state of northern Cyprus.

At all times (except where shown in the main text) he had been the chief Turkish Cypriot negotiator in the intercommunal talks and at all conferences both at home and abroad. Seen by many as the stumbling block to a negotiated settlement. Has opted for a policy of separation (since the early 1950s) and has stood by that choice for over 50 years.

# GREEKS

## Alexandros PAPAGOS 1883-1955

A distinguished soldier and statesman. He took part in the Balkan Wars of 1912-13, the Asia Minor adventure of 1919-1922 and fought the Italians and the Germans during World War II. He was taken to Germany as a hostage. Liberated in 1945, he directed postwar operations in Greece against the communist resistance fighters and was appointed Field-Marshal in 1949.

In May 1951, Papagos resigned as military commander-in-chief to form a new political party, the Greek Rally (*Ellinikos Sinagermos*), which soon became the strongest political force in Greece. Enjoying wide popularity and modelling himself on Charles de Gaulle, Papagos led his party to a decisive victory in the elections of November 1952 and became Premier. He died in office.

Papagos holds the distinction of being the first Greek Premier to take the Cypriot issue to the UN - in 1954. Public opinion was the decisive factor in such a decision.

## Constantinos KARAMANLIS 1907-1998

Born at Próti, near Serres in Macedonia. The oldest of seven children of a poor school master, Karamanlis was able, with the help of local benefactors, to attend secondary school and the University of Athens, receiving a law degree in 1932 and practicing law in the capital.

Launched into politics by the Populist Party, he was elected to Parliament in1935 for Serres, which continued to re-elect him. In 1952, he entered the government of Papagos as Minister of Public Works and when Papagos died in October 1955, Karamanlis was chosen by King Paul to succeed him. Also in 1952, he married Amalia Kanellopoulou, niece of Panagiotis Kanellopoulos, a prominent politician, whom he divorced in 1970.

He formed his own party (*The National Radical Union - ERE*) and served Greece as Premier until 1963

In July 1974 he was recalled from Paris to head the National Emergency Government. He founded the *New Democracy Party* which won the elections of November 1974. He served as PM to 1980 and as President of the Greek Republic from 1980 to 1985 and from 1990 to 1995. He oversaw Greece's entry into the European Community (1981).

Following acute pressure from the Greek Palace, NATO and the US, Karamanlis decided to disentangle the awkward Cyprus problem and was instrumental in setting up the infant republic in 1959-60.

# Evangelos AVEROFF-TOSSITZA 1910-1990

Born in Metsovo he was educated at the University of Lausanne, Switzerland where he studied law and economics.

He was active in the resistance movement 1939-45; imprisoned in Italy he escaped and continued to fight until the end of the War.

Elected MP in 1946 he served successfully as Minister of Supply, Minister of National Economy and Commerce and then as Foreign Secretary from 1956-63.

He was active in the resistance against the Greek dictatorship 1967-74 and was twice imprisoned. With the return of civilian government he served as Minister of National Defence 1974-81, Deputy Premier June-October 1981 and then leader of the new Democracy Party 1981-84.

On the Cyprus problem Averoff, like Karamanlis, was constantly functioning within the restrictive dictates of NATO and the US. He appeared to want enosis and later independence but his country which depended economically on the US had a limited range of options. He was unable to withstand the pressure too long; he was instrumental in guiding through the highly restrictive Zürich-London Agreements of 1959, which finally set up the Cyprus Republic in 1960.

His two-volume work in Greek entitled '*A History of Missed Opportunities*' published in 1981 records the chances which he believed were available to close the Cypriot chapter before the catastrophic coup and Turkish invasion of 1974.

A man of unsettled habits, inflammable temper and divided allegiances. However, Averoff had many talents and diverse interests. A politician, intellectual and literary man - an eminent figure in the affairs of modern Greece.

# George PAPANDREOU 1888-1968

Born in Kaléntzi Greece, Papandreou served his country well in several positions. He headed a Greek government in exile 1944, and then was leader of the national administration, 1944-45. He was again Premier, as head of the reformist Union Party in 1963 and 1964-65. Being under the vice-like grip of American, and to a lesser extent British geo-strategic and corporate interests, his range of options were somewhat limited. As far as he could however, Papandreou supported the legally elected government of Archbishop Makarios and did everything he could to prevent the subjugation and placing of Cyprus under the American and NATO military umbrella. Thus, he was instrumental in 'rejecting' the Acheson proposals of 1964. Papandreou is referred to as the grand old man (*o geros*) of Greek democracy.

# Andreas PAPANDREOU 1919-1996

The son of George Papandreou, he was born on the island of Chios and educated at the Athens University Law School, Columbia and Harvard. He became a US citizen in 1944 and served for two years in the US navy but resumed his Greek citizenship in the early 1960s.

Following the military coup of 1967 he was imprisoned and exiled but returned to Greece in 1974 and founded the Pan-Hellenic Socialist Movement (PASOK). In 1981 he was elected Greece's first Socialist Prime Minister; he was re-elected in 1985 and again in 1993.

As far as he could both in his earlier years and during his terms of office, Papandreou supported the policy of independence and territorial integrity pursued by the Cyprus government. In his book *'Democracy at Gunpoint'*, Papandreou condemned American involvement in the island's affairs. He openly defied the *'para-state'* that had ruled Greece since 1949. The principal institutions being the Palace, the Army General Staff, elements of the Church hierarchy and the US Embassy.

In November 1995 he was hospitalised with pneumonia and resigned soon afterwards.

# *TURKS*
# Adnan MENDERES 1899-1961

Born near Aydin he was educated in law but being the son of a wealthy landowner, he became a fairly successful farmer.

He entered politics in 1931/32, at first in opposition but later with the party in power under Kemal Ataturk.

In 1945 he became one of the leaders (together with Celal Bayar, Fuat Koprulu and others) of the Democratic Party and was Prime Minister in 1950. He was re-elected in 1954 and 1957 but in May 1960 he was deposed and superseded by General Cemal Gursel after an army coup.

He repeated more than once that Turkey would *'never'* accept a *'Greek Cyprus'*. He demanded federation and/or partition, depending on what suited his country best.

For the *'crimes'* of the 1950s he was hanged at Imrali (the prison island, Sea of Marmara) in September 1961. Pleas by world leaders failed to save him.

# Ismet INÖNÜ 1884-1973

Turkish soldier and politician born in Izmir, Asia Minor.

The first premier of Kemal Atätürk's new Republic 1923-24, 1925-37. He introduced many political reforms transforming Turkey into a modern state. He was unanimously elected President (Turkey's second) in 1938 on Ataturk's death and he served in that capacity until 1950.

From 1950 he was leader of the opposition but in 1961 he became premier with General Gursel as President. In 1965 he resigned after failing to govern effectively with minority support.

With Venizelos and Atätürk, Inönü was one of the architects of Graeco-Turkish friendship in the 1930s.

In the 1960s however, and conscious of the army in the background, the ageing Inönü was forced to seek the geographical separation of the two communities in Cyprus and his premiership was responsible for repeatedly violating the air space of the island. In his reply to President Johnson's letter on 14 June 1964 Inönü stated that the necessity of a military intervention in Cyprus had been felt *"four times since the closing days of 1963"*. Ten years later that became a reality.

# Bülent ECEVIT 1925 -

Born on 28 May in Istanbul he was educated in Ankara, London and Harvard.

A celebrated columnist, poet, scholar and politician. He was elected MP for the centre-left Republican People's Party in 1957 and served as such to 1980. From 1961 to 1965 he was Minister of Labour and Secretary-General of the RPP from 1966 to 1971. He served as Prime Minister for 9 months in 1974, 1 month in 1977 and from January 1978 to October 1979.

Conscious of the army and the partitionist policies of his country, NATO and the US behind him, he ordered the invasion of Cyprus in 1974. Nicknamed *'karaôglan'* (the Turkish Robin Hood) he became the idol of the masses.

Following the military coup of 1980 he was detained and barred from political life and then imprisoned for a short period of time. He later established the Democratic Left Party and in December 1998, he was asked to form a caretaker government. Following elections held in April 1999, he continued as Premier, leading a coalition government.

*BRITISH*

# Sir Antony EDEN  1897-1977

Educated at Eton and Christ Church Oxford. Elected MP for Warwick and Leamington in 1923, he held his seat till his resignation in 1957. Conservative politician with vast ministerial experience mainly at the Foreign Office from the early 1930s. On 6 April 1955 he succeeded Winston Churchill as Prime Minister.

Failing health coupled with the effects of the Suez fiasco of 1956, when he was abandoned by the Americans, resulted in Eden resigning the premiership on 9 January 1957. He was created 1st Earl of Avon in 1961. He died on 14 January 1977.

Over Cyprus and during such troubled times he had no positive policy and due to his prompting, Turkey was pleasantly hijacked into the Cyprus question as the third interested party. The policy of separation was henceforth firmly entrenched.

# Sir Maurice Harold MACMILLAN  1894-1986

Educated at Eton and Balliol College, Oxford. In the 1950s he served as Minister of Housing 1951-54 and as Minister of Defence 1954-55 and thereafter Foreign Secretary to the end of 1955 when he was appointed Chancellor of the Exchequer.

Macmillan succeeded Eden as PM in 1957. Like his predecessor his Cyprus policy was riddled with inconsistencies. It was a *non-policy* dictated by Middle Eastern strategic and economic interests and by the belief of a firm alliance with Turkey. Both leaders unashamedly played the *Turkish card to the detriment of Cyprus' unity. Partition,* as a way out of the Cyprus impasse, was always high on their list of priorities. Both Eden and Macmillan must have been aware of the dictum that *diplomacy* is *a multi-million pound business.* They practiced it to its fullest capacity! Over Cyprus morality, justice and fairness were way down their list of political perceptions.

He was created 1st Earl of Stockton in 1984 and died on 29 December 1986.

# Sir James CALLAGHAN 1912 - 2005

Educated at Portsmouth northern secondary school, he was elected Labour MP for South Cardiff in 1945. In 1964 he was appointed Chancellor of the Exchequer in Harold Wilson's government and from 1967 to 1970 he served as Home Secretary.

As Foreign Secretary from 1974 to 1976 he worked tirelessly at Geneva with his Greek and Turkish counterparts (Mavros and Gunes) to bring about a cease-fire and thus prevent further destruction following the Turkish invasion. As far as he could Callaghan supported the unity and territorial integrity of Cyprus. For this he had to bear the wrath of the Americans and the Turks. He served as Prime Minister from 1976 to 1979. He was created a peer in 1987 and took the title of Baron Callaghan of Cardiff.

## Sir John HARDING 1896-1989

He rose to the position of Chief of Staff of the Allied Army in Italy in 1944. From 1955 to 1957 he was Governor-General of Cyprus during the first two years of the national liberation struggle.

He re-organised the security forces to combat EOKA, re-established order through the imposition of martial law and press control, banished Makarios to the Seychelles and although he failed to bring about a political settlement he was widely respected and feared for his straight forward soldierly approach.

He was created a peer in 1958 and took the title of 1st Baron of Petherton. He died on 20 January 1989.

## Sir Hugh FOOT 1907 - 1990

Born on 8 October 1907, he was educated at St. John's College, Cambridge. He held many government administrative posts abroad - in Palestine, Transjordan, Jamaica, Nigeria and Cyprus.

He was the island's last Governor from 1957 to the time it achieved full statehood having already served there as colonial secretary from 1943 to 1945. A man of peace and great international understanding he was instrumental in bringing an end to the hostilities in Cyprus. From February 1959 he successfully guided the interim Cypriot administration into becoming a republic in August 1960. A major blot to his illustrious and statesmanlike career was the hastily-drawn Foot-Macmillan Partnership Plan of 1958 which finally laid the lid on Cyprus' enosis and unrestrictive independence dream.

He was awarded a life peerage in 1964 and assumed the title of Baron Caradon. He died on 5 September 1990.

# AMERICANS
## Dean ACHESON 1893 - 1971

A law graduate from Yale and Harvard.

Under-Secretary of State from 1945 to 1947 and Secretary of State from 1949 to January 1953. He acted as adviser to 4 Presidents. He became the principal creator of US foreign policy in the Cold War period following World War II. He helped to create the Western Alliance (NATO was the first peacetime defensive alliance entered into by the US), in opposition to the Soviet Union and other communist nations.

After leaving office he returned to private law practice but continued to serve as foreign policy adviser to the White House.

His partitionist policies regarding Cyprus had a profound affect on the island's survival. The famous '*Acheson Plans*' of 1964-65 were intended to lead to double enosis which would have meant the establishment of American and NATO bases there to serve the large western interests of the area. Although rejected at the time, Acheson persevered and he declared in 1966 that a solution could be imposed on Cyprus by the use of superior and more sophisticated arms. Such a policy was '*approved*' and finally achieved in 1974.

## John F. KENNEDY 1917 - 1963

Born in Massachusetts on 29 May, he graduated from Harvard in 1940 and then served with great gallantry during World War II.

In January 1961 he was inaugurated 35th. President of the US - the youngest man and the first Roman Catholic to be so elected.

As senator and then president until he was mysteriously assassinated on 22 November 1963, Kennedy earned the gratitude of the world for his constant reminders that all should fight against the common enemies of man: tyranny, poverty, disease and war itself.

During his three-year presidency, relations between the US and Cyprus were very cordial. In fact, Kennedy treated Makarios with the utmost respect and when the latter heard of Kennedy's assassination he openly wept because as he said "*Cyprus has lost a dear friend*".

# Henry Alfred KISSINGER 1923 -

Born on 27 May in Fürth, West Germany. His family emigrated to the US in 1938 to escape the Nazi persecution of the Jews.

He obtained his doctorate in government from Harvard University, became a professor there and served as a consultant on security matters to various US agencies during 1955-68, spanning the administrations of Eisenhower, Kennedy and Lyndon B. Johnson.

From 1969 to 1976 he was a major force in world diplomacy and served as Secretary of State from 1973 to 1977.

In 1973 he shared the Nobel Peace Prize.

Over Cyprus he took the view that US interests and global commitments dictated that the island should remain under NATO control and supervision and within the US's sphere of influence. Therefore, attempts by Cyprus to follow a non-aligned policy were resisted and in 1974 when Turkey invaded the island, following the Greece-inspired coup, the US did not raise a finger to stop her. America had achieved its aim by proxy. Its Cyprus policy was ill-considered, short-sighted and hopelessly dominated by military considerations. Its policies appear to have succeeded and it now has a large military base and other facilities in the Turkish-controlled northern part of Cyprus.

# UNITED NATIONS
# U THANT 1909 - 1974

A Burmese diplomat, born in Pantanaw on 22 January. When his country became independent in 1948 he took up government work and held several key posts.

U Thant began serving as acting Secretary-General of the UN on 3 November 1961, when he was unanimously chosen by the General Assembly and on the recommendation of the Security Council, to fill the unexpired term of Dag Hammarskjold who was killed in an air crash in September 1961. On 30 November 1962, he took the supreme post of Secretary-General for a term of office ending on 3 November 1966. He was re-appointed for a second term on 2 December. His term of office continued until 31 December 1971.

In 1964 he was instrumental in mobilizing a UN peacekeeping force in Cyprus plus a mediator for the purpose of promoting a peaceful solution and an agreed settlement for the island. The US and Britain as well, opposed the work of the UN designated mediator, the former President of Ecuador Galo Plaza, and lobbied for the suppression of the report. When it was finally issued in 1965 it remained a dead letter.

U Thant retired at the end of his second term in 1971 and he died on 25 November 1974 after a long illness.

# Kurt WALDHEIM 1918 -

Austrian statesman was born on 21 December in Sankt Andra-Wördern near Vienna. Waldheim joined the Austrian diplomatic service in 1945 and in 1972 succeeded U Thant as Secretary-General of the UN. He won a second five-year term in 1976 and tried for an unprecedented third term in 1981. China, however, vetoed his candidacy through 16 rounds of voting before he withdrew.

Waldheim paid three visits to Cyprus, in June 1972, August 1973 and August 1974 for discussions with government officials and to inspect UNFICYP. During his last visit and in the wake of the hostilities the Secretary-General arranged for talks to begin between Clerides and Denktash. He firmly believed in the unity and territorial integrity of the island.

Waldheim also served as President of Austria from 1986 to 1992.

# Javier PEREZ DE CUELLAR  1920 -

A lawyer and career diplomat who was born in Lima, Peru on 19 January.

At the age of twenty he joined the Peruvian administration and was a member of its delegation to the General Assembly at its first session in 1946. In 1973 and 1974, he represented his country in the Security Council, serving as its president at the time of the events in Cyprus in July 1974. On 18 September 1975, he was appointed special representative of the Security Council in Cyprus, a post he held until December 1977. Succeeding Kurt Waldheim, he served two terms as Secretary-General from 1 January 1982 to December 1991.

Associated with the Cyprus question for years he believes in the co-existence, harmony and unity of all peoples.

# Boutros BOUTROS-GHALI  1922 -

Born in Cairo, Egypt on 14 November, he was to become the first Arab and the first African to hold the leading UN post. He served as the 6th Secretary-General from 1 January 1992 to 3 December 1996. He had a long association with international affairs as diplomat, jurist, scholar and widely published author.

Boutros-Ghali vigorously supported UN mediation in post-cold war strife. His term saw lengthy and difficult peacemaking/keeping operations in Bosnia and Herzegovina, Somalia, Rwanda and Cyprus. In what was surely a bold initiative he presented in April 1992, his '*Set of Ideas*' which reaffirmed the UN's position that a settlement must be based on a state of Cyprus with a single sovereignty. Following further UN-sponsored meetings in the summer a revised version of the '*Set of Ideas*' took shape on which a map was also annexed reflecting UN proposals on the territorial issue. The Security Council duly approved the expanded version. The new state of Cyprus would be comprised of two politically equal communities in a bi-communal and bi-zonal federation. The '*political equality*' of the two communities would be exercised through '*effective participation*' in the government and its administrative organs. The proposals were accompanied by a map which would have reduced the Turkish-held area to about 28 per cent of the island. Parts of the city of Varosha and the town of Morphou in the northwest and over 30 villages along the Varosha-Nicosia-Morphou road would have been returned to Greek Cypriots for resettlement. Also, once the overall framework agreement was approved in separate referenda by the two communities, a programme of action to promote cooperation and close relations between the two sides would have been implemented.

In his '*Agenda for Peace*' (June 1992) Boutros-Ghali attempted to develop a coherent rationale for UN activities. He was also of the opinion that if every ethnic or linguistic group claimed statehood then there would be no limit to fragmentation. The US however, became dissatisfied with Boutros-Ghali's independent leadership and successfully blocked his bid for a second term as Secretary-General in 1996.

# Kofi A. ANNAN 1938 -

Born in Kumasi, Ghana, on 8 April Kofi Annan became the 7th. Secretary-General of the UN. He was also the first to be elected from the ranks of the UN staff. He began his term on 1 January 1997.

He used his good offices effectively in several political hot-spots and oversaw the creation of a *'situation centre'* that monitors UN peace-keeping operations around the clock. Regarding Cyprus he worked tirelessly to get the two sides together in what have been termed *'proximity talks'*. The promotion of durable peace via a negotiated settlement remained his primary objective.

In an effort to move the process forward Kofi Annan submitted a plan for a comprehensive settlement on 11 November 2002, with a first revision on 10 December and a second on 26 February 2003. The plan envisaged a reunited Cyprus with a federal government and consisting of two *"constituent states"* under a common state that would have a single international legal personality and sovereignty and would speak and act with one voice. Further amendments in March 2004 once more failed to bring the desired results. Although the island was admitted to the EU on 1 May 2004 it still remains *'divided'*.

Describing his job Kofi Annan said, *"I am a cheerleader, a promoter, a salesman, a debt-collector, a father confessor and there are other aspects I still have to discover"*. Lofty ideals but did they bring peace to Cyprus?

# APPENDIX – C
# Orthodox Archbishops of Cyprus 1570s-2005

| | | | |
|---|---|---|---|
| Timotheos | 1575 - 1587/8 | Damaskinos | 1824 - 1827 |
| Athanasios | 1600 - 1602 | Panaretos | 1827 - 1840 |
| Benjamin | 1602 - 1609 | Joannikios II | 1840 - 1849 |
| Christodoulos | 1609 - 1631 | Kyrillos I | 1849 - 1854 |
| Nikiforos | 1660 - 1673 | Makarios I | 1854 - 1865 |
| Hilarion Kigala | 1674 - 1678 | Sofronios II | 1865 - 1900 |
| James I | 1679 - 1689 | 'Vacancy | 1900 - 1909 |
| Germanos II | 1690 - 1705 | Kyrillos II,Papadopoulos | 1909 - 1916 |
| James II | 1710 - | Kyrillos III, Vassiliou | 1916 - 1933 |
| Silvestros | 1718 - 1731 | 'Vacancy' | 1933 - 1947 |
| Philotheos | 1734 - 1759 | Leontios Leontiou | 1947 (Jun/Jul) |
| Païsios | 1759 - 1766 | Makarios II, Myriantheus | 1947 - 1959 |
| Chrysanthos | 1767 - 1810 | Makarios III, Mouskou | 1950 - 1977 |
| Kyprianos | 1810 - 1821 | Chrysostomos I | 1977 - |
| Joakim | 1821 - 1824 | | |

NB: The dates shown above for the Ottoman supremacy (1571-1878) are not always accurate.

# APPENDIX – D
# Ottoman Sultans 1566 - 1924

| | | | |
|---|---|---|---|
| Selim II | 1566 - 1574 | Osman III | 1754 - 1757 |
| Murad III | 1574 - 1595 | Mustapha III | 1757 - 1774 |
| Mohammed III | 1595 - 1603 | Abdul Hamid I | 1774 - 1789 |
| Ahmed I | 1603 - 1617 | Selim III | 1789 - 1807 |
| Mustapha I | 1617 - | Mustapha IV | 1807 - 1808 |
| Osman II | 1618 - 1622 | Mahmoud II | 1808 - 1839 |
| Mustapha I | 1622 - 1623 | Abdul Mejid I | 1839 - 1861 |
| Murad IV | 1623 - 1640 | Abdul Aziz | 1861 - 1876 |
| Ibrahim | 1640 - 1648 | Murad V | 1876 - |
| Mohammed IV | 1648 - 1687 | Abdul Hamid II | 1876 - 1909 |
| Suleiman II | 1687 - 1691 | Mohammed V | 1909 - 1918 |
| Ahmed II | 1691 - 1695 | Mohammed VI | 1918 - 1922 |
| Mustapha II | 1695 - 1703 | Abdul Mejid II | 1922 - 1924 |
| Ahmed III | 1703 - 1730 | | (Caliph only) |
| Mahmoud I | 1730 - 1754 | | |

NB: The Sultanate was abolished and Turkey became a Republic in October 1923. The Muslim religion was disestablished and the caliphate abolished in March 1924.

# APPENDIX – E
## British Personnel - 1878 - 1960

**Administrators:-**

1878 Garnet Wolseley,
   later Lord Wolseley

1879 Robert Biddulph

1886 Henry Bulwer

1892 Walter Sendall

1898 William Haynes-Smith

**High Commissioners:-**

1900 William Haynes Smith

1904 Charles King-Harman

1911 Hamilton Goold-Adams

1915 John Clauson

1920 Malcolm Stevenson

**Governors:-**

1925 Malcolm Stevenson

1926 Ronald Storrs

1932 Reginald Stubbs

1933 Herbert Palmer

1939 William Battershill

1941 Charles Woolley

1946 Reginald Fletcher,
   later Lord Winster

1949 Andrew Wright

1954 Robert Armitage

1955 John Harding, later Lord
   Petherton

1957 Hugh Foot, later Lord Caradon

# APPENDIX – F
## Greek Monarchs 1833 - 1967*

| | |
|---|---|
| 1833 - 1862 | Otto, Prince of Bavaria (Wittelsback) |
| 1863 - 1913 | George I, Prince William of Denmark (Glucksburg) |
| 1913 - 1917 | Constantine I |
| 1917 - 1920 | Alexander |
| 1920 - 1922 | Constantine I |
| 1922 - 1923 | George II |
| 1924 - 1935 | 'Republic' |
| 1935 - 1944 | George II |
| 1944 - 1946 | 'Regency' |
| 1946 - 1947 | George II |
| 1947 - 1964 | Paul I |
| 1964 - 1967 | Constantine II |

* The monarchy was abolished by the junta. They proceeded to proclaim a *presidential parliamentary republic* on 1 June 1973.

# APPENDIX – G

## Presidents of Cyprus

Archbishop Makarios III ....................1960 - 1977
Spyros Kyprianou..............................1977 - 1988
Georgios Vassiliou.............................1988 - 1993
Glafcos Clerides.................................1993 - 2003
Tassos Papadopoulos.........................2003 -

# APPENDIX – H

## Population Statistics

### 1. Actual Population: 1881 - 1983 (to the nearest 1,000)

| | | | |
|---|---|---|---|
| 1881 | 186,000 | 1946 | 450,000 |
| 1901 | 237,000 | 1960 | 578,000 |
| 1921 | 311,000 | 1983 | 652,000 |

### 2. Comparative table (%): 1881 - 1983

| | 1881 | 1931 | 1946 | 1960 | 1973 | 1983 |
|---|---|---|---|---|---|---|
| Greek Cypriots | 73.4 | 79.5 | 80.2 | 76.6 | 78.9 | 80.1 |
| Turkish Cypriots | 24.9 | 18.4 | 17.9 | 18.1 | 18.4 | 18.6 |
| Others | 1.7 | 2.1 | 1.9 | 5.3 | 2.7 | 1.3 |

### 3. 1881 Census by Religion

| | |
|---|---|
| 136,629 ......... | Greek Church |
| 46,389 ......... | Mahomedan |
| 3,066 ......... | Various religious sects - (the majority |
| **186,084** | being Roman Catholic and Church of England) |

### 4. 1960 Census by Nationality

442,521 : Greek
104,350 : Turkish
3,628 : Armenian
2,708 : Maronites
3,351 : British
2,796 : Latins
18,261 : Others

**577,615**

NB: For all population figures (1-4) allow for counting, non-registration and other minor statistical errors. For the 1881 census see CO 456/3. The words/definitions/categories used are as per those used by the official colonial records.

# APPENDIX – I

## UNFICYP - Countries providing military and civilian police personnel (as at 4 May 2004)

| Country | Military Personnel |
|---|---|
| Argentina* | 403 |
| Austria | 6 |
| Canada | 1 |
| Finland | 3 |
| Hungary | 122 |
| Ireland | 4 |
| Slovakia | 276 |
| United Kingdom of Great Britain and Northern Ireland | 386 |
| **Total:** | **1,201** |

| Country | Civilian Police |
|---|---|
| Australia | 15 |
| India | 7 |
| Ireland | 20 |
| Netherlands | 4 |
| **Total:** | **46** |

* The Argentine contingent includes soldiers from Bolivia (2), Brazil (2), Chile (32), Paraquay (32), Peru (2) and Uruguay (3).

In pursuing its 1964 mandate, UNFICYP must perform two fundamental functions in Cyprus today. It must (a) maintain the military *status quo* in the buffer or dead zone and prevent the recurrence of fighting and, (b) must carry out humanitarian and economic activities to promote a return of normal conditions.

The buffer zone extends across Cyprus for some 180 km and comprises about 3 per cent of the island's territory. The area between the lines varies in width from 7 km to only a few yards on the infamous green line that divides the capital, Nicosia.

From mid-December 2004 and for the next six months, UNFICYP's strength will be reduced to 860 - a reduction of some 30%.

A Cypriot peasant girl painted by the great artist Adamantios Diamantis

# APPENDIX – J

## Other personalities "involved" in the making of 20th century Cyprus

Creativity, courage, determination and initiative are all deep-set aspects of the proud inhabitants of Cyprus. Worldwide, the islanders, be they Greek, Turkish, Armenian, Maronite or Latin have excelled themselves in many fields.

The arts have benefited from the growing interest on the part of the government which has established and supported art galleries, public libraries, a state orchestra and a state theatre. At this level Cyprus has also profited from the activities of 'foreign' organisations such as the British Council, the Goethe Institute, the French Cultural Centre and the American Centre. Frequent visits by internationally-known artists, orchestras, ballet and theatrical companies have stimulated public awareness. A useful contribution has also been made by the various TV networks which make generous use of imported educational and cultural film material. Local productions are not only plentiful and colourful but highly popular.

Some talented local artists have emerged and their work has appeared in many European exhibitions. **Angelos Markides**, for example, has represented Cyprus at prestigious events worldwide and is noted for the mastery of his inspiration and materials. Everything is measured and has an inner rhythm and in this lies the expressive power and imposing presence of his compositions - works of art which are tender and poetic in their expression of the tragic. Other artists, just as expressive, have made their name on the international stage. **Diamantis,** for example, is regarded as the *"father of modern Cypriot painting"*. Other prominent artists include **Stass Paraskos,** who has established the first school of painting in Paphos, **Andreas Charalambides, Kanthos, George Kotsonis, Renos Lavithis, Skoteinos,**

Stass Paraskos in front of one of his works

Telemachos Kanthos

Adamantios Diamantis

*Left:* George Kotsonis' *"In front of the Sea"*

**George Georgiou, Mary Plant, Hambis** the engraver of Cyprus and **Kasialos. Nicos Kotziamanis,** an internationally-renowned sculptor and artist, has few equals in his profession. **Ritsa** and **George Kyriakou** have worked very hard to establish Gallery K in Hampstead, London and so has **George Evgeniou** with *'Theatro Technis'* (Art Theatre) also in the British capital.

In the field of poetry and prose-writing, the Cypriots have again made great strides. **Manos Kralis** born in Nicosia (1914), is talked of as being one of the *'rejuvenators'* of Cyprus' poetry. His collection of poems called *'Taste of Freedom'* and published in 1974 have as a central theme the tragic events of that year - events which have been explored by many other distinguished writers. Undoubtedly, **Vasilis Michaelides** is the undisputed *'Cypriot national poet''* yet others have contributed immensely to the island's cultural development. **Azinos, Germasiotis, Liasides, Paleshis, Tziapouras. Charalambides, Montis, Libertis** and

Mary Plant's
*Aphrodite of the shells*

Pavlos Liasides

Loukis Akritas

Vasilis Michaelides                          Demetrios Libertis

**Loukis Akritas** whose work *'The Plain' (o Kambos)*, should be set amongst the two or three best prose-writings left to us by the generation of the 1930s. Local Cypriots and those in the diaspora have also excelled in other fields and have received international recognition and fame:

**Dr. Vassos Karageorghis** is an eminent scholar, writer and archaeologist. *"The father"* of Cyprus' archaeology is certainly an apt description.

In the realm of property, speculation and international finance **Sir Reo Stakis** achieved unprecedented success; **Stelios Hadjioannou** of *'Easy Jet'* etc is a consumer-orientated market-manipulator with an extraordinary rate of continuous growth; **Theo Paphitis** is not only highly successful in business but in soccer management as well, being chairman of Millwall FC for several years. Cyprus also boasts probably the largest research and consultancy organisation in the eastern Mediterranean region, called the *'Middle East Marketing Research Bureau'* it was established in the 1960s. Arguably the largest construction company of the Middle East, *'J & P'*, established by the energetic **Joannou** and **Paraskevaides** and Cyprus is still their headquarters. **Haris Sophoclides** is a high achiever in the realm of business and as the President of the UK and worldwide Federation of Cypriot's has contributed admirably to the promotion and awareness of the island's problems.

Reo Stakis              Theo Paphitis

*Right:* Haris Sophoclides

Constantinos Spyridakis

*Right:* Tefkros Anthias

**Katsouris Foods (UK)** is also very prominent in the European markets. **Chris Lazaris** - property and investments - **Andreas Panayiotou** and **Giorgos Partakis** - hotelier, are also highly successful.

Cypriots have also made great strides in medicine, in the other sciences and arts. The talented and hardworking islanders are to be seen in leading hospitals, universities and research organisations all over the world. To mention just a few: **A.K. Emilianides** was a leading constitutional jurist and writer; **Theodoros Papadopoulos** and **Constantinos Spyridakis** are historians and scholars with few equals. In medicine, **Professor A. Nicolaides** is a leading heart surgeon and **Professor Kypros Nicolaides**, the founder of the Fetal Medicine Foundation, is justifiably seen as a world authority in this field. He was the first doctor to perform laser surgery on an unborn child, the first to drain excess fluid from a foetal heart and a pioneer of ultrasound scanning. **George Christofinis** is a microbiologist with many authoritative papers to his name. *'Interferon'*, a protein substance which restrains the replication of virus particles, is associated with his hard and efficient work over many years.

*Left:* Stelios Hadjioannou, founder of the "Easy" group of companies

*Right:* Professor Kypros Nicolaides

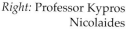

In music, talent is again plentiful. **Michalis Violaris, Marios Tokas, Anna Vissi** and **Constantia** are highly successful artists of popular Greek songs. **George Michael** is one of the great mega-stars of the world's pop scene. **John Themis,** is a gifted composer and songwriter. In 2004 he composed the music for the BBC's transmission of the highly successful Olympic Games held in Athens. The UK's Eurovision entry for 2005 *'Touch My Fire'* is also written by him. **Solon Michaelides** is a very talented conductor and **Marios Papadopoulos** is a conductor and soloist of major international standing. **Michael Cacoyiannis**, the man behind *'Zorba the Greek'* and *'The Cherry Orchard'* is one of the world's most respected directors. **Pantazis** is also a film director of rising reputation.

The list is large; space does not allow me to mention them all. And, to compound my difficulty, new talent (as expected) is emerging, in all fields, from the younger generations. It must not be forgotten that Turkish, Armenian and Maronite personalities have added much to Cyprus' rich culture in many fields.

One may wonder why is the list dominated by men! Without making any excuses, we can confidently say that women from Cyprus and of Cypriot origin are emerging very strongly in most fields of life not only in the arts and music but in journalism and writing and in commerce, science and the law. It is important to mention that since the 60's London and the UK became an important centre of Cypriot achievements as mentioned in this text.

Solon Michaelides

Pavlos Liasides

A short selection of available books in **English.**

M.A. Attalides (Ed.)........... – Cyprus: Nationalism and International Politics.1979

D.S. Bitsios ......................... – Cyprus: The Vulnerable Republic. 1975

A.C. Chrysafis ..................... – Who Shall Govern Cyprus - Brussels or Nicosia? 2003

V. Coufoudakis (Ed.) .......... – Essays on the Cyprus Conflict. 1976

N. Crawshaw...................... – The Cyprus Revolt: An account of the struggle for union with Greece. 1978

R.R. Denktash..................... – The Cyprus Problem. 1986

L.G. Durrell........................ – Bitter Lemons. 1959

C.M. Foley........................... – Legacy of Strife: Cyprus from Rebellion to Civil War. 1964

H.M. Foot ........................... – A Start in Freedom. 1964

V. Fouskas &
H.A. Richter (Eds).............. – Cyprus and Europe: The long way back. 2003

A.C. Gazioglu ..................... – The Turks In Cyprus. A Province of the Ottoman Empire (1571-1878). 1990

G. Gregoriou ....................... – Cyprus: A View From the Diaspora. 2000

D. Hannay........................... – Cyprus: The Search for a Solution. 2005

M. Harbottle........................ – The Impartial Soldier. 1970

M. Harbottle........................ – The Blue Berets. 1971

P.T. Hart.............................. – NATO Allies at the Threshold of War: Cyprus, a Firsthand Account of Crisis Management, 1965-68. 1990

C. Hitchens.......................... – Cyprus. 1984

R. Holland........................... – Britain and the Revolt in Cyprus, 1954-59. 1998

D. Hunt (Ed.) ...................... – Footprints in Cyprus. An illustrated History. 1982

A. James............................... – Keeping the Peace in the Cyprus Crisis of 1963-64. 2002

J.S. Joseph........................... – Cyprus, Ethnic Conflict and International Politics: From Independence to the Threshold of the European Union. 1991

V. Karageorghis................... – Cyprus: From the Stone Age to the Romans. 1982

R. Katsaounis...................... – Labour, Society & Politics in Cyprus during the second half of the 19th. century. 1996

G.H. Kelling........................ – Countdown to Rebellion: British Policy in Cyprus, 1939-1955. 1990

S. Kyriakides...................... – Cyprus: Constitutionalism and Crisis Government. 1968

C. Kyrris ............................. – History of Cyprus. 1986

Y. Leventis .......................... – Cyprus: The Struggle for Self-Determination in the 1940s. 2002

P. Loizos ........................... – The Greek Gift: Politics in a Changing Cypriot Village. 1975

H. Luke ................................. – Cyprus: A Portrait and an Appreciation. 1965

D. Markides ......................... – Cyprus 1957-1963: From Colonial Conflict to Constitutional Crisis. 2001

K.C. Markides ...................... – The Rise and Fall of the Cyprus Republic. 1977

S. Mayes ............................... – Makarios: A Biography. 1981

L.C. Moseley (Ed) .............. – Research for Social Welfare: Six case studies in Cyprus. 1979

F. Mirbagheri ...................... – Cyprus and International Peacemaking. 1998

T.R. Mockaitis ..................... – British Counterinsurgency, 1919-60. 1990

Z.M. Necatigil ..................... – The Cyprus Question and the Turkish Position in International Law. 1993

B. O'Malley & I. Craig ....... – The Cyprus Conspiracy. 2001

S. Panteli ............................. – Historical Dictionary of Cyprus. 1995

S. Panteli ............................. – A History of Cyprus: From Foreign domination to troubled independence. 2000

A. Papandreou ..................... – Democracy at Gunpoint: The Greek Front. 1973

P.G. Polyviou ...................... – Cyprus: Conflict & Negotiation, 1960-80. 1980

J. Reddaway ......................... – Burdened with Cyprus: The British Connection. 1986

H.I. Salih ............................. – Cyprus: The Impact of diverse Nationalism on a State. 1978

S.R. Sonyel ........................... – Cyprus: The Destruction of a Republic - British Documents 1960-65. 1997

K. Spyridakis ...................... – A brief History of Cyprus. 1974

I. D. Stefanidis .................... – Isle of Discord: Nationalism, Imperialism and the Making of the Cyprus Problem. 1999

R. Stephens ........................... – Cyprus, a place of arms. 1966

L. Stern ................................. – The Wrong Horse: The Politics of Intervention and the Failure of American Diplomacy. 1977

A. Theophanous ................. – The Cyprus Question and the EU: The Challenge and the Promise. 2004.

C.G. Tornaritis .................... – Cyprus and its Constitutional and other Legal Problems. 1980

K. Tofallis ............................. – A History of Cyprus: From the ancient times to the Present. 2002

P.N. Vanezis ......................... – Makarios: Life and Leadership. 1979

P.N. Vanezis ......................... – Cyprus: Crime without punishment. 2000

V.D. Volkan ......................... – Cyprus: War and Adaptation. 1979

K. Waldheim ......................... – The Challenge of Peace. 1980

C.M. Woodhouse ................ – Karamanlis: The Restorer of Greek Democracy. 1982

C.M. Woodhouse ................ – The Rise and Fall of The Greek Colonels. 1985

S.G. Xydis ............................. – Cyprus: Reluctant Republic. 1973

C. Yennaris ........................... – From the East: Conflict and Partition in Cyprus. 2003

*Left:* Clerides and Denktash during one of their many meetings.

*Right:* Kofi Annan and Clerides – in the background *(centre)* is the UN chief negotiator, Alvaro de Soto

*Above centre* between Denktash and Clerides and *below right* the chief UN negotiator, Alvaro de Soto

*(Photos Christos Theodorides)*

A symbolic photograph: *from the left,* Spyros Kyprianou, Constantinos Karamanlis, Mrs Kyprianou and Andreas Papandreou.

Photographic material supplied by: the author, the publishers, P.I.O. (Cyprus), the National Archives (Kew), Doros Partasides, Christos Theodorides and by many other private collections.